CAMILLE GUTT AND POSTWAR
INTERNATIONAL FINANCE

FINANCIAL HISTORY

Series Editor: Robert E. Wright

TITLES IN THIS SERIES

FORTHCOMING TITLES

CAMILLE GUTT AND POSTWAR INTERNATIONAL FINANCE

BY

Jean F. Crombois

LONDON AND NEW YORK

First published 2011 by Pickering & Chatto (Publishers) Limited

Published 2016 by Routledge
2 Park Square, Milton Park, Abingdon, Oxfordshire OX14 4RN
711 Third Avenue, New York, NY 10017, USA

First issued in paperback 2015

Routledge is an imprint of the Taylor & Francis Group, an informa business

BRITISH LIBRARY CATALOGUING IN PUBLICATION DATA

Crombois, Jean-Francois.
Camille Gutt and postwar international finance. – (Financial history)
1. Gutt, Camille, 1884–1971. 2. International economic relations – History – 20th century. 3. Diplomacy – History – 20th century. 4. Finance ministers – Belgium – Biography.
I. Title II. Series
337'.09044-dc22

ISBN-13: 978-1-138-66134-9 (pbk)
ISBN-13: 978-1-8489-3058-2 (hbk)

Typeset by Pickering & Chatto (Publishers) Limited

CONTENTS

ACKNOWLEDGEMENTS

The project of writing this book started about ten years ago when I embarked on a Wiener-Anspach Postdoctoral Fellowship at Balliol College and at the Faculty of Modern History at the University of Oxford. It would not have succeeded without the support of a number of people and institutions. My thanks include the American University in Bulgaria for granting me a leave of absence in order to complete my research in Belgium and in Britain. I would also like to thank the Modern European History Research Centre at the University of Oxford for hosting me in spring 2010 as a Senior Visiting Research Fellow. A number of people have given me their support and have expressed interest in this book project. Among them, I would like to thank especially Martin Conway, Patricia Clavin and Guy Vanthemsche who agreed to review some chapters of this book and whose advice has been particularly helpful. Any remaining mistakes and errors are of course entirely my own. Last but not least, I would like to express my deepest gratitude to my wife, Clemena, for her patient and rigorous proof-reading of the manuscript.

LIST OF TABLES

INTRODUCTION

Just after his appointment, in 1946, as the first managing director of the International Monetary Fund (hereafter IMF) *Fortune Magazine* depicted Camille Gutt in the following terms:

> There is little to suggest the international banker in Camille Gutt's outward appearance. He lacks the impressiveness of a J. P. Morgan, the aloof dignity of a Montaigu Norman. A wiry little man with quizzically arched eyebrows and an irrepressible beard, he looks more than an unshelled turtle than anything else. Yet, despite his appearance, Camille Gutt is one of the most outstanding financial authorities on the international scene today.[1]

The rise of Gutt to the pinnacle of financial diplomacy certainly owed less to a well planned career than to the result of a succession of unpredicted events and meetings that formed the landmarks of his impressive accomplishments. Indeed, very little in his early life suggested that Gutt would embrace the career of an international businessman, international negotiator and Belgian finance minister in 1934–5 and again during the Second World War as a leading member of the Belgian government-in-exile in London. And yet, if Gutt could easily be considered as one of the most influential Belgian political figures of the first part of the twentieth century, biographical information about him is rather scarce. Though Gutt published two short books recounting his first experience as finance minister in 1934–5 and his war experiences,[2] he has not attracted much attention of Belgian economic and political historians.

Three reasons may account for this neglect. The first was the fact that, until very recently, there were no real archives relating specifically to Gutt. The very nature of his professional activities on the fringes between private and public life did not lead to the production of public papers usually available for an individual of such historical importance. The second was certainly due to his unusual career which made him difficult for historians to define as either *politician* or *businessman*. Indeed, until the 1980s, Belgian and international historians were still reluctant to grasp fully the importance of what would be referred to as business history, let alone financial history, for the understanding of the evolution of twentieth-century international history.[3] The third reason relates to relationship between the international and the national aspects of Gutt's career and activities. Indeed, if the interwar period is sometimes defined as one of 'hypernationalized geopolitics',[4] it was also a period of intense transnational activities especially in the form of a new kind of financial diplomacy that reflected a great fluidity between the domestic and the international dimensions of financial matters that has been overlooked in much traditional diplomatic history.[5]

This book proposes to address this neglect by examining the role played by Camille Gutt in shaping postwar international finance. It will address this role in the context of three major questions.

The first relates to the involvement of private businessmen in financial policy either in its domestic or international dimensions and how to account for the role of such private interests in the conduct of public policy. It is true to say that despite the substantial analysis of this period the existing scholarship provides few examples of the role of individual actors in this process.[6]

The second question relates to the influence of private interests in shaping national interest.[7] In other words, to what extent did private interests contribute to shaping the national interests as expressed in national diplomacy? This book will address this question through the specific case of Belgium focussing essentially on Belgian diplomacy during the Second World War in the framework of the Belgian contribution to the Allied war effort.

The third question concerns the construction of the postwar monetary order that consisted of multilateral economic cooperation as embodied in the creation of the Bretton Woods institutions and of regional cooperation as reflected in the creation of the Benelux agreements between Belgium, the Netherlands and Luxembourg. Based on new material and new scholarship it will raise the following question: to what extent were the discussions on the postwar monetary order more concerned with the problems inherited from the interwar period rather than laying down the basis for a *new* departure?

In view of these questions, this book goes well beyond a traditional biographical approach. Rather, it will try to position Gutt's career in the transformations of the relations between finance and politics with a focus on the Second World War and the direct postwar era, especially in its international monetary and financial aspects. It will be argued that Gutt's case reflects the extent to which the period from the end of the First World War to the 1950s, could be considered as part of a single historical sequence of events. This process was marked by the attempts of a generation of political and economic elites to come to terms with the political and economic transformations generated by the First World War, the consequences of the Great Depression of the 1930s and the new situation created by the Second World War and the subsequent nascent Cold War.

Therefore, this book has to be regarded primarily as a case study in international financial history. Such an approach has indeed led to the emergence of a new way of looking at the history of financial and economic diplomacy. This new scholarship is important for two main reasons. In the first place, it emphasizes the role of individuals in the process in terms of both perceptions and decisions.[8] Indeed, if economists and economic historians have tended to neglect individuals in favour of institutions, structures, and complex arithmetic models, international financial history deals with individuals and tries to understand the factors that may have contributed to their decisions, whether they proved successful or not. Secondly, it is because it leads to a re-assessment of European history in the era from the 1920s to the 1950s and in particular emphasizes the impact of financial diplomacy on the relations between states.[9]

Indeed, international financial diplomacy reflected a new way of dealing with relations between states. If such a form of diplomacy already existed in the nineteenth century, it became much more visible and influential after the First World War. As such, it was characterized by a number of features that made it a specific form of diplomacy. In his book published in 1935, the financial journalist Paul Einzig defined its main forms as conferences that brought together experts rather than diplomats, though these experts had also to take account of their respective countries' positions.[10]

More recent scholarship has attempted to refine Einzig's assumptions. One view highlights the interwar period as a period of transition from the control over financial diplomacy in the 1920s by businessmen to central bankers.[11] Another view stresses the role already played by central bankers in the 1920s in stabilizing currencies through international cooperation.[12]

Not surprisingly, Belgium and Belgians do not feature as central figures in this literature as their role quickly became marginal. At occasions, some Belgian personalities are even mistakenly presented as having been French.[13] Nevertheless, they were not only witnesses but also active actors in this international financial diplomacy that arose from the ruins of the First World War even if the international scholarship has not been very generous about them.[14]

As far as Gutt's career was concerned, his positions as an international businessman and negotiator made him a perfect example of the transnational economic elite that emerged during the interwar period. Some recent scholarship has emphasized the importance of transnational communities as important factors for the understanding of the shaping of international cooperation, or the lack of it, since the First World War. In this perspective, transnationalism is not to be understood as a one-way street leading almost naturally to greater international cooperation. Instead, it may also lead to the strengthening of national sovereignty and the defence of specific interests within the different countries.[15]

In some respects while also underlining the way in which perceived national interests played an important role in international financial diplomacy, this book will contribute to this field by emphasizing the impact of transnationalism on international cooperation. It will suggest that the case of Gutt should not be differentiated too much from a more collective transnational experience of the First World War and its direct aftermath that affected a whole generation of Belgian elites. For these elites, the First World War was seen as a double blow. Despite having emerged on the winning side of the First World War, the outcome of the conflict precipitated the decline of her economy. In the second half of the nineteenth century, the Belgian economy that was able to take full advantage of the country's political neutrality, emerged as one of the most successful ones on the Continent. Though a small country, it had secured a vast overseas colony, the Belgian Congo, and its banks were major investors in Russia, South America and China. In 1918, however, the Belgian economy emerged devastated from the First World War and had to undertake a painful and expensive process of reconstruction. To finance this process, the Belgians counted on the payment of German reparations while they resented their status as junior political actors in the peace negotiations and the subsequent international arrangements sealed in the 1920s.[16] As a result, Belgian political and economic elites shared the feeling that the country had been unfairly treated even though it had paid a heavy price as a result of the First World War. Finally, the Belgian economy suffered from the fragmentation of the international and the Continental economy during the 1930s. In turn, Belgian political and economic elites tried to push for the opening of their neighbours' economies but without much success.

During the Second World War, Gutt was finance minister in the Belgian government-in-exile in London. There is no doubt that because of his past experiences, international connections and close relationship with George Theunis, he became the most important figure among the Belgians in exile in London. However, his role should not only to be understood in the light of individual choices. It has also to be put in the context of his functions as Belgian finance minister confronted with the need to redefine Belgium's international economic policy as a result of the Second World War. These two dimensions, the personal and the national, are indeed inseparable. Essentially this book will also propose a fresh view on Belgian diplomacy that hitherto has not attracted much attention from international historians.[17]

In the context of the Second World War, many among Belgian elites, such as Gutt, had to find a way of reconciling two opposing objectives. One the one hand, as representatives of a small nation, they sought to defend their national sovereignty. And on the other hand, they were acutely aware of the need for their country to secure outlets for its exports and to protect it from the evils of monetary instability. Because of this they had to enter into some forms of economic cooperation at the risk of compromising their country's sovereignty. In this respect, in addressing these issues, this book will re-assess the existing literature on Belgium's foreign policy during the Second World War. It will argue that

Belgian wartime international financial diplomacy was based on the defence of national sovereignty as the precondition of international cooperation rather than the acceptance of possible outright limitations of sovereignty for the sake of international cooperation as it is often presented in the literature.[18]

Finally, this book also deals with the political decisions made by representatives of governments-in-exile during the Second World War in shaping the postwar financial and monetary order. Such experiences have been until recently rather neglected by twentieth-century historians.[19] For sure, the impact on these governments-in-exile's policies on postwar Europe remained largely minimal.[20] Nevertheless, this book will present a fresh assessment that takes into account two important dimensions. First, the experiences of exile constituted, at the level of elites, an intensive form of transnationalism among allied officials, businessmen and politicians. Secondly, the experience of exile also led these elites to start a process, however incomplete, of a re-assessing their interwar foreign, financial and monetary policies.

In this context, this book deals with the case of Camille Gutt and his role in all the questions mentioned above while encompassing not only his role in Belgian history but also to some extent in European history as well. It will attempt to place Gutt's experience in the wider picture of the relationship between warfare, economics and finance. There is indeed no doubt that, if wars represent an extreme situation, they often reveal some deeper socio-economic trends. For Marxists and neo-Marxists, these are analysed from the view of the construction of a military–industrial complex in which wars are just seen as a class struggle by other means.[21] More historical research on the subject has been rather rare with some notable exceptions such as the seminal book by Alan S. Milward's *Economy and Society* or Niail Ferguson's *The Pity of War*.[22]

In this book, the argument will be made that wars contribute to making the relationship between business and politics both more visible and more complex. If business interests participate in the definition of national interests, business people have also their own views on what they consider to be the national interest. In other words, national interests are not fixed in a permanent way. They also evolve as the result of specific personal and collective experiences as shown in the case of Gutt.

This book can be considered as a sequel of an early book consisting of the author's doctoral dissertation and published in French in Belgium in 1999.[23] Nevertheless, it proposes a different angle that emphasizes the international dimensions of Gutt's career over his domestic ones. This book has also taken account of new materials, including an updating of the Belgian and international historiography on the different issues covered. Indeed, in the last decade, a series of biographies of some important actors during the period such as Paul van Zeeland, Paul-Henri Spaak and Hubert Pierlot have been published in Belgium.

Other recent valuable works of reference are the two volumes on the history of the National Bank of Belgium. The first volume covers the Second World War while the second deals with Belgian postwar monetary policy.[24] There has also been a renewed interest in financial history, especially in its international dimensions in the last few decades. To the already mentioned books by Ferguson and Milward can be added the scholarship produced by Barry Eichengreen, Patricia Clavin and Harold James, without forgetting Robert Skidelsky's biography of John Maynard Keynes.[25]

In terms of sources, this book relies mostly, but not only, on Gutt's personal archives that were deposited in the Centre d'Etudes et de Documentation Guerres et Sociétés Contemporaines (hereafter CEGES) in Brussels by his son Etienne Gutt. These archives concern Gutt's activities during the Second World War as well as his experience as managing director of the IMF alongside other documents and correspondence of a more personal nature. They also contain the complete private correspondence between Gutt and Theunis during the war, which offers a unique insight into the Second World War and the issues covered in this book. If these archives do not contain significant material concerning Gutt's activities during the interwar period, this gap can be filled by the Theunis papers that contain some interesting documents. The latter were not accessible at the time of the French publication but have been used for this book. Finally, these archives were supplemented by other available documents in the American, British and French archives.[26]

Finally, a brief overview of each chapter follows below for the reader's benefit: Chapter 1 deals with Gutt's career during the interwar period. It includes a descriptive section dealing with Gutt's early life and career. It also analyses Gut's career path in the context of the changing relations between business and politics in Belgium's interwar financial policy in both its domestic and international dimensions.

Chapter 2 addresses Gutt's role in the negotiations over the Belgian contribution to the Allied war effort. It will emphasize the importance of these discussions as they reflected both the difficulties experienced by the Belgians in exile in revising the old paradigms of Belgian interwar foreign policy and the legacy of failed attempts at providing free trade in Western Europe.

Chapter 3 is concerned with Gutt's participation in the discussions that took place in London with respect to postwar international monetary cooperation. It emphasizes the extent to which the Allies continued with a negotiating framework that already demonstrated its shortcomings during the interwar period. It also underlines the difficulties for Gutt as well as other Europeans in exile in adhering to the principles of the 'Keneysian revolution'.

Chapter 4 deals with Gutt's attempt to resolve the dilemma between the need for international cooperation and free trade and the safeguarding of national sovereignty as reflected in his plans for a monetary and trade agreement between Belgium, the Netherlands and Luxembourg, known as Benelux. In doing so, it will propose a new approach to these agreements while highlighting both the legacy of Gutt's interwar experience and his scepticism towards the universalist approach adopted by John Maynard Keynes and Harry Dexter White as well as the need for a gradual regional approach to economic cooperation, albeit one restricted to Western Europe.

Chapter 5 addresses Gutt's participation in the discussions that led to the Bretton Woods conference of July 1944. If the Belgian minister did not play a central role in these discussions, his views on both Keynes's and White's plans were very specific. In these discussions, Gutt's positions were also determined by the legacy of his interwar experience and the dilemma between international cooperation and the defence of Belgium's sovereignty.

Chapter 6 deals with Gutt's immediate postwar experiences, first as Belgian negotiator of the settlement of the Lend-Lease agreements with the Americans, then as participant in the Savannah conference and finally as the first managing director of the IMF from 1946 to 1951. The main contribution of this chapter is to include Gutt's personal views on the different issues relating to the IMF policy towards the reconstruction of the Western European economies.

1 CAMILLE GUTT, FINANCE AND POLITICS (1919–40)

This chapter will offer a biographical sketch of Camille Gutt's pre-1940 career. It will not, however, follow a strictly biographical approach but will instead address his career in the context of the changing nature between finance and politics in interwar Belgium. More precisely, it will be argued that the interwar period reflects not only the growing fluidity between business and politics, but also the first tensions and divisions over financial policy, especially in terms of domestic economic policy.

The following chapter will be divided into three main sections. The first section will offer a brief survey of Gutt's early life and career. The second will posit his multifaceted role within the context of the rising of big business in politics in interwar Belgium. The third section will address the experiences of Gutt as Belgian finance minister in 1934–5 and in 1939–40.

Camille Gutt's Early Life and Career, 1884–1919

Very little is known about Gutt's family origins. Gutt was born in Brussels on 14 November 1884. His father Max Guttenstein came from Neuzedlish, a city included in the district of Tachau (now Tachov in the Czech Republic) on the remote edges of Bohemia, then part of the Austrian–Hungarian Empire. His mother, Marie-Pauline Schweizer was from Alsace. In the early 1920s, Camille Guttenstein decided to change his name to Gutt. The name Guttenstein resurfaced in the 1930s in a climate of rampant xenophobia and anti-semitism in Belgium, but there is no evidence of him belonging to Judaism (see below) and in reality both Gutt's parents were Protestant (see Chapter 2).

The few available documents suggest that Max Guttenstein established himself in Brussels in 1877. He made his living as a journalist and director of a journal called *Le Nord* [*The North*]. This journal was financed by Russia in order to restore the image of the country in Western Europe after the disaster of the Crimean War. In 1886, Max Guttenstein acquired Belgian nationality. He died in Brussels in 1891.[1] Left with his mother and his half-sister, Hélène ,[2] the young Gutt managed to pursue his studies in Brussels thanks to scholarships. In 1906, he completed his university education by getting a double degree in political and social sciences in 1904 and in law in 1906 from the Free University of Brussels where he had among his professors the future Belgian foreign affairs minister, Paul Hymans. It is presumably during his studies that Gutt met Claire Frick, whom he married in 1906. The couple shared the same interest in theatre and developed a very intimate relationship. Claire Frick's father, Henri-Charles Frick, was not only a lawyer but also prominent local liberal political figure in Brussels and the owner of a newspaper called *La Chronique* [*The Chronicle*]. It is therefore not surprising that Gutt started his professional career as both a barrister and a journalist. The subjects covered by the young journalist who signed some of his articles using the pseudonym of *Silly* were extremely varied but already reflected his main centers of interests such as theatre, literature but also the first steps of the automobile industry and more importantly of avia-tion. Before the war, Gutt also contributed to other local newspapers where he met a number of prominent Belgian political and literary figures. In 1911, Gutt became editor of the Belgian equivalent of Hansard in Britain. This gave him a unique observation point on Belgian parliamentary political life on the eve of the First World War.[3]

In any case, it is fair to assume that had it not been for the First World War, Gutt's path would not have changed much. He would certainly have gone down in history as a talented journalist and an acute observer of Belgian cultural and political life. When the war broke out, Gutt was in the Belgian Parliament cover-ing the speech of King Albert I on 4 August 1914 to both Houses of Parliament, announcing Belgium's declaration of war to the German Empire. On the same day, another event of a more private nature took place with the birth of his first son, Jean-Max Gutt.

On the following day, 5 August, Gutt enrolled in the first cyclist regiment as a volunteer. After three months, when its regiment became short of supplies, he decided to join the Spahis following a meeting with one of his French friends who was captain in the same regiment. In April–May 1915, Gutt fought at Ypres where the Germans first made use of their deadly gases.[4]

Following the battle, Gutt decided to go to the French city of Le Havre where the Belgian government-in-exile was established. There, he met a number of important figures of the Belgian colony in exile such as political figures and journalists. His signature can even be found on a manifesto written by a number of Belgian personalities in favour of a future extension of the national territory to the Grand Duchy of Luxembourg, the Dutch Limburg and to the so-called Eastern districts of Eupen and Malmédy as Belgian war aims. The author of this manifesto was Pierre Nothomb, a well-known lawyer and advocate of the ideas for a 'greater Belgium' during the First World War.[5]

In October 1915, the Belgian government sent Gutt to London to work with the Belgian War Material Purchasing Commission. At the time the Belgian Commission was headed by a colonel who showed little interest in the economic aspects of his work. Eventually, the Belgian government-in-exile in France decided, in December, to send the colonel back to the front and to replace him with Georges Theunis. Upon arrival, Theunis got particularly upset when he saw that none of his staff apart from a young lieutenant was present. This young lieutenant was Gutt who had taken the habit, unlike his colleagues, to have lunch in his office with sandwiches prepared by his wife. Theunis was led to Gutt's office and the two men talked for more than two hours. As Gutt would recollect much later: 'We talked ... But the conversation did not finish. It lasted exactly 50 years'.[6]

The two men, who up to that day had never met or heard each other's names, could not be more different. Gutt was a lawyer interested in literature, in horseracing and an atheist: Theunis was an engineer, mostly interested in figures, not particularly keen on lawyers and a committed Catholic. In reality, these differences more than making any collaboration between them impossible, worked exactly in the opposite way. According to Gutt: 'I have always thought that these divergences, instead of pushing us apart, established the complementarity that united us'.[7]

This meeting with Theunis constituted certainly the first important turn in Gutt's career. Theunis was already a powerful Belgian business figure. Educated as an engineer at the Belgian military school, he had become a close associate of the Belgian businessman Edouard Empain who was the head of one of the most important business groups in the sectors of transports and electricity in Europe, building tramway lines across the Continent including the famous *Métropolitain* in Paris.[8] The position of Theunis in London reflected the strong alliance made during the First World War between big business and politics.[9]

In London, Gutt, who was still referred to as a man of letters, was developing in a completely new world made of businessmen from the allied nations working for their respective governments such as Jean Monnet, Arthur Salter, and many others whom he would later meet again in the interwar period and during the Second World War. On a more personal level, Gutt's wife managed to leave occupied Belgium with their first son, Jean-Max . A second son, Francois, was born in London in 1916.

Camille Gutt and Financial Policy, 1919–34

At the end of the First World War, Gutt thought naturally of resuming his double career as journalist and barrister. But as soon as August 1919, he was offered by Theunis the position of secretary general of the Belgian delegation to the Reparations Commission. The Commission became the main political focus of inter-Allied discussions concerning the determination of the amount of the German reparations to be paid as war damages in execution of the Treaty of Versailles. This Commission included some high profile personalities such as Raymond Poincaré, Charles Jonnart for France or Sir John Bradbury for Britain.[10]

When in 1921, after a year as finance minister, Theunis was led to combine this position with that of prime minister; Gutt followed him to Brussels and became his chief of Cabinet at the Finance Ministry. As finance minister, Theunis was put in charge of the negotiations over the German reparations. As a result, the Belgian foreign affairs ministers were given a merely nominal role in these discussions. In January 1924, Gutt returned to Paris to replace Arthur Bemelmans as Belgian deputy-delegate to the Reparations Commission. This move to Paris was also strategic. Indeed, in 1924, a new settlement was to be negotiated under the supervision of the American banker, Charles Dawes, in order to put an end to the French–Belgian occupation of the Ruhr. As main negotiator, Theunis decided to appoint another important Belgian business figure in the person of Emile Francqui. The latter had expressed misgivings at Theunis's domestic policy and, more particularly, his fiscal policy to come to grips with the increasing budget deficits and rising inflation (see below). From the point of view of Theunis sending Francqui to Paris considerably decreased Francqui's potential nuisance effect at home. But sending Gutt to Paris ensured a tight control over his actions.[11]

It was also during this period, in 1921, that Gutt decided to change his name from Guttenstein to Gutt. This change was justified by Gutt's fear that his name had a too 'Germanic' consonance which would expose him while negotiating with the Germans.[12] It would only be during the 1930s that Gutt was attacked by some newspapers with the accusation of being Jewish (see Chapter 2).

The important roles played by both Theunis and Francqui in Belgian politics after the First World War reflect the increasing influence of business interests on both Belgian domestic politics and international financial diplomacy.

In the late 1920s, Theunis entered the powerful group of the Société Générale de Belgique, Belgium's number one universal bank until 1934.[13] Theunis was also close to the Catholic party without being a member. In the early 1930s, and following growing tensions with Francqui, Theunis decided to resign from the Société Générale while remaining active in the Empain group and a close observer of Belgian financial policy. But Theunis was much more than a national political figure. He played an important international role within the League of Nations. In 1927 he presided over the International Economic Conference convened in Geneva and was subsequently appointed as president of the Economic Consultative Committee to the League of Nations. Finally, from 1929 to 1931, he became president of the International Chamber of Commerce.[14]

Francqui was another extremely influential Belgian business figure. Having joined the army, he entered in the service of the Independent State of Congo whose head was King Leopold II of the Belgians before it became a Belgian colony in 1908. After a career as both a consul and a businessman in China, Francqui became in 1910 the head of the Belgian Banque d'Outremer, one of the main Belgian overseas banks. In 1912, Francqui finally joined the Société Générale de Belgique where he became vice-governor in 1923 and then governor in 1932 until his death in 1935.[15]

Francqui was certainly a more colourful and perhaps a more controversial figure in Belgian politics than Theunis. Gutt wrote of him:

> The supreme joy of Francqui was to topple and form governments. I think he did it often with the national interest in mind but also with his own interest in mind. He would have equally done it without any interest at stake, just for the fun of it.[16]

Surely, there was no love lost between the two powerful figures, Theunis and Francqui. In reality, only Gutt, who succeeded in winning Francqui's trust, was able to act as a bridge between them.

This rise of business people to political prominence should not hide the fact that, at the time, very few national rules dealt with any possible conflict of interests. In most cases, such rules were only confined to civil servants. Therefore, it would be naïve to believe that such businessmen who were involved in government completely ignored their own business interests. The only guarantee for their conduct lied in their personal integrity. This exposure of business interests, both at the domestic level and then at the international level, also had some potentially damaging effects. These would only be revealed later in the 1930s when big business was blamed for the economic difficulties during the Great Depression.[17]

However, this takeover of big business over Belgian financial policy would not go completely unchallenged. If in foreign policy, and especially with respect to the handling of the issue of the German reparations, the involvement of Belgian businessmen was widely supported across the Belgian political spectrum, in domestic monetary and financial policy cracks appeared as early as the middle of 1920s to reach a breaking point during the crisis of 1934–5.

Gutt and the 1926 Stabilization of Belgian Currency

When sent to Paris in late 1924, Gutt knew that his mission would be short as Theunis had just accepted a caretaker mission in waiting for the elections scheduled for April 1925. In this context, the question of Gutt's future was still unresolved. Then, in early 1925, Gutt was invited for lunch in Paris by Empain, also known as the *General*. The object of the meeting was to discuss Gutt's plans beyond politics. Empain told Gutt how happy he would be to introduce him to his business activities. In the same conversation, Empain also mentioned the extent to which Francqui had thought of proposing to Gutt to enter the board of the directors of the Banque d'Outremer.[18]

Once again, though, Gutt's career took an unexpected turn when Francqui asked him, in May 1926, to work as one of his special advisers when appointed minister without portfolio in the newly formed government led by Henri Jaspar. This government went down in Belgian history as the triumph in the taking-over of financial and monetary policy by Belgian big business.[19]

Indeed, the general elections of April 1925 had given Belgium her first left-wing governing coalition made of Socialists and Christian-Democrats. The main objectives of this coalition had been to stabilize the Belgian currency and to resume its link with the gold standard while dealing with the growing public deficit inherited from the four years of German occupation of Belgium and financial policies led since 1918.

In short, under the Conservative government led by Theunis, from 1921 to 1924, Belgian financial policy was essentially based on the need to restore public finances and to ensure the payment of the German reparations. But the faith that the Belgians put in the German reparations led them to borrow considerable amounts of money on the international markets. To make matters worse, when facing German reluctance to fulfil their obligations in terms of reparations, the Belgians joined the French in 1923 in the costly occupation of the Ruhr. As a result, the government had to find ways to close the widening financial gap created by the continuing rise in borrowing and the lack of revenues. These ways consisted of issuing Treasury bonds which considerably worsened the external liability of the country while creating taxes such as a new value added tax.[20]

The government formed in the aftermath of the elections in 1925, included a new finance minister, Albert-Edouard Janssen, at the time director at the Belgian Central Bank, who designed a plan to salvage Belgium's public finances. This plan was based on two main measures. The first consisted of devaluing the Belgian franc towards the sterling at a rate of 107. The second consisted of financing the budget deficit through the adoption of new taxes and more importantly, the negotiation of a 100 million dollar international loan. Then, Janssen tried to negotiate this loan with a consortium of international private bankers led by the American banker, John Pierpont Morgan but without success. Indeed, the same bankers, aware of Francqui's objections, declined the offer. As a result the government that was already under tremendous pressure from Belgian Conservative and financial circles fell in May 1926, just over a year after the elections. A new government of national unity was then constituted with the participation of the three main political parties in Belgium (Catholics, Liberals and Socialists) led by Jaspar as prime minister. In reality, the real head of the government was Francqui who was appointed as special minister with a mission to resolve the financial crisis.[21]

In order to carry out his mission, Francqui decided to call on Gutt whom he appointed as secretary and sent him to London to lay down the ground for the negotiation of the loan with the consortium of American and British banks. The position had no official definition and was especially created to suit Francqui's wishes.[22] Once the loan agreement was completed, the government unveiled the new parity of Belgian currency at 176. On this occasion Gutt took full measure of the lack of economic cooperation between the different European countries. When he accompanied Francqui to Paris to discuss the new exchange rate of the Belgian currency, the two men were received at the private residence of the French Prime Minister Poincaré, so as not to attract too much attention to the planned operation. The visit was justified by Francqui's willingness to stabilize both the French and the Belgian currencies simultaneously at a common exchange rate. Nevertheless, the return of Poincaré to office ruined Francqui's effort. Indeed, the new French prime minister was eager to preserve France's financial independence while cautious not to set an inappropriate rate for the French franc.[23] Therefore the meeting proved disappointing as Francqui and Poincaré barely touched upon the question of the new parity and instead had a general discussion on different international questions.[24]

During his brief tenure as minister, from May to November 1926, Francqui also seized the opportunity to reform the statutes of the Belgian Central Bank, the National Bank of Belgium, which led to strengthening of the business representation within its main decision-making structures. Francqui's triumph, however, was not complete. Indeed, his plan included offering Theunis the position of governor of the Belgian Central Bank. By such an appointment, Francqui wanted to make sure that Belgian monetary policy was made independent of politics like in Britain. Naturally, he first explored the possibility with Gutt who told him that according to him, there was little chance that Theunis, still recovering from his five years in office,[25] would contemplate such an offer.[26] Instead the position went to Louis Francq, a second choice candidate and second-tier liberal politician, who revealed to be unable to cope with the crisis of 1934–5 (see below).[27]

The Belgian devaluation of 1926 can be considered as a first important moment in Belgian financial history for two main reasons: Firstly, because it considerably enhanced the national and more importantly international prestige of Belgian bankers such as Francqui who made the Société Générale de Belgique the main intermediary of the Treasury when negotiating international borrowings.[28] As such it opened an unprecedented speculative boom in the Belgian economy. The total capitalization of Belgian companies was multiplied by four in less than two years following the operation. According to Belgian economists, this financial boom only concealed the fact that the Belgian economy became more reliant on domestic demand rather than on international markets. The problem would arise when, following the collapse of the international economy

in 1929, domestic demand would reveal to be insufficient to overcome the recession at the beginning of the 1930s.[29] Secondly, the 1926 monetary stabilization
reflected some cracks in the consensus over Belgian financial and monetary policy. These cracks became visible in the growing divergence of views between the
professional economists working at the Belgian Central Bank and the private
bankers. These economists, amongst which included the future Belgian Prime
Minster Paul van Zeeland and others belonging to the so-called Leuven School
of Economics, objected to the extent of the devaluation on the ground that it
only suited the interests of the private bankers.[30] These divergences would have
some lasting consequences especially when in the mid-1930s the government
was confronted with a new crisis resulting from the Great Depression.

Gutt and Private Business Interests 1926–34

As mentioned above, Gutt's transformation as a businessman was already on
track before the events of 1926. Bearing in mind the closeness between Gutt
and Empain on the one hand and with Francqui on the other, it should come
as no surprise to see Gutt entering a sector in which the two businessmen were
particularly involved. This sector was the one of the non-ferrous metals. In this
respect, it is worth noting that business did not lead Gutt to politics but rather
the reverse – politics led him to business (see Table 1.1).

The non-ferrous sector was then seen as full of promises, as a result of the combination of a number of factors. First, the First World War led to the demise of the
Metallgesellschaft, a German company that was the main provider of raw materials
for the European market. With the dismantling of the Metallgesellschaft's quasi-
monopoly, the field was opened for new players, in Belgium and in Europe, to step
in.[31] Secondly, the British were especially eager to seize the opportunity to ensure
that the British Empire became self-sufficient in non-ferrous metals.[32]

Finally, the Société Générale de Belgique which controlled the powerful
mining giant of the Union Minière du Haut-Katanga, one of the world's leading
suppliers of copper, had the project of creating non-ferrous production capabili-
ties in Belgium using the mining resources extracted in the Belgian Congo.[33]

These factors led the Société Générale de Belgique, together with national
and international investors, such as the British Metal Corporation of Sir Cecil
Budd, to the creation of a number of important companies such as, in 1920,
the Société Générale des Minerais.[34] In 1928, Gutt entered the board of this
company and found himself alongside Francqui, Gaston Blaise, Fernand Pisart,
Theunis but also Oliver Lyttleton, future Viscount Chandos[35] and member of
the War Cabinet during the Second World War, among others.

Gutt, however, was not an engineer but a lawyer. As such, he specialized in
the negotiation of selling contracts in both sectors of copper and tin. In this field,
he worked mainly with Pisart with whom he developed a long-term friendship.

In 1926, the two men presided over the creation, in New York, of the African Metals Corporation. Its shareholders included some Belgian companies, such as the Union Minière while its board of directors comprised a number of prominent Belgian businessmen such as Francqui, Edgar Sengier and the financial journalist and expert in non-ferrous metals, Guy Franklin Creveling.[36] The African Metals Corporation, which was merely a trading syndicate, would play a crucial role during the Second World, in the context of the Belgian–American negotiations over the question of Belgian uranium from the Congo (see Chapter 2).

The establishment of this New York-based company took place in the context of the struggle between the two main cartels in the field of copper. On the one side, the Belgian-Anglo-American cartel regrouped around the Rokhana and managed by the American (though later naturalized British citizen) copper magnate, Alfred Chester Beatty and, on the other side, the American cartel of the Anaconda mostly active on the American continent. Beatty was a well-known figure in the Belgian Congo as the key shareholder of the Société Internationale Forestière et Minière, known as the Forminière which became one of the world's largest diamond producers.[37]

Table 1.1: Business activities of Camille Gutt during the interwar period.

Companies	Positions	Main Shareholder(s)	Sector
African Metals Corporation	Board member: 1926–34 and 1935–9	Société Générale de Belgique and Union Minière du Haut Katanga	Non-ferrous and mining
Ford Motor Cy (Belgium)	Board member: 1927–34; CEO: 1936–9	Ford and Lord Perry	Automobile
Cie des Métaux d'Overpelt-Lommel	Board member : 1927–34 and 1935–9	Bank Philippson; Cie and Société Générale de Belgique	Non-ferrous
Société Générale des Minerais	Board member: 1928–34; managing director: 1935–9	Société Générale de Belgique and British Metal Corporation (since 1920)	Non-ferrous and mining
Société Générale Industrielle et Chimique du Haut Katanga	Board member: 1930–4 and 1935–9	Sovay & Co.; Société Générale de Belgique; Philippson Bank; Empain.	Non-ferrous, mining and chemicals
Electrorail	Board member: 1930–9	Empain	Electricity and transports
Cie Belge des Mines, Minerais et Fonderie du Zinc de la Vieille Montagne	Board member: 1935–9	Société Générale de Belgique	Non-ferrous and mining
Société Générale Métallurgique d'Hoboken	Board member: 1935–9	Société Générale de Belgique; Union Minière du Haut Katanga; British Metal Corporation since 1920	Non-ferrous and mining

During the first half of the 1930s, the fall in commodity prices led the main producers to conclude international cartel agreements such as the international copper and tin cartels established in 1935.[38] Owing to his involvement in both sectors, Gutt participated in these negotiations alongside Pisart but also Francqui and another important colonial business figure, Félicien Cattier, who actively defended the interests of the Union Minière du Haut-Katanga.[39]

The involvement of Gutt in these cartel negotiations may be surprising to some who might view him as a proponent of free trade (see Chapter 3). In reality, the two were not seen incompatible at the time. Indeed, at the 1927 Geneva International Economic Conference presided over by Theunis, the delegates did not reject outright the existence of cartels and just mentioned the need for greater publicity to prevent abuses.[40] Later, in 1933, at the London Monetary and Economic Conference, calls were made for the conclusion of such international agreements especially with respect to copper.[41]

Hence, in Gutt's mind as in other peoples', in the absence of other forms of international economic cooperation, cartels had to be considered a good thing both for producers and consumers. In a conference before a local Belgian business association in 1938, Gutt explained:

> In the present complexity of economic life, where all the problems are interconnected, where international aspects impact on domestic aspects, and finance on economics, these cartels are indispensable regulators and it is absolutely necessary that their role should be known precisely by the public.[42]

In 1927, Gutt also entered the board of directors of Ford Belgium Cy that had been created in 1922 by Lord Perry, first importer of Ford cars into Europe. In 1936, he became the CEO of Ford Belgium. This last activity was not related to the ones regarding non-ferrous metals and found its main explanation in Gutt's passion for cars. However, this did not prevent Gutt from taking an active part in the defence of Ford's interests in Belgium. For instance, when facing the adoption of rising import duties, Gutt did not hesitate in November 1932 to get in touch with Fernand van Langenhove, general secretary of the Belgian Foreign Affairs Ministry, in order to send him a note on the subject.[43] However, the note did not change anything as the import duties were adopted in 1933 harming Ford's business activities until the 1935 devaluation.[44] Finally, in 1930, Gutt entered the board of directors of Electrorail, one of the flagship companies of the Empain financial and industrial group.[45]

In any case, Gutt was always very careful not to define himself as a banker, but rather as an industrialist. When he realized that his name had been put down as a banker on the registry of the International Chamber of Commerce, he instantaneously wrote back to Pierre Vasseur, the ICC's general secretary, in saying: 'I am not a banker, I am just simply an industrialist and a trader'.[46]

In the meantime, Gutt's business activities enabled him to enlarge his circles of business acquaintances to people such as Lyttleton, Budd and Beatty, while at the national level he imposed himself as a key figure within the non-ferrous activities of the Société Générale de Belgique.

Gutt and International Financial Diplomacy: German Reparations and Monetary Conference 1919–33

When asked after the Second World War about the number of international conferences in which he participated, Gutt answered that he stopped counting them after sixty-three.[47] Owing to his former assignment at the Reparations Commission, it was almost natural for Gutt to remain involved in the issue during the 1920s and in the early 1930s. As chief of Cabinet of Theunis, Gutt's functions included not only the supervision of the Belgian experts taking part in all these conferences but also the task of serving as press officer for them when he did not himself decide to take his pen to publish articles in Belgian newspapers in order to work up the Belgian public opinion against the positions of one or another great power.[48]

In 1924, Gutt was appointed as expert and worked alongside Francqui within the Dawes Committee that proposed a new settlement of the German reparations after the French–Belgian occupation of the Ruhr region. In these negotiations Gutt played a crucial role in two ways. Not only was he instructed to watch Francqui but also to control him during the discussions within the Committee of Experts. The problem came when Francqui, too eager to seal a deal, became a bit too close to endorsing the British proposals that would cut considerably the amount due to Belgium. Eventually, Gutt, alongside other advisers, succeeded in convincing Francqui to resist these demands and, ultimately, to considerably limit the damage for Belgium. For the Belgians, the Dawes plan was seen as a retreat from the Versailles commitments. But the Belgian government, facing monetary instability and rising inflation, was just not in a position to provoke a failure of the negotiations.[49]

In 1929, when the question of renegotiating the Dawes settlement arose, Gutt was appointed with Francqui to the Committee of Experts gathered under the aegis of the American businessman, Owen D. Young. In the margins of the discussions, Gutt succeeded in reaching a settlement on the question of the marks owed by Germany to Belgium as a result of the occupation during the First World War. Gutt received a special message of acknowledgement from King Albert I of the Belgians on this occasion.[50] In connection with the Young settlement, Gutt also took part in the Hague conference of 1929 that laid down the basis for the establishment of the Bank for International Settlements (hereafter BIS) in charge of the commercialization of the payment of the German reparations.[51] Finally, Gutt, again with Francqui, was also involved in the discussions connected to the Hoover Moratorium that led to the final renegotiation of the German Reparations in Lausanne in 1932.[52]

In these discussions, Gutt appears as a skilful tactician, as custodian of Belgium's best interests and as a canny negotiator. In 1929, a French newspaper, *Le Petit Parisien*, depicted Gutt as follows:

> Since 1924, there has been indeed no inter-Allied Commission nor international conferences in which he [Gutt] has not represented Belgium and in which he [Gutt] did not get noticed for his deep knowledge of the questions, the fairness of his views, and in case of difficulties, the resources of his imagination.[53]

For Gutt, as for the other Belgian experts, the negotiations over the German reparations left a bitter feeling of injustice caused. They remained with the impression that Germany had been able to take advantage of the division among the Allies – the French and the British more particularly. The impact of these negotiations was also to be felt during the Second World War. Indeed, they would continue to obsess people like Gutt and Theunis about the need, after winning the war, to not lose the peace as was felt to have been the case after 1919.

In reality, this assessment would be later rejected by more contemporary research that challenged the idea that the Belgians, compared with the French and the British, were unsuccessful with respect to the settlement of German reparations. More recent scholarship has suggested that not only did Belgium receive proportionally more that the French and the British but it also got a bigger share than the 8 per cent that had been negotiated right after the Armistice. The reasons for such success have been identified as follows: the continuity in terms of the appointment of Belgian negotiators that formed a cohesive group with perhaps the exception of Francqui; their willingness to address the negotiations from a business-like view rather than from a political one; and, finally, the wide public support of these negotiators as well as the other Belgian political parties.[54]

Finally, Gutt also took part in other important gatherings where he was able to expand his international experience. In 1933, he was one of the Belgian experts to the preparatory Commission in charge of setting up the agenda of the International Monetary and Economic Conference convened in June in London in which he also participated alongside Francqui, Hymans and Jaspar. There Gutt found himself at the forefront of what remained in history as one of the greatest failures of international monetary diplomacy that led the world to trade and monetary fragmentation (see Chapter 3).

In all these negotiations, Gutt appeared as an *expert*, working mostly in the shadow of imposing figures such as Theunis and Francqui.[55] But as such he acquired first-hand knowledge of the failure of international economic cooperation during the interwar period. As a result there was certainly no idealism left for Gutt as this experience made him highly sceptical of the possibility of such cooperation. True, Gutt completely understood the limitations of Belgium as a small power, but this knowledge taught him how to take advantage of divisions between the great powers. This required a staunch defence of Belgian sovereignty seen both as a precondition of international cooperation but also as a possible means of reinforcing it (see Chapters 2, 4 and 5).

At a more personal level, these activities enabled Gutt to come across all the major players in both diplomacy and international financial affairs. In 1922, he witnessed Benito Mussolini's first and last appearance in inter-Allied discussions when meeting in London at prime ministerial level. Then Gutt took measure of the gulf between the new Italian fascist leader and politicians such as Lloyd George and Poincaré attached to the principles of liberal parliamentarianism. He also met with Aristide Briand, Louis Loucheur, Walter Ratheneau and Gustav Stresemann. Among these political figures, there is no doubt that David Lloyd George and Arsistide Briand impressed him the most. Of Ratheneau, Gutt was amazed at his language skills, while he witnessed Stresemann's poor health on seeing him a few months before his death in 1927.[56] But this list of figures does not only include people who passed away before the Second World War, it also encompassed a great number of people whom Gutt would meet again when he arrived in London in August 1940, such as Winston Churchill, Arthur Salter, Montaigu Norman, John Maynard Keynes, Andrew McFadeyan, Frederick Leith-Ross, to mention just a few.

Finance Minister 1934–5 and 1939–40

In the 1930s, Gutt was not yet a well-known name in Belgian politics, even if his involvement in the negotiation of the German reparations gave him a certain exposure both in the national and international media as shown above. Surely nothing destined Gutt for high political office if not the deep friendship and respect he had won from Theunis and Francqui.

Finance Minister in the So-Called 'Government of Bankers' (1934–5)

After a spell in the worlds of business and financial diplomacy, Gutt was called back in 1934 to domestic Belgian politics. If Belgium had witnessed since 1926 a period of relative economic prosperity, the devaluation had failed to address the structural weaknesses of the Belgian economy in terms of modernization.[57] The new economic difficulties following the Wall Street Crash and more particularly its consequences in Germany and Austria as soon as 1931, changed the situation completely. The real blow, however, to Belgium occurred when the sterling fell sharply following the British decision to sever its link with gold; almost overnight, the sterling reserves that had been accumulated in the Belgian Central Bank reserves lost 30 per cent of their value.[58]

In this context, Belgian financial policy-makers opted for the defence of the existing rate of the Belgian currency. This involved a harsh policy of deflation. But the successive governments proved unable to restrict the budget deficits caused by a tremendous increase of public spending, notably to cope with growing unemployment. This combination between the need to defend the parity of the currency and unstoppable rising public spending put the country on the brink of economic ruin.[59]

Worse, the banking sector which was characterized by the existence of universal banks combining traditional banking activities and investments was also on the verge of collapse owing to massive immobilization of assets. In the summer of 1934, the Belgian government had to rush to adopt the first decrees that put an end to the existence of universal banking by restricting banking activities to short-term credit and deposit while excluding long-term investment activities from them.[60]

In short, the country was confronted not only with economic depression, but also with a financial and banking crisis. To this, a political crisis was added following the defection of the liberal party from the ruling coalition a few months after the accidental death, on 17 February 1934, of King Albert I. It was therefore up to a young and inexperienced new king, Leopold III, to cope with the situation.[61]

In November 1934, after endless political discussions, King Leopold III on Francqui's suggestion appointed Theunis as prime minister and gave him *carte blanche* for the constitution of a Cabinet whose mandate would be limited to the resolution of the economic and financial crisis.[62] Theunis was unaware of the fact that his name had been proposed by Francqui but decided to include the latter in his Cabinet as special minister without portfolio as well as Gutt as finance minister. Most certainly, the lessons of the 1920s were learned. Indeed, Theunis remembered that leaving Franqui in the cold could be risky. At the same time, to include Gutt in the Cabinet as well presented the advantage of restoring a triangular relationship in which Gutt was put at the centre.

This appointment, however, took Gutt completely by surprise. At the time, he was cruising on a steamer in the middle of the Atlantic after having spent most of the year in the US. On 16 May 1934, he was included in the Belgian delegation sent to announce the accession to the throne of King Leopold III and was invited by Franklin D. Roosevelt to the White House for luncheon.[63]

In late 1934, the monetary and financial situation could not be more difficult. In less than two months, assets worth up to 2 billion francs left Belgium, the public deficit was estimated for the fiscal year up to 300 million francs and banks were on the brink of collapse despite the adoption of the new banking legislation. As a first measure, Gutt and Francqui rushed to Amsterdam to negotiate a loan of 100 million francs with Fritz Mannheimer, the head of the Dutch branch of the Mendelshson Bank. The conditions to which the loan was granted led to some strong criticisms on the part of the officials on the Belgian Central Bank.[64]

What made the situation even more difficult was that the deflationary measures fuelled popular anger and the threat of a big demonstration in Brussels orchestrated by some young socialists lead by Paul-Henri Spaak, future Belgian prime minister and minister of foreign affairs. This put additional pressure on the government. But behind the scene, socialist leaders struck a deal with some officials at the Belgian Central Bank and with the same economists who had objected to the 1926 monetary stabilization of a possible devaluation of the national currency.[65] In March 1935, the new fall of sterling followed by unprecedented decrease of the gold reserves of the Belgian Central Bank led to the fall of the government. The events of 1935 marked not only the spirits of the times but would confirm some important antagonism between the two worlds of private and central banking in Belgium.

The formation of government that occurred in the aftermath of the Stavisky affair in France attracted the hostility of public opinion towards bankers and financiers. Skilfully nicknamed 'the government of bankers'[66] by its opponents owing to the background of most of his members, the Theunis-Francqui Cabinet was exposed to ferocious press campaigns denouncing the 'Wall of Money'.[67] As Gutt pointed out, if the formula was inaccurate, it was nevertheless quite effective. For the record, Gutt was always eager to mention that only Francqui could be defined as a banker while Theunis only occasionally touched upon banking. He himself never did and never claimed to have done so.[68]

Among the three main members, Gutt attracted most of the public anger which flirted in some cases with anti-Semitic rhetoric with reference to the rediscovery of his original surname.[69] The experience proved so unpleasant that Gutt felt obliged to take his own defence. First, he sent a long note to King Leopold III, who in a subsequent meeting agreed with Gutt's version of events.[70] Secondly, following the fall of the government, he spent most of his time justifying and correcting information published in Belgian newspapers. For example, rumours spread that Gutt has embezzled 20 million francs to buy properties, that Theunis went to Cannes with his gold and Francqui to Barcelona where he committed suicide![71] If all these rumours were quickly proved baseless, the climate became so bad that a judiciary investigation was opened on the losses in the gold reserves of the Belgian Central Bank. In this context, it is not surprising that Gutt, as a former journalist, felt the compelling need to put the records straight and decided to publish a book where he gave his own version of events.[72]

For sure, Gutt was unrepentant that the Belgian currency could have been saved. But to his mind, three reasons led eventually to the fall of the Cabinet.

The first reason was that the non-inclusion of the Socialist party in government of national unity like in 1926. There Gutt did not spare the Belgian socialist leader, Emile Vandervelde who became fixated on a plan for structural reforms drafted by Henri de Man.[73] This plan would only be very partially implemented in the new government led by van Zeeland who succeeded Theunis as prime minister in March 1935. As finance minister, another businessman, Max-Léo Gerard, succeeded Gutt, which considerably contained the reformist ambitions of the new government.[74]

The second reason was that the financial and economic challenges caused the banking crisis that required urgent bailout measures by the government to prevent the collapse of the whole financial sector. Here again, Gutt blamed mostly the Belgian Central Bank's governor, Francq, for not having kept the government sufficiently informed of the situation of the Belgian banks. The third reason lay in the lack of support from the Belgian Central Bank and other economists close to the Leuven School, who advocated a devaluation of the Belgian currency. Amongst, these, Gutt particularly blamed the then vice-governor of the Belgian Central Bank, van Zeeland, not only for his lack of support but for also the fact that he drafted a plan for a devaluation with some Socialist figures such as de Man (see below).[75]

The last aspect of the experience of 1934–5 lay in the decision by the new government to establish, in April 1935, a parliamentary inquiry into the heavy losses of gold from the Belgian Central Bank's reserves. Francqui, Gutt and Theunis had to testify and defended their policy. For this reason, Gutt had to delay the publication of his book as he wanted to reserve his comments for the inquiry commission. Meanwhile, the judiciary investigation led to a dismissal of any accusation against the three ministers apart from Francqui who was accused of having taken advantage of his position to protect his assets. However, the Belgian businessman's sudden death a few months later cut short any further actions.[76] It is worth mentioning that if the three Belgian business figures resigned from their positions in the private sector to take over their political responsibilities, their association with business interests arouse considerable suspicion. In this light, the Belgian government decided to set up another inquiry, this time in 1936, on the relationship between big business and politics. This enquiry led to the drafting of the first legislation dealing with possible conflicts of interest. But these measures were never properly enacted due to the start of the Second World War.[77]

Another important consequence, this time on a more personal level, of Gutt's experience as finance minister during 1934–5 was the considerable deterioration of his relations with Paul van Zeeland, almost to a breaking point. The two men did not know each other very well but had met on several occasions. The first time was in 1925, when van Zeeland had been invited by Gutt for lunch at his home in Brussels to discuss the issue of the future relations between the Soviet Union and Belgium. Both agreed then, against the position of the majority of Belgian political and economic elites, on the need to put an end to the isolation of the Bolshevik regime. The second time was in 1929 at the Hague Conference in which van Zeeland participated as an expert of the Belgian Central Bank in the discussions over the establishment of the BIS. Later in 1932, the two men met again when the first political difficulties appeared as a consequence of the beginning of the Depression in Belgium. Then, both agreed on the need for a deflationary policy in order to safeguard the stability of Belgian currency.[78] On 16 March 1935, on the following day of the government's resignation, Gutt learned from van Zeeland that the latter had already prepared a governmental programme based on the devaluation of the Belgian currency of 28 per cent. Gutt then realized than van Zeeland had negotiated this plan behind his back while showing his support for the government.[79]

Needless to say that Gutt was opposed to the idea of such a devaluation which presented, according to him, the danger of increasing Belgium's external debt, mostly subscribed in foreign currency and of increasing the climate of defiance of investors, especially in the light of future borrowings by the Belgian Treasury. More fundamentally, the meeting of 1935 marked a real turning point in the relationship between the two Belgian political and financial figures. It would plant the seeds of a deep climate of distrust and rivalry between the two that would reach its climax during the Second World War.

Indeed, on a personal level nothing could reconcile Gutt and van Zeeland. To start with, Gutt liked to define himself as a man of letters or even a writer and would describe van Zeeland as an economist. According to Gutt: 'I am fundamentally a writer. He is fundamentally an economist. I am attracted by words, he finds concepts charming. I am a sceptic and an enthusiast; he is a believer and a quiet man.'[80]

But while Gutt went down in Belgian history as a partisan of orthodox financial and fiscal management, van Zeeland appeared as the saviour of the Belgian economy and an emulator of Roosevelt's New Deal. It is true that van Zeeland's economic policy, when Belgian prime minister from 1935 to 1937, was based on his plan for a devaluation of which the new rate had been calculated using the purchasing power parity principles suggested by the Swedish economist, Gustav Cassel. This earned him praise from Keynes in person.[81] Nevertheless, van Zeeland's tenure ended sadly when the prime minister was forced to resign following his mishandling allegations of having received some illicit remuneration from the National Bank of Belgium.[82] In any case, van Zeeland's stand against the Belgian extreme-right leader and future collaborationist, Léon Degrelle, at the Brussels by-election of 1937 made him a household hero.[83]

As we will see, however, these distinctions may be somewhat exaggerated, sometimes for political convenience. The Belgian historiography has praised van Zeeland stewardship of the economy as an example of the application of the New Deal's principles, as modernist reformist policies as opposed to the old deflationary policies of the 'Government of Bankers' and even as a an early partisan of Keynesian economics.[84] (see also Chapter 5).

This thesis can partly be traced back to a small book attributed to van Zeeland's brother, Marcel van Zeeland, on the *Van Zeeland Experience in Belgium* published in French in 1940.[85] In reality, while van Zeeland may have introduced some important social innovations, his policy did not lead to a deep transformation of the Belgian economy and it is doubtful whether it could be considered as counter-cyclical. First, van Zeeland's tenure as prime minister was too short, less than two years, in order to make a significant impact. Secondly, he did not go as far as to leave the Gold Bloc but only changed the parity of the Belgian currency and led Belgium alongside the other gold countries to join the Tripartite Monetary Agreement concluded between France, Britain and the US (see Chapter 3).[86]

Finally, there is no doubt, that if big business left the foreground of Belgian politics as a result of the 1935 crisis, they were still actively resisting any serious attempts at reforming the economy in the shadows.[87]

A year after van Zeeland came in to power Gutt gave an assessment of his achievements in a note not destined for publication.[88] In this long note, he praised van Zeeland for the progress made but remained unrepentantly against the idea of devaluation. Gutt's reasoning was very much based on the illusory short-term effects of such a measure. According to him, monetary depreciation would lead to nothing less than an increase of prices offsetting quickly its advantages and requiring new deflationary measures thereafter.[89]

In effect, Gutt's views were vindicated as soon as 1937 when the economic downturn led Belgium to face financial problems once again, this time in an increasingly difficult international context. When he returned to the government as minister of finance in 1939, Gutt had to deal with that legacy, which in turn made him even more sceptical about van Zeeland's achievements.

Finance Minister 1939–40

In February 1939, while Gutt had retired entirely from politics to resume his business activities in the non-ferrous sector and his passion for aviation – leading him to fly non-stop from Brussels to Elizabethville in the Belgian Congo to spend the Christmas of 1938 with his third son, François, King Leopold III asked once more for his services. At first, Gutt, who still had in mind the painful memories of his experience of 1934–5, refused the King's offer to appoint him as finance minister. But the King's insistence and the vivid memories of the young

King's support during that period led him to accept that demand. As Gutt would declare later during the War:

> Before, the King had behaved very nicely with me, when, in 1935, I had left the government and I had been the target of unspeakable attacks ... Then, I had ensured him of my total devotion. It was at that time [in 1939] that he called me and I had to accept his demand.[90]

In February 1939, Gutt therefore entered the new government led by the Catholic Prime Minister Hubert Pierlot with the participation of the Socialists and the Catholics. If the first days of the Cabinet were marked by the impact of some political problems such as some disputes over some linguistic issues, the agenda shifted quickly to financial policy.[91]

Indeed, if by 1937, Belgium's financial situation had been restored, it did not withstand the sudden reversal of the economic conjuncture. Worse, the budgetary situation was left in complete disarray after the resignation, in 1937, of de Man, the Belgian finance minister. In May 1938, Belgium also suffered from the deterioration of the international situation marked by the annexation of Austria by Adolf Hitler's Germany. Even more worrying from a financial point of view for Belgium was the consequence of the French devaluation decided by French Prime Minister Edouard Daladier, in the same month. This decision provoked a flow of gold, of up to 4 billion francs from the Belgian Central Bank. Charged with forming a new government in the spring of 1938, the young Socialist leader Spaak called upon another businessman, Gérard, as finance minister. But the latter proved unable to convince his fellow ministers of the need for a harsh financial policy and decided to resign. As a successor, Janssen, the failed finance minister of 1925–6, was appointed. However, he did not succeed to reassure the financial markets. In the second half of 1938, Belgian financial situation was in a deadlock. Solutions were needed urgently not least following the decision to trigger the first phase of the army mobilization in the aftermath of the September's Munich crisis.[92]

In this context, the most prominent business figures in Belgium agreed on the need to replace Janssen by a stronger personality. The Royal Palace was also pushing for the appointment of Gutt who had been contacted by the King and who finally accepted, but not without some reluctance (see above).

Politically speaking, the year 1939 would see a succession of three governments all led by the same Catholic Prime Minister Pierlot, but with different coalitions and in which Gutt remained as finance minister. With the declaration of war following Hitler's invasion of Poland in September 1939, Belgian financial policy became highly linked with the hope of the King and of large sections of the public opinion of the possibility for the country to escape the conflict.

Indeed, following Hitler's decision, in 1936, to remilitarize the Rhineland, the Locarno system completely collapsed. As a result, Belgium's security was now based on some provisional French and British guarantees and the even vaguer League of Nations's commitments in terms of collective security. In this context, the government adopted a new policy referred as the policy of independence. This policy consisted of the country giving up her obligations contracted in Locarno, in other words: the adoption of self-declared neutrality. Eventually, in 1937, the British and the French agreed, not without reluctance, to release Belgium from the terms of Locarno while reaffirming their own guarantees.[93]

In public, and mainly before French audiences, Gutt appeared as a supporter of this policy.[94] As finance minister, however, and as early as 1939, he also believed strongly in the need to prepare the country for the war while maintaining the link between the Belgian currency and gold, and ensuring budgetary discipline. The first was argued on the ground of foreign policy of independence. The second was argued on the ground of preparing the country for war in the best possible manner.

In September 1939, before his colleagues in the government, Gutt emphasized the need 'for the country to prepare itself to live in a war economy'.[95] This implied for him the need for additional fiscal resources and the refusal of a devaluation of the national currency. This policy was attacked by some business circles who believed that instead of preparing the country for war, Belgium should take advantage, from an economic point of view, of her self-imposed neutrality. The clash between these two views was reflected in the discussions over Gutt's measures for new taxation.

The most controversial measure of all was certainly the project of tax on exceptional profits. For Gutt, that measure had to fulfil two purposes: First, it was to target revenues that were still untouched by taxation; and secondly, through such a tax, to avoid these revenues fuelling inflation. Needless to say, the project attracted a lot of opposition, mostly from right-wing political circles and from the representatives of Belgian big business interests. Faced with such opposition, Gutt did not budge, and apart from some amendments, the new tax was approved on 3 January 1940.[96]

In many ways, Gutt's fiscal policy anticipated and followed Keynes's recommendations expressed in a series of articles in 1939 and later gathered in a book entitled *How to Pay for the War*.[97] There is no doubt that these views comforted Gutt in his decisions and led him to revise more favourably his opinion about Keynes himself (see Chapter 3).

Finally, Gutt was also involved in some important initiatives that would prove to have important consequences in the context of the Second World War. In March 1939, he decided with the agreement of Georges Janssen, head of Belgium's Central Bank, to move the Belgian gold reserves to safety to France,

Britain and the US (see Chapter 3). More contested was the decision to appoint an ambassador-at-large to the US with the special mission of promoting Belgian exports in America and defending the Belgian foreign policy of independence. The creation of this mission was suggested to the King by the Belgian prime minister, Pierlot. At first, Pierlot thought of sending the former prime minister, van Zeeland, who had just completed his mission on behalf of the American, British and French governments to propose a solution aimed at restoring international economic cooperation between the main industrialized nations (see Chapter 3). The proposal to send van Zeeland to the US was rejected by Gutt who feared that the former would use his new mission to strengthen his credibility abroad and to undermine the actions of government at home. Gutt even threatened to resign if this project was carried through. Finally, Pierlot, who was aware of Gutt's importance within the government, gave in and proposed instead Theunis as an alternative. On 18 September 1939, Theunis was then appointed as Belgian ambassador-at-large to the US. In addition to his official mandate, Theunis also received the mission to act as the personal messenger of King Leopold III to President Roosevelt.[98] To this effect, he would be joined by another of Gutt's old business acquaintances, Pisart. The appointment of Theunis would prove to be of a considerable importance for Belgium and for Gutt during the Second World War. In New York, Theunis would deploy considerable efforts to save the image of the country tarnished after the defeat and more importantly after the decision of King Leopold III to remain in occupied Belgium, officially as a 'prisoner'. For Gutt, the presence of Theunis in New York would prove useful as it opened a direct and personal channel with American and Belgian business and political figures (see Chapter 2).

Conclusion

In addition to providing a biographical sketch of Gutt's early career, this chapter has addressed Gutt's path in the context of the growing role played by big business in Belgian politics during the interwar period. Indeed, the three main aspects of Gutt's activities during the interwar period – financial negotiator, finance minister and businessman – should not be treated separately from each other. Rather, they reflect the great fluidity between politics and business in interwar Belgium. Such fluidity can be considered as the legacy of the First World which projected big business to the forefront of politics, both domestically and internationally.

At the international level, Gutt's participation in international financial diplomacy reflected the importance of transnational networks that were made of businessman and national experts to address postwar economic and financial issues. More specifically, Gutt was involved in the negotiations over the German reparations. This transnational experience would reveal to be important for Gutt as it would shape his views on international cooperation, especially in the context of the Second World War.

At the domestic level, Gutt participated in the complete takeover by big business representatives such as Theunis and Francqui over Belgium financial and monetary policy. As Gutt's experiences showed, however, this takeover was by no means unchallenged. If big business enjoyed a widespread support in their handling of the negotiations over German reparations and other international monetary questions, the situation was different when dealing with domestic Belgian financial policy. As early as 1926, the first cracks appeared between big business and professional economists, either academics or officials of the Belgian Central Bank. In 1935, these cracks reached a breaking-point, as reflected in the divergences between Gutt and van Zeeland over financial policy.

In this context, the experience of 1934–5 represented a real watershed in Belgian financial policy. It consecrated the looming divorce between the central bankers, professional economists and big business in the management of domestic monetary and financial policy. More precisely, big business faced a real crisis of legitimacy at the time. As a result, a new generation of professional economists emerged to deal with Belgian financial policy. This process was everything but painless, especially with respect to Gutt.

The tensions that then emerged between Gutt and van Zeeland have to be understood in this context, apart from some additional personal aspects. However, one should perhaps not overstate the differences in terms of economic policy between two Belgian political figures. This could only lead to exaggerating the reformist agenda of the first, and the conservatism of the second. What these differences may tell us, however, is that there was the gap between a policy of fiscal discipline and a policy of easiness such as the one led by van Zeeland, based only on short-term benefits and neglecting its long-term effect. There is no doubt that as a politician, van Zeeland was more interested in capitalizing on quick political gains unlike Gutt, who did not have to be concerned with the state of public opinion. Surely, the reasons of their growing antagonism have to be found in this fundamental difference. Interestingly enough, these discussions over economic policy would resurface during the war both in their domestic and international dimensions (see Chapters 3 and 5).

As the events of 1939–40 highlight, the retreat of big business was merely strategic as showed in the return of Gutt as finance minister in 1939. When called back to the government as finance minister, Gutt had this time to confront the legacy of the van Zeeland experience in a particularly challenging international context for Belgium. Moreover, his financial policy met the opposition of a substantial part of the Belgian business community eager to take advantage of the country's self-declared neutrality instead of preparing the country for the event of war.

2 BELGIAN WAR FINANCIAL DIPLOMACY: NEGOTIATING THE BELGIAN CONTRIBUTION TO THE WAR EFFORT

It may be surprising but Belgian historians have tended to overlook the issue of the Belgian contribution to the Allied war effort, not only in its economic and financial aspects, but also in its political and diplomatic aspects. Only recently have several biographical works have shed some (though insufficient) light on this problem.[1] Otherwise, Belgian Second World War historiography has remained dominated by two sensitive issues, namely King Leopold III's attitude during the war (see below) and economic collaboration with the Nazis in occupied Belgium.[2]

In this context, the question of the Belgian contribution to the Allied war effort has been neglected in the national diplomatic history. This chapter will argue that precisely this question is important as it compelled the Belgians in exile to confront the paradigms inherited from interwar foreign policy. In this process, economic and financial issues played a significant role as they would allow the Belgians to postpone the political decisions on the future of Belgian foreign policy.

In the autumn of 1940, the Belgian government-in-exile was finally reconstituted. It consisted, however, of only four ministers, as a result of the complex chain of events of the previous summer. Consequently, the Belgian government-in-exile in London was weak and therefore found it difficult to impose its will on the remainder of the Belgian community-in-exile. This weakness proved to be a crucial aspect of the Belgian positions regarding the negotiations over the contribution to the Allied war effort.

It would not be surprising to see Gutt, as a former businessman and finance minister within the Belgian government-in-exile, playing an important role in these negotiations. However, there were more fundamental reasons explaining his involvement. First, if the Belgians did not have a lot to offer to the British and then later to the Americans in terms of troops, their gold reserves sent before the Second World War to London and the rich resources of the Belgian Congo, constituted their main assets. This put financial diplomacy at the heart of Belgian foreign policy during the Second World War. Secondly, Gutt quickly emerged as one of the very few Belgians in London to have a clear view of Belgian war aims and, more importantly, of the strategy to adopt in the negotiations with the British and the Americans.

Indeed, the use by the Belgians of their valuable economic assets as bargaining chips for possible postwar demands entailed a number of unresolved issues. The first question was the one of defining the war aims: to what political aims could these resources be used? The second question was the one of consensus among the Belgians outside occupied Belgium, not only politicians but also business representatives, especially in the Belgian Congo itself: how to reconcile political objectives with particular business interests? With the coming of the Americans, a third question arose, which concerned the choice between the main Allies: whom to favour, the British, the Americans or both?

Gutt played an important role in shaping most of the decisions of the Belgian government-in-exile on these issues. In the process, he also experienced the limits of the devotion of the Belgian business community-in-exile towards the Allied cause. Finally, he had to deal with a complex situation of multiple centres of decision-making – in London, in New York and in the Belgian Congo – working at times in different directions and, worse, with conflicting objectives.

This chapter will be devoted to the three main issues mentioned above with a focus on Gutt. The first part deals with the reconstitution of the Belgian government-in-exile in London. The second addresses the negotiations over the Belgian contribution to the British war effort while the third looks at the negotiations led with the Americans. In each of these three parts, the interplay between private interests and national interests as shaped by the policy of the Belgian government-in-exile will be emphasized.

Reconstituting the Belgian Government in London

The events that led a handful of ministers to reconstitute a Belgian government-in-exile have given rise to abundant literature in Belgium, usually centred on the King's position and his relations with his ministers. These events proved to play an important role in Belgian history as they contributed to the well-known 'Royal Question' or the question of the future of Leopold III as the King of the Belgians in 1949.[3]

In short, on 28 May 1940, Leopold III decided to capitulate the Germans and declared himself a prisoner against the will of his ministers who begged him to follow them and leave the country. This decision raised a number of constitutional issues and created some real difficulty for the Belgian government. Indeed, in leaving Belgium, the Belgian ministers cut themselves from the King. As a solution they decided, with the support of the Belgian members of Parliament present in Limoges, to vote a resolution declaring the impossibility for the King to reign and their intention to continue fighting alongside the Allies. These dramatic events led to an irremediable divorce between King Leopold III and Prime Minister Pierlot.

On 18 June, the news of the French capitulation considerably undermined all remaining Belgian hopes. However, on the previous day, in Bordeaux, Gutt had met his former colleagues of the Société Générale de Belgique who asked him to go to London with Albert de Vleeschauwer, the Belgian minister of colonies. For such business representatives, the stakes were indeed high as far as their foreign assets were concerned let alone their strategic interests in the Belgian Congo. On 18 June, the Belgian ministers met again and only two pronounced themselves in favour of continuing the struggle alongside the British. These two ministers were Gutt and Marcel-Henri Jaspar. The latter decided to leave France in haste to London and tried to constitute a Belgian legal entity with the support of some other Belgian politicians who had already arrived in the English capital (see below). But at same cabinet meeting, the Prime Minister Pierlot warned his ministers of the need to safeguard Belgian interests in the Congo. He suggested to them to send the Belgian Minister of Colonies to the Congo with extended powers. This idea was rejected by Gutt who thought that it would divide the government. On the same day, de Vleeschauwer met this time with Cattier, another important business figure linked with the colonial interests of the Societé Générale de Belgique, who repeated the message of the evening before of the need to send a limited number of ministers to London. However, as far as the government was concerned, the decision was taken to abandon the fight.[4]

At this moment, Gutt was very discouraged. After having fought his colleagues unsuccessfully, he decided to follow the majority. In this context, he had to think about his future and his family's future. A return to Brussels looked increasingly impossible to envisage. His wife, Claire Gutt, had managed to send him a message in which she warned him of the situation in occupied Belgium and the fear of racist persecutions.[5] According to Gutt, even if he considered that his reputation as 'banker, liberal and a Jew'[6] (see Chapter 1) was unfounded, there was no doubt that the Nazi could declare 'Jewish anyone they want'.[7] In reality, Gutt learned in 1943 that his wife had been several times summoned to the *Kommandantur* in Brussels where she had been interrogated as to her husband's membership of the Freemasons as well as whether he should be considered Jewish. Claire Gutt had confirmed that her husband's family was Protestant.[8]

In any case, and as far as his future was concerned, Gutt thought of going to New York or London and resuming his business activities either for the copper cartel or for an important Belgian bank such as the Banque Belge pour l'Etranger or even for the Belgian multinational Solvay.[9] Then, a number of key events revived Gutt's conviction of the need to go to London in order to continue fighting alongside the British.

Instead of the Congo, the Belgian minister of colonies decided, after a stop in Lisbon, to go to London. There he met with a number of Belgian business figures and several British Cabinet ministers including Churchill who asked him: 'Where is the government? Why isn't it coming?'[10] As a result of these meetings, the need was felt to send at least a limited number of Belgian ministers to London, more particularly, the Prime Minister Pierlot, Foreign Affairs Minister Spaak and Finance Minister Gutt. At that time the latter, who was staying in Vichy, made a last attempt to contact Leopold III in order to convince the King to reconsider his views and to support the government in the possibility of continuing the war.[11]

When Gutt met his wife, Claire, in late July in Vichy, she asked her husband why the ministers had not yet gone to London to continue to fight alongside the British. In the meeting, the two also made a series of private arrangements concerning their three sons who were to be sent to England. As for Gutt's wife, she decided to return to Brussels in order not to give the impression of fleeing.[12]

Gutt also received a series of letters from some high-profile Belgian economic figures, such as Raoul Richard and Hubert Ansiaux, all prompted by Theunis and all leading to the same idea: that the war was not over. Therefore, Gutt was urged to go to London. These messages also informed Gutt of the manoeuvres in London to form a new Belgian legal entity and the need to have at least several ministers in Britain.[13]

So, towards the end of July, Gutt was resolved to go to London. However, he agreed to postpone his trip in order to meet de Vleeschauwer, the Belgian minister of colonies, along with his colleagues, Pierlot and Spaak, at a secret meeting on the Franco-Spanish border at a place called Le Perthus. At this meeting, the three ministers listened with attention to de Vleeschauwer who told them about the importance for all of them to be in London. The four agreed and decided to go in two stages. At first, only Gutt and de Vleeschauwer would leave, via Spain and Portugal. Spaak and Pierlot were to follow but not before meeting a last time with their colleagues of the government remaining in Vichy. On 8 August, Gutt and de Vleeschauwer arrived in London. They would be reunited on 22 October with their two colleagues.[14]

A final aspect of Gutt's activities during the period between May and July 1940 concerned the financial and monetary relations with Britain and France. On 14 May 1940, the Belgians concluded with the French a payment agreement very similar to the Reynaud–Simon financial and monetary agreement of December 1939 but with a new parity for the Belgian currency at 100 Belgian francs for 144,44 French francs. In the aftermath of Belgium's capitulation, however, the French demanded that the Belgian franc be further devalued to be put it at parity with their currency. The Belgians and the French also agreed to extend their agreement to the British on 25 May 1940. Later in June, and as a consequence of the new parity between Belgian and French currencies, a new parity between the pound and the Belgian franc was established at the rate of 176,625. The French capitulation led to a further change in these parities. On 9 July 1940, the previous parity of May 1940 between the Belgian franc and the French franc was restored while the new parity between the Belgian franc and the pound was only changed in October, from 176,625 to 123. This change allowed the Belgian Central Bank to pay much less for the French francs that the Belgian refugees would convert to Belgian francs when back in Belgium.[15]

When Gutt and de Vleeschauwer arrived in London on 8 August, both Belgian ministers had to face a series of difficulties. With respect to their former colleague, Jaspar, they had to deal with his attempt at creating a new Belgian legal entity with the members of Parliament who had already arrived in the British capital. In New York, some high-profile Belgian business and political figures such as van Zeeland also tried to organize themselves in some sort of Belgian National Committee. Finally, the two ministers were also confronted with Leopold III's reluctance to acknowledge their legitimacy. In messages sent to them in October via the Belgian Ambassador in Berne, the King conveyed the position that, according to him, the war was over and that from that point on, the Belgians had to show the Germans courtesy and respect. Eventually, in January 1941, the King gave in and abstained from directly challenging the legitimacy of the Belgian ministers in London.[16]

Thanks to British support, however, the two ministers were able to impose themselves progressively on the rest of the Belgian political figures in London. In return, the Belgian members of Parliament residing in the British capital were given a number of tasks and were regrouped into a Consultative Committee with almost no real powers. Nevertheless, the two Belgian ministers found it difficult to be fully acknowledged as the legal Belgian government by the British. But on 3 October, Gutt and de Vleeschauwer won their first battle when authorized to express themselves on the BBC as the only legal Belgian authorities.[17]

Only Spaak's and Pierlot's arrival in London on 22 October clarified the situation. The Belgian government then consisted of four ministers and was enlarged to include additional former ministers arriving in London during the war and other Belgian high-profile personalities who were given the position of under-secretary of state. However, because of the links established during the summer of 1940 and the compelling necessity to stick together, it was the four ministers, Pierlot, Gutt, Spaak and de Vleeschauwer, who constituted the backbone of the Belgian government-in-exile in London during the Second World War (see Table 2.1).

Table 2.1: Composition of the Belgian government-in-exile in London.

Name	Positions within the Belgian government-in-exile
Hubert Pierlot	Prime minister (1939–45); Minister of education (1939–44); Minister of defence (1942–4)
Camille Gutt	Finance minister (1939–45); Minister of economic affairs (1940–4); Minister of defence (1940–2)
Paul-Henri Spaak	Foreign affairs minister (1939–45); Minister of propaganda (1940–2); Relief and refugees minister (1940–4)
Albert de Vleeschauwer	Minister of colonies (1939–44); Minister of justice (1940–2)
Antoine Delfosse	Minister of justice and propaganda (1942–4)
August De Schryver	Home Office minister (1943–4)
Herman Balthazar	Minister of communications (1943–4)
Henri Rolin	Undersecretary of state for defence under Gutt's authority in 1942
Gustave Joassart	Undersecretary of state for relief under Spaak's authority (1942–3)
Julius Hoste	Undersecretary of state for education under Pierlot's authority (1942–4)
Joseph Bondas	Undersecretary of state for relief and work (1943–4) under Pierlot's authority
Raoul Richard	Undersecretary of state for relief (1943-4) under Spaak's authority

As for Gutt, he had to constitute his own team of advisors. Fortunately, he could rely on some qualified staff working for the Belgian Economic Mission established in London in May 1940. First, Gutt called upon two officials from the Belgian Central Bank, Adolphe Baudewijns and his junior colleague, Ansiaux, who were given responsibility over the Belgian gold reserves. To deal with other economic issues such as shipping, Gutt recruited André van Campenhout, a Belgian jurist trained in Britain. Finally, he decided to turn to the current head of the Belgian Economic Mission, René Boël. This last appointment proved to be the most challenging one for the Belgian minister. Indeed, Boël was not only an important business figure as the inheritor of the Boël group active in the fields of chemicals and steel production in Belgium. He was also related to the Solvay family, and in this respect had been entrusted the control over the Solvay assets in the Free World. These assets were of considerable importance as Solvay had imposed itself as a major Belgian multinational in the fields of chemicals and banking.

In London, Boël solicited the minister to be appointed at a position reflecting his expertise and rank. In addition to a high function, Boël also asked for a nice title. Finally, after many exchanges of letters, Gutt agreed to propose the appointment of Boël as Advisor to the Belgian government on a temporary basis. If Gutt appreciated Boël's skills and expertise, he was always aware of his advisor's inclination to play his business interests over his political missions (see below).

Finally, Gutt was still looking for a trustworthy Chief of Cabinet. He finally found the solution when in April 1941 he hired Ernest de Selliers de Moranville, a young Belgian diplomat in Canada who also had a strong legal background.

The Belgian Contribution to the British War Effort

As soon as Gutt arrived in London, he paid special attention to the question of Belgian war aims. In reality, some first small steps had already been undertaken prior to the minister's arrival in London. In the English capital, Boël worked within the Anglo-French Coordination Committee headed by Jean Monnet and Arthur Purvis[18]. In July 1940, he was appointed the Head of the Belgian Economic Mission. Other Belgian officials from the Belgian Central Bank such Ansiaux and Baudewijns had to wait, first for the coming to London of de Vleeschauwer and then of Gutt, to see their power over the Belgian gold reserves recognized by the British. During Gutt's absence, the main negotiations concerned the Belgian contribution to the British war effort in terms of shipping. During his first visit to London, de Vleeschauwer confirmed the first agreements regarding shipping and agreed to give the British the gold from the Belgian Congo. Both agreements gave rise to numerous objections from the Belgian business community, especially in the Congo, but also from occupied Belgium and from the King himself, who considered the war over and thought that the Belgian Colony should remain neutral.[19]

With Gutt's arrival, the real negotiations could start. The Belgian minister was well aware of the two main cards that the Belgians had at their disposal in their negotiations with the British – the Belgian gold and the resources from the Congo. Gutt was strongly involved in the first issue while the second was handled mostly by the minister of colonies and the authorities in the Belgian Congo. In contrast to the other governments-in-exile or representatives in London, the Belgians had indeed the great advantage of relying on such resources. For example, Charles de Gaulle and the Free French were completely dependent on British financial support to carry out their activities.

Under the regime of Cash and Carry established by the Americans in September 1939, the British had to pay for their supplies of vital war materials. The Treasury, which found itself short of gold and hard currencies, did not have another choice but to turn to Britain's European allies, who had gold reserves in London. By far, the Belgian gold reserves transferred to the Bank of England and amounting to more than 10 billion Belgian Francs or 59 million pounds were the most important and soon the only ones available (see below).

If Gutt played an important role in these negotiations, it is not only because of his ministerial responsibilities but also owing to the important number of old acquaintances he met in the corridors of Whitehall and at the Bank of England. Besides the fact that he was by far the most fluent in English in contrast to Pierlot and especially Spaak whose English was almost non-existent while de Vleeschauwer undertook to learn it while in London. At the same time, Gutt, who was obsessed by Belgian experience at the end of the First World War, was not ready to do any favours and was determined to bargain for what he considered Belgium's best interests. In doing so, however, he had to participate in the discussions aiming at defining a new foreign policy doctrine with respect to the future relations between Britain and Belgium for the postwar period.

Gutt in London: Old Acquaintances and First Contacts

When Gutt arrived in London, in August 1940, he was by no means in *terra incognita*. In contrast to the rest of his colleagues within the Belgian government-in-exile, he had already a rich experience in Britain. In London, Gutt was reunited with a number of old acquaintances in Whitehall, especially at the Treasury. Among these, a number had served during the interwar period such as Leith-Ross, Richard Hopkins and David Sigismund Waley also known as 'Sigi'. At the Bank of England, Gutt had already met with its governor Montagu Norman and his main adviser, Arthur Siepmann. But if a number of old-timers were still active in the corridors of power in London, the civil service had undertaken reforms as early as 1938 that led to opening Whitehall to the experience of outsiders such as academics and high-profile businessmen. These people represented the *irregulars* in the British civil service. Amongst these included a number of people whom Gutt knew already from its interwar activities such as MacFadeyan[20] and Lord Perry, his former boss at Ford, as well as some old acquaintances in the non-ferrous metals sector such as Beatty, Budd and Lyttleton, without mentioning Keynes himself.[21] In short, Gutt resumed contact with that transnational elite that had haunted the corridors of interwar international financial diplomacy.

It is no surprise that a few days after arriving in London, Gutt first met with Salter, Leith-Ross and the new chancellor of the Exchequer, John Kingsley Wood. The first issue that Gutt wanted to raise was the one of a possible British relief to occupied Belgium.[22] Two weeks later, on 26 August, Gutt alongside his colleague, the minister of colonies, met with Churchill at 10 Downing Street. At the meeting, the two Belgian ministers confirmed their willingness to put the Belgian resources, including the ones of the Belgian Congo, at the disposal of the British war effort. They also told Churchill about their project of setting up a small Belgian military force of about 1,000–2,000 men. In exchange, the Belgian ministers asked, on top of restoring Belgian independence, to make the country the closest possible associate of the British Empire. At this stage, however, the British, who still questioned the position of the two ministers, refused to commit themselves to the Belgian demands.[23]

Belgian War Aims and Anglo-Belgian Relations

If Gutt was well aware of the importance of the Belgian Congo for the British war effort, he preferred nevertheless to concentrate his attention on the Belgian gold reserves kept at the Bank of England. Several reasons may explain this decision. First, there is no doubt that, as finance minister, Gutt had more leverage in the negotiations with the British Treasury than with respect to the Congo. Secondly, Gutt knew very well how badly the British needed the gold belonging to the Allied governments for their purchases in the US under the Cash and Carry System especially after the Dutch and the Norwegians refused to part with their own reserves.[24] There was, however, for Gutt no question of relinquishing these gold reserves without taking account of Belgian demands. Indeed, the memories of the aftermath of the First World War were still vivid in his mind. Then, with Theunis, he had had to fight hard to have Belgium's rights acknowledged by the two big Allies – France and Britain – not mentioning the issue of the German reparations that left a bitter taste of injustice with both of them. The question remained, though: which demands?

In this respect, the Belgians decided to resort to a old document dating back to 1916 and called the Sainte Adresse Declaration. It was used by the Belgian government as soon as the German offensive on Belgium on 10 May 1940.[25] This Declaration had been drawn after considerable discussions amongst the Belgians in exile as to Belgium's war aims at the end of the First World War. The documents included four demands: first, the restoration of Belgium's political and economic independence; second, the guarantee of a seat at the table of the peace negotiations; third, compensations for the war damage; and fourth, Allied support of Belgian post-conflict rehabilitation. An annex to this document related to the extension of these guarantees to the Belgian Congo.

The way the document was used is also telling of the lack of thinking of the Belgian political circles in terms of foreign policy objectives during the interwar period. However, for Belgians like Gutt, the Sainte Addresse Declaration was considered insufficient. Indeed, the Declaration concerned mostly political objectives and not enough possible economic ones. This can be explained by the legacy of Belgium's interwar economic situation. With respect to trade, Belgium had severely suffered from the greater economic and monetary fragmentation of the Continent. The only Belgian achievement in this field was the conclusion, in 1932, of the Ouchy convention by which its three signatories, Belgium, Luxembourg and the Netherlands committed themselves to tariff reduction. The three countries, however, failed to include both France and Britain in the scheme. As a result, Belgium and the Belgian Congo were hit hard by the Ottawa agreements, concluded in the same year. A consequence of these agreements was the closing off of the Commonwealth to Belgian trade while the Congo, in compliance with the Berlin agreements of 1885, had to keep a regime of open-doors (see Chapter 4).

There is no surprise then that the Belgians in exile in London, including Gutt, saw the negotiation over the Belgian gold as an unique opportunity to put forward some additional economic demands to the British government. The main one that quickly met with a large consensus in London was that Belgium's economy was to be included in the Commonwealth. In September 1940, this demand was formally drawn by the Belgian Foreign Affairs Ministry in London asking for Belgium to be offered a similar trading status as the one offered to the countries part of the Ottawa agreements of 1932.[26]

The negotiations over Belgian gold began at the beginning of October. The Treasury did not make a secret of its interest in these precious reserves. It even proposed to the Belgians to buy them. In exchange, the Treasury would supply the Belgians with sterling and dollars. But Gutt was not duped and rejected the offer on two grounds. On the one hand, in exchange for its gold, Belgium would inherit sterling whose postwar value was still far from certain. On the other hand, it would make the Belgian Treasury completely dependent on British control.[27]

When receiving the letter from the Treasury confirming the British position, Gutt was well aware of the strategic importance of the Belgian gold. Therefore, when replying to his British opposite number, he decided not to restrict his letter to the issue of the Belgian gold but to include also demands for closer economic ties with Britain. Interestingly, Gutt's letter mostly emphasized the Belgian demands in the field of economic cooperation but not the more political ones. The letter was indeed based on a memo written by van Langenhove in which the Belgian diplomat explicitly insisted on the need to preserve Belgium's freedom in her relation with a bigger power such as Britain.[28]

As a result, in his letter, Gutt made the British aware of his conviction that as the post-First Wold War period had shown, Belgium would not be able to count on hypothetical German reparations. At the same time, the British economy, even weakened as a result of the war, would still be able to maintain her supremacy. In this light, Gutt reminded the chancellor of the failed efforts of Belgium towards trade liberalization during the 1930s and concluded that an economic association with Britain would be natural in the context of the cooperation between the two countries. In other words, the Belgians were considering nothing less than entering the Ottawa agreements of 1932. This possibility was based on a double rationale. First, the Belgians were eager for Belgium to participate in a multilateral trading scheme and feared to find their economy at the end of the Second World War isolated as had been the case during the 1930s. Second, there was an important dimension linked to the situation in the Belgian Congo. It was indeed imperative for the colonial products to be treated on an equal footing with the ones produced in the British Empire.

Addressing finally the question of the Belgian gold, Gutt proposed instead of selling it to the British, to lend it to them. In exchange, the British would supply the Belgians with the needed dollars and sterling.[29]

The first reply to Gutt's letter came from Waley who told him that the Belgian demands could not be addressed by the Treasury but would be instead handled by the Board of Trade. As to Gutt's proposal about a possible lending offer of Belgian gold, Waley was clear in his refusal and repeated the British offer for a purchase agreement.[30] Only on 14 November did Gutt receive a response from the chancellor of the Exchequer, Kingsley Wood, who restricted his letter to the financial aspects of the question while repeating his refusal of Gutt's proposal to lend the Belgian gold and leaving the rest to be dealt with the Foreign Office. Meanwhile, Lord Halifax, who had met with Pierlot and Spaak, freshly arrived from France, discussed with the Belgian ministers only some general aspects of Belgian–British relations.[31]

In reality, the Foreign Office was extremely reserved about the Belgian demands. The lack of commitment in favour of foregoing the old principles of the *policy of independence* was very much regretted. As for Belgium's entry with the Congo in the Commonwealth, the issue raised a number of problems. First, the Americans were set against the preferences system as it would show in the negotiations on the Atlantic Charter in August 1941. Second, the other Dominions had also to give their agreement. Finally, there was a clear risk for the British to see themselves swamped with similar demands from their other European allies.[32]

However, in his reply to the Belgians, Halifax did not seem to completely reject their demands even if he still remained vague as to any commitment for the postwar period. For Gutt, there was no doubt that Halifax's reply was a perfect example of *Foreign Office style* empty of any real commitments but having the merit of slightly opening the door for future discussions. As he emphasized: 'this is an opportunity that we have to seize. To get results in these discussions would mean to achieve what no other government has been able to do since 1919.'[33]

From November onwards, the discussions were to be divided between the two Belgian ministers. The financial and technical aspects of the operation concerning the Belgian gold were devolved to Gutt and his team and to Spaak its political aspects.

On 26 December, Gutt had a meeting with Kingsley Wood and Hopkins at the Treasury to discuss the modalities on which the British could use the Belgian gold. It became clear that the two sides still disagreed on the best formula to choose. In the following days, the Treasury through Arthur Siepmann tried to put some pressure on Gutt's advisor, Baudewijns, threatening the Belgians with a possible British requisition of their gold reserves in London.[34] The British government, though, aware of Gutt's strong position, agreed on the lending formula instead of a purchasing one.[35] So, in February 1941, the Belgians and the British finally discussed the different aspects of the lending solution. After some more discussions, the two sides agreed on a loan of the Belgian gold to the British. It was up to the British to refund the Belgians in monthly instalments for a period up to 5 years. The agreement was finally signed on 4 March 1941.[36]

On the political front, the discussions between Spaak and Halifax proved to be even more difficult. When meeting Halifax's successor, Antony Eden, Spaak gave him a new Belgian memo containing the same demands as the one included in the former letter to Kingsley Wood. The question was settled by the British War Cabinet on 10 February with the approval of the memo drafted by Sir Alexander Cadogan, permanent undersecretary at the Foreign Office. The Cadogan Memorandum was even less encouraging in terms of a possible postwar economic and political cooperation between the two countries than Halifax's letter. If it contained a number of commitments regarding the restoration of Belgium's sovereignty and territorial integrity, including the Belgian Congo, it subjected any future postwar cooperation to the prevailing conditions at the end of the war.[37] A few days later, Spaak had no other choice that to accept the Cadogan Memorandum.[38]

As far as the Belgian Congo's contribution to the British war effort was concerned, Gutt also took part in the negotiations that led to the conclusion of two agreements, both signed on 21 January 1941. The first agreement covered the financial aspects of the relations between the Belgian Congo and Britain. Its main clause confirmed the parity between the Congolese currency and sterling back to 176,625 as well as the entry of the colonial economy in the sterling zone. This led to a situation of two different parities, one of 123 for the Belgian currency and one of 176 for the Congolese currency, towards the sterling. The second agreement concerned mostly the purchasing conditions of Congolese products by Britain on the same basis as the ones coming from the other Dominions.[39]

To the British, these two agreements ensured that both the supplies of gold from the Belgian colony and the entry of the Congo in the British change control mechanism.[40] For the Belgians, these agreements reflected their desire of seeing the Congo enter the Ottawa agreements without having to commit themselves too much with respect to Belgium's future foreign policy.[41]

Nevertheless, the implementation of these agreements would prove to be a constant source of problems owing to the complex division of power within the Belgian government-in-exile between Gutt and de Vleeschauwer and between the Belgian government and the colonial authorities and business representatives. In short, the latter, supported by their own minister, were dragging their feet in supplying the British as well as the Belgian Treasury. The Belgian business representatives in the Congo were indeed relying on the fact that they possessed their own central bank and currency to oppose the idea of a financial solidarity with the Belgian government-in-exile in London as well as with Britain.[42] In fact, these formal reasons concealed some deeper political and economic realities. From a political point of view, many in the Belgian Congo, including the apostolic vicar, Mgr de Hemptine, were very much set against the Belgian government in London. Instead, they voiced their support for King Leopold III and for a neutral position for the Congo in the conflict. From an economic point of view, the big extracting colonial companies were complaining about the prices set by the British for the purchase of their production. The situation reached such a low point that Belgian Prime Minister Pierlot deemed necessary, in August 1942, to go to the Belgian Congo in order to discuss these issues with the local political and business representatives, but without producing any concrete results.[43]

In reality, the US entry in the war, in December 1941, opened new perspectives for colonial businesses as well as possibilities of acquiring dollars rather than accumulating sterling balances. In this context, the British and the Americans decided in 1942 to organize their supplies from the Belgian colonial supplies through the negotiation of a new tripartite agreement. However, the project failed owing to the reluctance of the Belgian colonial authorities. As a solution, the British proposed the establishment of a Tripartite Committee in the Belgian Congo which entailed the further weakening of the grip of London on Belgian Congolese interests.[44]

More concretely, these negotiations showed the extent to which the Belgians in London were unable to use the Congo as a political levy in their relations with the British. As a result, the Belgian gold proved to be the only card for the Belgians, even if the final agreement fell short of their demands. Despite such setbacks, the British option remained high on the agenda of the Belgian government-in-exile and of Gutt in particular (see Chapter 4).

British–Belgian wartime relations were also marked by other important issues, such as the organization of relief for occupied Belgium, the pooling of resources and a special agreement defining the relationship between the Belgian Congo and the Allies. As far as the first issue is concerned, the Belgians were quite unsuccessful. For Gutt, the failure to secure British relief for the Belgian population in the occupied country had equally to do with Churchill's intransigence and with the lack of opportunism of his colleagues, especially the prime minister, in their handling of the question. Indeed, when meeting with Churchill in the direct aftermath of the conclusion of the two agreements sealing Belgian–British wartime economic and financial cooperation, the Belgian prime minister failed to win over his British counterpart on the issue of possible relief for the population in occupied Belgium. With respect to the pooling of resources discussed in the aftermath of the adoption of the Atlantic Charter by the Allies at the St James conference of 24 September 1941, Gutt advocated further cooperation between the Allied nations. He had to face, however, the reluctance of countries like the Netherlands and Norway to fully participate in such a cooperation.[45]

Belgian Contribution to the War Effort: American–Belgian Relations

The wartime relationship between the Belgians in exile and the Americans presented a very different picture from the one with the British. At first, the Belgians put great hopes in the US, especially with respect to a possible relief in the occupied territory. For this, they relied on the experience of the First World War when American relief was channelled to Belgium under the aegis of Herbert Hoover and his Commission for Relief. At the same time, the Belgians in exile remained extremely suspicious of the Americans. Here again, the experience of the First World War and of its direct aftermath played an important role. The Belgians indeed remembered how the Americans asked their allies to repay the loans contracted in the US during the conflict.[46] In short, they lived in the fear of a repetition of such an episode at the end of the Second World War.

When Theunis was appointed, in September 1939, as Belgian ambassador-at-large in the US, he first lived for a few months in Washington. However, with the outbreak of the war, his mission changed completely (see Chapter 1). Aware of the need to strengthen the economic relations with the US, Theunis decided in June 1940 to settle in New York. In the financial metropolis, he only found a moribund Belgian consulate. He also had to face an important community of Belgians in exile, consisting of former Belgian ministers and businessmen. Among them, the presence of van Zeeland revealed to be the most problematic. When leaving Belgian politics in 1938, van Zeeland had accepted the offer made by the American businessman and president of the originally Belgian–British multinational Société Financière de Transports et d'Entreprises Industrielles (SOFINA) Dannie Heinemann, to enter the Board of the Compania Hispano-Americana de Eletricidad (CHADE), the main affiliate company of SOFINA in South America. But van Zeeland had not lost hope of regaining some high-profile position in the Belgian government. Indeed, it was rumoured he was lobbying to be appointed as the new Belgian Ambassador in Washington or at least a special Belgian representative responsible for Belgian colonial interests in the US.[47] The threat was all too real when Spaak, Belgian foreign affairs minister, on a trip to US, mentioned his willingness to replace the Belgian ambassador in Washington. As a result, Theunis ended up defending the current ambassador, even though he considered him inadequate, in order to prevent his possible replacement by van Zeeland (see below).[48]

During the war, Theunis remained in New York. In doing so, he was naturally cut off from the political circles in Washington. To make matters worse, Wall Street bankers, such as Winthrop Aldrich and James Warburg were still highly critical of the New Dealers in Washington.[49] In time, however, and following the adoption of the Lend-Lease legislation, in March 1941, the Roosevelt administration opened itself to business circles by appointing people such as William S. Knudsen in charge of the new Office for Production Management, Edward Stettinius Jr, as head of the Lend-Lease administration and Donald Nelson at the War Production Board.[50]

Nevertheless, Theunis still found it difficult to deal with a new generation of lawyers and economists proposing a higher regulation of the economy. On occasion, he did not hesitate to refer to them as 'the dictators of economic life in the USA'. [51] At a more personal level, Theunis's acquaintances in New York consisted of people that had been active during the preceding Coolidge and Hoover administrations such as Dawes and Young and who had almost retreated from politics.[52] His only politically active friend was no less than Hoover himself. However, Hoover, who still nourished the hope of taking his revenge on Roosevelt since his unexpected defeat of 1932, proved quickly to be a huge liability for the Belgians. Indeed, Theunis was deeply involved in the Belgian efforts to convince the Americans to organize some forms of relief for the population in occupied Belgium. In this respect, Hoover (who had been at the origin of a vast American relief effort during the First World War) was trying to set up a similar system but not without political aims of a hypothetical revenge against Roosevelt. However, his association with controversial personalities such as the pilot Charles S. Lindbergh, a well-known isolationist and Nazi sympathizer considerably contributed to tarnishing his reputation and he was considered by some as a Germanophile.[53] Even Hull who had some sympathy for Hoover quite straightforwardly rejected his proposals. As he put it in his memoirs: 'I further believe that it was the duty of the occupying nation, Germany, and not the United States, to feed the conquered peoples. We could not afford to assist Hitler by relieving him of his obligations.'[54]

In 1941, Gutt tried unsuccessfully to convince the Americans to allow relief in occupied Belgium. In a meeting with Roosevelt in May he realized the extent to which the situation had become hopeless.[55] Later in October, Spaak would reach the same conclusion after meeting the US President. In December, the US entry in the war ruined all remaining Belgian hopes for American relief. Some further initiatives were taken, and further meetings took place in 1942 and 1943, all producing the same result of the American refusal.[56]

Among the Republicans, Theunis was well acquainted with the lawyer and future Eisenhower's secretary of state, John Foster Dulles, who, as senior partner in the prestigious law firm, Sullivan & Cromwell, had the reputation of the being the best paid lawyer on Wall Street. Theunis had known Dulles since the Versailles Peace conference, where the latter served as junior member of the American delegation of the Reparations Commission

In New York, Dulles was also defending Belgian business interests such as, for example, the ones of the Belgian multinational Solvay. In 1941, Theunis also asked Dulles to represent the Belgian Central Bank in its lawsuit against the French central Bank (see Chapter 4). Contrary to the other American acquaintances of Theunis, Dulles was also working for the Roosevelt administration which was eager to foster some bipartisanship consensus, mostly with respect to foreign policy.[57]

In short, Theunis's position in New York contrasted greatly with that of Gutt in London. If the latter could rely on numerous contacts – at the Treasury, the Bank of England and even within the Cabinet – the former was much more politically isolated and still prisoner of old networks built during the 1920s whose members had either retired from politics or were even opposed to the Roosevelt administration. This situation that could be subsumed as knowing the wrong men at the wrong places considerably affected the relations between Belgium and the US during the Second World War.

At a more political level, things did not look much better. First, Theunis complained repeatedly about the lack of liaison with Spaak, Belgian foreign minister, who replied that as the first was in constant touch with Gutt, there was no need for him to write to Theunis too frequently. Secondly, Theunis considered that Robert Vander Straeten-Ponthoz, the Belgian ambassador in Washington, who was at the end of his career, showed considerable weakness in his handling of Belgian–American relations. In the aftermath of the US declaration of war to Japan, the Belgian diplomat only told the Americans that Belgium had just broken its diplomatic relations with Japan. Finally, it would take 19 days for the Belgians to formally consider themselves at war with Japan.[58] Much worse was still to come. In the autumn of 1941, when Spaak made his first trip to the US, his meetings with both Cordell Hull and Roosevelt proved to be rather unsuccessful. Not only did the President create a bad impression on him but Spaak's lack of English was an additional problem – he was unable to say anything to his American counterpart, Hull.[59]

All these problems reflected the political neglect of the US by the Belgians in exile during the Second World War. In April 1944, Spaak's main advisor, van Langenhove, concluded in a memo that Belgian–American relations just consisted of economic questions linked with the discussions relating to the issue of the Belgian assets in the US, the Lend-Lease agreement and the negotiation of the future Bretton Woods agreement.[60] In short, the Belgians completely overlooked the political aspects of their relationship with the US, preferring to concentrate on their relationship with Britain which they considered as their main partner for postwar reconstruction. In this context, American–Belgian wartime relations could be defined under the concept of privatization. Under this concept, we refer to the overall importance of private interests in the shaping of foreign policy decisions. This dimension has been somewhat overlooked by traditional diplomatic history that failed to capture the stakes and political implications of these negotiations.[61] Apart from the question of relief, this privatization can be found to different degrees in the three following issues: the issue of Belgian assets in US; the Lend-Lease negotiations; and the negotiations over Belgian uranium.

First Case of Privatization: The Question of the Belgian Assets in the US

With the adoption of the Trade with the Enemy Act of 1940 and the First President Act of 1941, the Roosevelt administration froze all assets, first the ones belonging to belligerent nations and then to enemy nations in order to make sure that they would not be used towards the German war efforts. This meant that Belgian assets in the US were blocked.[62] The question of their release was of primary interest to their owners in the Free World. The Belgian government was also concerned with them as they could be useful for the country's war effort or its postwar reconstruction. The Belgian assets in the US and in Canada were estimated at 750 million dollars out of the total of more than 8 billion seized.[63] It would take more than two years for the Belgian authorities to recover the more than 5 billion dollars worth of Belgian gold held at the Federal Reserve Bank in New York.[64] To reassure the American authorities, the Belgian government adopted new legislation in February 1942 dealing with the situation of Belgian assets outside occupied Belgium. In the direct aftermath of the adoption of this measure, the Belgian government, on Gutt's suggestion, also decided to send a mission to the US with the objective of negotiating the release of the Belgian assets. The mission was directed by Boël and van Campenhout. The former was particularly interested in the issue as the official representative of Solvay's interests in the Free World while the latter was a lawyer and civil servant. For the Belgian businessman, eager to defend his own interests, there was no doubt that the Americans were just waiting to seize the opportunity to take possession of the Belgian assets in their territory.[65]

In the US, the two Belgian negotiators had to face a rather hostile climate. The Americans had already given the FBI the mission to check Sengier's activities in New York while Belgian assets such as the one belonging to the Société Générale de Belgique were considered highly suspicious (see below). In addition, the Belgians suffered from the lack of insider contacts within the Roosevelt administration and could only rely on a list quickly compiled by Dulles. Finally and to make matters worse, Boël's insistence on the situation relating to his own Solvay assets became such a source of embarrassment that Dulles had to tell him to stop his personal pursuit.[66]

In reality, the two Belgian negotiators experienced the existing rivalries between the different agencies within the Roosevelt administration. The Treasury was eager to retain full control of these foreign assets in the US while the State Department was ready to contemplate their release while raising some legal concerns about the possibility of applying Belgian legislation in the US. Finally, Adolf Berle for the State Department suggested that the Belgian assets be submitted a positive control only. In other words, the American authorities would recognize the authority of their Belgian owners if they complied with American legislation.[67] But, on their return to London, the two Belgian negotiators were forced to acknowledge that they had not succeeded to convince the Americans to release fully the Belgian assets even though they remained hopeful of a possible reversal of the American position.[68]

In June 1943, when Gutt left for the US to discuss Belgian monetary policy and the Keynes–White monetary plans, he decided to bring up the issue with the US officials. But this time, and after meeting with White and then with Acheson, Gutt learned that the problems came in fact from the State Department and not from the Treasury. Indeed, Acheson told him that for the time being the administration wanted to keep its right of control over all foreign assets in the US. In this light, any recognition of Belgian legislation by the Americans would deprive the US administration of such preventive control.[69] Gutt was quite amazed at the American position. As he wrote in a memo addressed to Spaak:

> It does not seem believable to me that, after a war fought for the rule of law and for democracy over dictatorship, the United States would neglect such an important right as the one that would allow Belgians, who sought refuge within the USA, to reclaim assets that were rightly theirs.[70]

In October 1943, Boël and then the diplomat Hervé de Gruben tried again to negotiate the issue but without much success despite of some assurances given by Pehle from the FFC that the Belgian assets would not be used as guarantees for future Belgian war debts.[71] In the immediate term, however, this still unsettled question considerably shaped Belgian attitudes towards the negotiation of the Lend-Lease agreement with the Americans.

Second Case of Privatization: Mutual Aid Agreement with the US

In November 1940, when the US Congress finally consented to amend the Neutrality Act, the British were able to buy supplies from the US on condition of paying for them and ensuring their shipping to Britain. After Roosevelt's third election, the American administration designed a new regime that would alleviate the British from their lack of hard currency and gold. In this view, the US Congress, in March 1941, adopted the Lend-Lease Act. This new legislation enabled the President not only to sell but also to transfer and lease war materials needed by the British without the latter having to pay for them. Such legislation was presented by Roosevelt as a national security law that succeeded to resist the pressure of the isolationists in Congress. With the US's entry in the war in December 1941, the Lend-Lease legislation was complemented by the Reverse Lend-Lease aimed at fixing the conditions of Allies' assistance to the Americans. The two mechanisms constituted the Mutual Aid regime between the US and its allies.[72]

If the practical modalities of the Mutual Aid regime were still vaguely defined, over time they took three main forms. The first consisted of direct lending of war supplies or straight Lend-Lease with a commitment of restitution at the end of the war. The second included services to be paid in cash or cash reimbursable Lend-Lease. As a result of the growing needs by the Allied nations, the US administration defined a third form that consisted of delaying these reimbursements through the so-called delayed reimbursement Lend-Lease.[73]

As soon as the Belgians in exile heard about the conclusion (in the autumn of 1941) of the Lend-Lease agreement between the US and Britain, they began thinking about a possible participation in the Mutual Aid regime. At first, scepticism prevailed. In a long memo, Boël considered that the Belgians had no interest in such an agreement. Politically, it would put Belgium in the position of a debtor towards the US, which would weaken its status in the likelihood of a future peace conference. But Boël also had some personal interest in the matter. Indeed, as Gutt pointed out to Theunis, his adviser was still haunted by the situation of the Solvay assets in the US and more concretely by the possibility that these assets could be seized by the Americans when settling their account with the Belgians at the end of the war. Gutt was not insensitive to Boël's first argument. According to him, the Belgians should avoid being too much indebted to the Americans and should, therefore, limit the agreement to supplying the Belgian Congo only in military materials. In the US, some Belgian diplomats did not share the points of view of their counterparts in London. After all, according to them, the Belgians had nothing to fear. When settling with the Americans, they would certainly not be put in a less unfavourable position that the other Allies.[74] Still, Boël continued sticking to his position. In the end, Theunis eventually made the balance tip in favour of a Belgian participation in the Mutual Aid mechanism aid. Indeed, he never made a secret of his vision of the war that he saw as very long and protracted conflict comparable to a new 100 years war. In this case, Africa would constitute the real central focus of the conflict and it was likely to believe that the needs of the Belgian Congo would by far exceed its resources.[75]

Finally, Belgium signed two Lend-Lease agreements with the US. On 16 June 1942, the general Lend-Lease agreement was signed. As a main provision, the Belgians decided to limit its scope to the cash reimbursable Lend-Lease in order to limit the risk of indebtedness towards the US.[76] In 1943, and following the entry of American troops in the Congo, another agreement, this time of Reverse Lend-Lease was signed with the Belgian Congo also based essentially on cash reimbursable form. In March 1943, the Office of Economic Warfare decided to cancel the cash Lend-Lease and to include Congolese supplies back to the normal trading circuits. Even though it remains difficult to understand this decision, it is possible to assume that it resulted from an intense lobbying by both American and Belgian colonial business interests in order to resume normal trading relations between the two countries without any public control. At the end of 1943, the total US Lend-Lease amounted to more than 2 million dollars restricted to military purchases. Under the cash reimbursable Lend-Lease, the Belgian Congo received a little less than 2 million dollars. Finally, in terms of Reverse Lend-Lease, the Congolese contribution amounted to almost 300,000 dollars. These given figures are just indicative and may not reflect the total of the Mutual Aid agreement to be settled at the end of the War.[77]

Third Case of Privatization: The Negotiations over Belgian Uranium

The last aspect of Belgian–American relations during the Second World War concerns the negotiations over the Belgian Congolese uranium. This question has already been covered by historians, in Belgium and in the US, but without consensus. The American historian, Jonathan E. Helmreich, has approached these negotiations and concluded that the Belgian government's strategy was typical of the one of a small state negotiating with bigger partners. This, according to him, explained the fact that the Belgians were trying to gain time in order to secure the best advantages possible.[78] Belgian historians preferred to emphasize the disproportionate importance played by private businessmen such as Sengier in the negotiations at the expense of the Belgian authorities.[79] In reality, while both views are true to some degree, they still miss not only the role played by Gutt in the negotiations, but also his close wartime acquaintance and relationship with Sengier.

Sengier had been in charge of the interests of the Société Générale de Belgique in the Free World since September 1939. These included those of the Union Minière du Haut Katanga of which he had been the CEO since 1924. However, it was only in July 1940 that he decided to settle in New York. In addition, as Sengier served also as representative of the Belgian Congo, he benefited in the US of the status of foreign government official. In any case, Gutt knew

Sengier quite well. The two men had met on numerous occasions while Gutt worked for a subsidiary of the Union Minière. In 1926, they were also involved in the creation of the African Metals Corporation (hereafter AMC). On a more personal level, however, Gutt did not have a high opinion of Sengier, especially after he suspected him of trying to get rid of his good friend, Pisart.[80]

In New York, the AMC proved to be particularly useful for Sengier and it quickly became the main supplier of the British and then of the Americans in non-ferrous metals. Cobalt, for example, took an increasing importance as it was used for making engines for long-range military planes. In 1941, the African Metals Corporation even struck a partnership with Union Carbide for the construction of a refinery in Niagara Falls. In New York, Sengier also tried to reactivate the old cartel agreements with the Union Minière's partners such as Rokhana. As a result, he succeeded in entering the Board of the American Metals Corporation.[81]

Sengier's activities in New York, apart from the ones directly related to uranium (see below), were known by Gutt as the two exchanged a regular correspondence during the war. They also discussed the possible resurrection of the cartel agreements for the postwar period. Old ideas resurfaced such as the one of Beatty to constitute an African bloc that would negotiate prices with an American bloc even if Gutt did not pay too much attention to such a plan.[82]

In the US, Sengier's activities were carefully watched by the Americans. For example, Theunis learned as soon as 1942 that Sengier's offices were bugged by the FBI that was investigating one of Sengier's former employees who fled to Guatemala and whose son-in-law and close associate was suspected of being pro-Nazi. Sengier himself knew that he was under close watch. He even realized that his phone conversations were being recorded. Nevertheless, he did not pay too much attention to it. In 1942, probes were launched by different American agencies. In January 1942, the Justice Department suspected the AMC of breaching the anti-cartel legislation. Later in March, Sengier was interviewed by the State Department about the activities of the AMC in the US. More particularly, the structure and the assets of the company aroused considerable attention.[83] In 1943, a thick report by the Office of Strategic Services of OSS investigated both the Société Générale de Belgique and the AMC. If the latter was relieved of all charges, the report was much more severe about the first, which was accused of 'playing both sides'.[84]

In reality, all this interest was also triggered by the involvement of the African Metals Corporation with the ultra-secret Manhattan Project, aimed at making the first atomic bomb. Indeed, in addition to the non-ferrous metals, the Union Minière du Haut-Katanga was also a major producer of uranium. As involved in the uranium-related business activities of the Société Générale de Belgique during the interwar period, Gutt knew very well about the scientific advances linked with such new metals. Scientists like Marie Curie and her son-in-law Frédéric Joliot-Curie got their supplies from Belgium where the Congolese uranium was treated.[85]

In May 1939, Sengier was approached by Sir Henry Tizard who offered him on behalf of the British government a pre-emption contract for the Congolese uranium. The same year, Sengier proceeded to the first shipping of uranium to the US where the precious mineral was stored in warehouses in Staten Island. So, before the outbreak of the war, the AMC had some 451 tons of uranium stored in the US. In June 1940, Sengier was approached by the American businessman and Roosevelt's close adviser, Alexander Sachs. Sachs's initiative directly followed the initiative taken by Albert Einstein and Leo Szilárd to warn Roosevelt of the importance that uranium might play in the war. By his offer, Sachs tried to convince Sengier to increase the shipping of uranium to the US with the commitment, on Sengier's part, not to re-export it. The Belgian businessman refused the offer, which, at the time, did not pose a serious problem to the Americans as they could get their supplies from Canada.[86]

It was only with the launch of the Manhattan Project, in August 1942, that the Americans set their eyes more firmly on Belgian uranium. In September, General Groves instructed his collaborators to get in touch with Sengier and the first contracts with the AMC were signed. Until 1944, the AMC was committed to providing the Americans with more than 29,734 tons of the strategic minerals.[87] These first contracts were signed without informing the Belgian government in London. In November 1943, Sengier sent Spaak a particularly evasive report about the growing importance of uranium for the Americans, just emphasizing the idea that:

> the Americans pay a special attention to radium, due to its uses as lighting raw material needed for the war production and industrial radiography. The needs in radium are ensured by refineries in Canada and in the USA. Supplies are shipped to America and to Britain.[88]

With the rapid progress of research, however, the question of the Belgian uranium took a highly strategic dimension. The Americans asked for further guarantees. They proposed to Sengier to include in their contracts a first-refusal clause by which the Americans would pre-empt all supplies of uranium while controlling the supplies to other partners. Sengier, however, rejected the American offer. The situation was getting very serious indeed. A few weeks earlier, in their meeting in Quebec City, Roosevelt had informed Churchill of the progress of the bomb. In February 1944, the Anglo-Americans decided to set up the Combined Policy Committee (CPC) whose first aim was to secure all supplies of Congolese uranium. Also, for the CPC, negotiations were to take place at the governmental level and not at the private level.[89] The CPC then charged Anderson, the chancellor of the Exchequer, himself a nuclear physicist and co-director of the British nuclear research programme, to get in touch with the Belgian government-in-exile to discuss the issue.[90]

The chancellor decided to get in touch with his Belgian counterpart, Gutt, with utmost discretion. As Gutt explained to Sengier, it was not surprising that the chancellor decided to approach him as a top priority. Indeed, Gutt's business connections with the AMC's activities, especially in the field of non-ferrous metals were well known by the British (see above).[91]

On 23 March 1944, Gutt only received a brief note from Anderson asking to see him on the same day at the Treasury. The meeting also included John Winand, the US ambassador. After the usual introductions, Anderson asked Gutt whether he knew anything about the Congolese uranium. The Belgian minister answered that he knew about it and that he had some distant knowledge of the research of Marie Curie on the atom. Satisfied with Gutt's reply, Anderson addressed the real object of the meeting still covered in a veil of mystery. He told Gutt that the issue at stake was only known to him, the US ambassador, the British prime minister and the American president. In concluding, he mentioned:

> This metal could constitute a frightening danger for humanity in the future. And this is why the President of the United States and the Prime Minister consider that their countries should have control over this metal. I was asked to come to see how this control may be ensured.[92]

To Gutt, the use of the word 'control', whose meaning in English is much stronger than in French, raised some deep concerns. Anderson, however, reassured him that the question might perhaps be on the agenda of the discussions at the peace conference that had to be resolved by an agreement on 'international control'.[93] Gutt was completely taken aback when he heard the chancellor and the US Ambassador mentioning the possibility of putting the Belgian uranium under international control. A last point of the meeting related to the possible inclusion of the general governor of the Belgian Congo.

However, Gutt said that, according to him, the question should be handled at the level of the Belgian government-in-exile only. Interestingly too, when asked about his own knowledge of the current research on the use of uranium, Gutt told his hosts: 'All I remember is what I was told, i.e. that an infinitesimal quantity of that metal would replace – if the experiences proved successful – all the coal necessary to the Queen Mary for 50 trips'.[94]

On the same day, later in the evening, Gutt told his three colleagues of the government about his meeting with the chancellor. Then the four ministers agreed to reply favourably to the British–American demand but under two conditions. The first related to the possibility for Belgium to share the know-how in terms of research in this field with the exception of its military applications. The second concerned the conclusion of a selling contract defining all the conditions in terms of pricing and deliveries. The reply was sent to the chancellor two days later.[95]

Meanwhile, the question was raised within the government whether or not to share these secret conversations with Sengier in New York. The ministers were divided. Nevertheless, Gutt insisted on the need to get in touch with Sengier. Indeed, the Belgian minister realized that Sengier was serious enough to keep a secret. In addition, to keep Sengier in the dark might very well arise his suspicion and render him even less keen on showing some flexibility in the negotiation of contracts with the Americans. So Sengier was not only told about these secret conversations but was also asked to come as soon as possible to London with all the relevant documentation related to uranium.[96]

On 4 May, Gutt met again with Anderson but in a much less favourable atmosphere. The Belgians as well as the other European allies were particularly upset when they learned that the British government had suppressed the secret codes and the diplomatic mail of the Allies with the exception of the Americans and the Soviets. In addition, Sengier who had arrived in London the evening before gave him a memo refusing the Anglo-American conditions.[97]

During the discussions, Anderson tried hard to convince Gutt about the Allies' intentions but the Belgian minister was adamant that Belgium should also benefit from the progress in the possible use of uranium. The chancellor also tried to downplay the importance of the Congolese uranium when mentioning the Canadian reserves. Gutt was not impressed as he knew very well that the Canadian uranium was much less rich than the uranium from the Congo.[98]

From May onwards, and with Sengier's arrival in London, the negotiations continued but at two different levels. The political aspects were discussed at the level of the Belgian government, while the purely commercial aspects of the agreement were handled by Sengier. In this dual process, Gutt played a central role as the link between the two discussions. As far as the political questions were concerned, the demands of the Belgian government were limited to the future applications linked with the use of the new energy. As far as the commercial questions were concerned, Sengier was adamant that the first refusal clause was not acceptable while making new demands in terms of financial support for the reopening of the main uranium production site in Shinkolobwe in the Belgian Congo. The negotiations continued during the whole of June and July, but in the absence of Gutt who had gone to the US to attend the Bretton Woods conference.[99]

The final agreement was finally signed on 25 September 1944. By its terms, the Anglo-Americans succeeded in including the first refusal provision, and the right of the Belgians for an equitable participation in the commercial use of uranium was recognized, should the metal become a new source of energy. The agreement was also interesting for its financial aspects as it would bring the

Belgian government an important quantity of hard currency such as dollars and pounds.[100]

Nevertheless, one could be struck by the little political use the Belgians made of their uranium reserves. In reality, Gutt's insight in these discussions showed that, in the absence of real policy towards the US for the postwar period, the Belgians revealed to be unable to capitalize on the importance of the strategic metal. The combination between the choice for the British card and the complicated relations between the Belgian government in London and the business colonial representatives made any different approach difficult if not impossible to contemplate for Belgian war diplomacy. As a consequence, the negotiations were mostly dominated by private interests.

Conclusion

If there is no doubt that economic considerations played an important part in the decision of at least a number of Belgian ministers to leave France for Britain and to continue the war alongside the British, the chain of events also shows the extent to which Belgian political and economic elites were reading the events through the lenses of their First World War experience. As the events unfolding under their eyes quickly took a very different turn, a great degree of confusion came to the fore and presented the different possibilities in a fundamentally new light.

The experience of the First World War and of its direct aftermath constituted also the template on which Gutt and the other ministers envisaged the Belgian contribution to the war effort. It explained the reliance on the Sainte Adresse declaration as a starting point for the Belgian thinking for discussions with the British. However, the insistence on economic issues also reflected the difficulties for the Belgians in exile to put in question the principles of the policy of independence inherited from the mid-1930s and their willingness to avoid committing the country politically to either the British or the American Allies.

The first question that the Belgians in exile and Gutt had to ask themselves in these negotiations related to the definition of Belgium's war aims. In this field, the Belgians appeared to have been completely unprepared.

Very quickly, however, a wide consensus emerged on the need to strengthen Belgium's links with Britain for the postwar period. These links, however, were much more of an economic nature than of a political one.

The agreement in Belgian circles also derived from more personal experiences of Belgians of their failure to create an open trade system at the level of the Continent in the 1930s. At the same time, this did not lead as far as the Belgians giving up the gold standard (see Chapter 4). In the negotiations on the Belgian gold reserves, Gutt played a central role. Here, his interwar experience played certainly an important role in shaping his negotiating strategy. His objective was to defend Belgian interests at best while convincing the British of the Belgian goodwill. Certainly, this strategy met with some criticism on the British side about the Belgians' real intentions. In any case, these negotiations would show the way for Belgium's wartime diplomacy that was mostly and almost exclusively focused on the British option.

However, if the British option met with a large consensus among the Belgians in exile, this consensus was far from complete. This leads us to the second question raised in this chapter, namely the extent to which business interests fully supported that political objective. In this case, businessmen, particularly in the Belgian Congo, voiced a number of misgivings to this approach. Politically, they only followed the Belgian government's decisions with great reluctance, taking advantage of the legacy of the constitutional arrangements that gave large economic autonomy to the Belgian Congo. This became even clearer when the US entered the war. It was then that the colonial business community took the full measure of all the advantage they could derive from playing on both Allies, especially in the context of their supply contracts as shown in the failed attempts, in 1943, to secure a tripartite agreement.

After the US entry into the war, the Belgians continued to focus all their attention on Britain. The reasons for this neglect of the American dimension in Belgium's wartime diplomacy may be explained by the following reasons. First there was the legacy of the 1920s when Belgium was asked to repay its wartime debts in the US. Secondly, the Belgians never succeeded in renewing their networks in the US after Roosevelt's first presidential election. This was all too visible for Theunis and the other Belgians in exile who still had a unfavourable opinion of the new American administration.

As a result, Belgian–American wartime relations were dominated by the defence of private interests, or the privatization of Belgium's foreign policy as reflected in the question of the Belgian assets blocked in the US, the reluctance to make use of the Lend-Lease mechanisms and the negotiations over Belgian uranium. The discussions on these different issues contributed to further the misunderstandings between Belgians and Americans during the Second World War.

3 FINANCIAL DIPLOMACY IN LONDON DURING THE SECOND WORLD WAR: TOWARDS A NEW MONETARY ORDER?

On 17 June 1942, at a dinner hosted by Gutt at the Berkeley Hotel in London to which his most important collaborators were invited, Keynes declared:

> During the last War, everybody had only one idea: to restore the situation exiting prior 1914. At present, nobody believes anymore in the possibility of restoring the pre-war situation. There is on the contrary, an undeniable will to build something new.[1]

This 'undeniable will to build something new' would not be without its paradoxes. First, it rested on the shoulders of men who had been involved in the failures of the past. In other words, the agenda of postwar monetary reconstruction had to lay down the basis for the future while addressing unresolved issues from the interwar period. Secondly, this new economic order had to take account of the emerging new system of international relations after the Second World War. If the interwar period witnessed a transition from one great economic power, i.e. from the UK to the US, the Second World War completed this transition. Finally, this new order could not entirely discount the divergences and convergences between the US and the UK in terms of international economic policy and objectives for the postwar order. These divergences were essentially dictated by the very different lessons the two big powers drew from their interwar experience. Consequently: 'Britain became more "nationalist", the United States, more "internationalist".[2]

The present chapter deals with Gutt's participation in the first stages of discussions on postwar international monetary cooperation. These discussions started in London at the initiative of the Treasury. Even if they did not achieve much, it will be argued that they revealed both the endurance of the practices inherited from the interwar experience in international financial diplomacy and the difficulty for some actors, such as the Belgian finance minister, to convert to the new paradigm in economics embodied in the Keynesian revolution.

This chapter will be divided into four sections. The first section will recall the main aspects of the failure of interwar international monetary cooperation. The second part will address Gutt's views on the postwar economic order through his reaction to the van Zeeland mission of 1943 agreed on by the European Allied governments in London and addressing postwar international cooperation. The third part will assess the first round of negotiations that took place among the Allies in London in which the Keynes's plan for an International Clearing Union was discussed for the first time. The final section will attempt an appraisal of Gutt's views on Keynes and on Keynes's economics.

The Failures of the Past

While the purpose of this section is not to relate the details of the history of international monetary cooperation during the interwar period, it may be useful to highlight some crucial aspects. From 1919 to 1933, political leaders in Europe seconded by the economic elites tried unsuccessfully to restore the pre-war international monetary system based on the gold standard. This period was characterized by a series of monetary conferences that culminated in the failure of the London Monetary and Economic conference of 1933.[3]

In 1920, the first monetary conference convened in Brussels under the aegis of the League of Nations led to a consensus on the need to balance budgets and to return to the pre-war monetary parities. As for the gold standard, the delegates agreed on the need to adapt it to the new realities. To this effect, the question was submitted to a group of experts. The discussions, however, quickly collapsed on the question of the German reparations. These two problems – the gold standard and the German reparations – were in fact linked. From a political point of view, both French and Belgians made the agreement on German reparations a condition for the discussions on the new monetary system largely because they relied on the German reparations to finance reconstruction. Two years later, in 1922, another conference convened in Genoa allowed a resumption of the discussions started in Brussels. On a diplomatic level, the Genoa conference led to the reintegration of Germany and the acceptance of the USSR in the European concert of nations. On a monetary level, the conference led to the adoption of a new monetary system defined as gold exchange standard. In this system, currencies were divided into two groups. The first group of currencies defined as key currencies were deemed to be convertible into gold. The second group consisted of the currencies that were only convertible through the 'key currencies' and were defined as 'dependent currencies'. With such a system, the participating nations tried to limit the use of gold to international settlements by alleviating the pressure on the gold reserves. Soon enough, the Genoa resolution became a dead letter. This failure can be explained by two dilemmas that characterized international economic cooperation during the 1920s.[4]

The first dilemma was reflected in the monetary stabilizations that were mostly undertaken on a case-by-case level in the absence of genuine international cooperation. Indeed, at Genoa a resolution calling for a better international cooperation between central banks had been adopted but failed to materialize owing to the French veto to any reopening of the discussion on German reparations.[5] As a result, monetary stabilizations were just orchestrated by the two main world central bankers, Norman, the governor of the Bank of England and Benjamin Strong of the Federal Reserve Bank of New York, who supervised the negotiations of the so-called stabilization loans.[6] If these operations led to the restoration of the gold standard in most European countries, they also reflected an increasing asymmetry between those countries that decided to devalue their currencies against gold and the others, like Britain, that decided to return to pre-war gold standard.[7] For example, France with an undervalued currency was able to sustain economic growth and to insulate herself from the worst effects of the depression at least until 1931. Conversely, Britain suffered from an overvalued currency which impeded her export trade and led to high levels of unemployment.[8]

The second dilemma concerned the liberalization of trade. In 1927, the International Economic Conference was convened in Geneva where the delegations agreed on the need to liberalize trade by a general application of the Most Favored Nation Clause. This unanimity, however, meant little when faced with the economic realities on the Continent where a growing number of governments were under considerable pressure to protect their domestic market from international competition by either raising tariffs or by promoting the formation of international cartels. Such cartels concerned not only commodities and raw materials but also semi-finished or fabricated goods such as cement, steel rails and also high-value added goods such as pharmaceuticals and electrical equipment.[9]

These two dilemmas became even more visible in the context of the worsening of the economic conditions as result, first of the credit crunch in the US at the end of the 1920s and the Wall Street Crash of 1929. The combination of tariffs, exchange controls with declining prices of commodities and agricultural products fed a downwards spiral leading to a major contraction of demand in the world economy. The value of world trade fell by staggering levels, by 20 per cent in 1930, a further 29 per cent in 1931 and 32 per cent in 1932.[10]

In this context, the leading industrialized nations were aware of the need for restoring international economic cooperation to mitigate the effects of the recession. In 1932, the Lausanne conference put an end to the payment of the German reparations in order to avert a complete collapse of the German economy. In Lausanne the participating nations agreed on the idea of convening an international conference to address world economic problems.

The international economic and financial conference was then convened in London in June 1933 with the purpose of addressing rising protectionism and reconstructing the already shattered gold standard since the British and American decisions to leave it, the former in 1931 and the latter in April 1933. After a few days of meetings, the conference lost its entire objective with the bombshell message of the newly elected American President, Roosevelt announcing his refusal to stabilize the dollar in order to concentrate his priority on the resolution of domestic economic problems.[11]

The period starting from the failure of the London Conference to the outbreak of the Second World War led to a growing economic and monetary fragmentation of Europe, shattering all hopes of economic multilateralism. Different European nations took the initiative to constitute a number of currency blocs, the sterling area centred on Britain with the participation of the Scandinavian countries, the Gold Bloc with France, Belgium, the Netherlands, Italy, Poland and Switzerland. Finally, the Nazi zone was centred on a system of clearing with essentially Central and Eastern European countries. These monetary blocs were in part overlapped by trading blocs, the Ottawa Bloc uniting the UK and the Commonwealth and the Ouchy Bloc between the smaller European countries such Belgium, the Netherlands and Luxembourg.[12]

As a result, monetary policy was led mostly from the point of view of domestic economic policy aimed at countering the effects of the Great Depression. The period then opened on a series of competitive devaluations (Belgium, 1935; France, 1936, etc) which had as a main consequence the export of economic problems from one country to another in relying on the advantages of depreciated exchange rates. This option became infamously known as *beggar-thy-neighbour* policy. An alternative system was designed by the UK and consisted of severing the link between gold and sterling while letting the latter slide within the framework of the Exchange Stabilization Fund.[13]

The second half of the decade witnessed two last attempts at restoring some forms of international economic and monetary cooperation. In September 1936, the Americans, British and French signed a tripartite agreement meant to provide a framework of cooperation for the devaluation of the French franc. It also provided for the commitment of subjecting any new devaluation of the French franc to international cooperation between the countries concerned. The agreement was also dictated by important political motives. The aim was, from the point of view of the Americans and the British, to avoid the economic collapse of France in the context of rising German assertiveness which was reflected in Hitler's decision to militarize the Rhineland. A few weeks later, the other countries of the Gold Bloc such as Belgium, the Netherlands and Switzerland adhered to the tripartite agreement. This agreement, however, proved to be unable to prevent another unilateral devaluation of the French franc in May 1938.[14]

Nevertheless, in the aftermath of its conclusion, the three powers decided, in 1938, to charge the former Belgian prime minister, van Zeeland with the League of Nations' sponsored mission to study the possibilities of the reduction of tariffs across the Western world. The van Zeeland mission led to a report that was quickly forgotten by the same three powers too busy to deal with the coming of the Second World War.[15] In his report, the former Belgian prime minister suggested the formation of a Pact of Economic Collaboration to be centred on the UK, the US, France, Germany and Italy.[16]

The collapse of international economic cooperation during the interwar period has given rise to a wide literature. Historians and political scientists have been eager to explain the failure of interwar monetary cooperation through the lenses of hegemonic stability theories. In a nutshell and, as Kindleberger pointed out, international economic cooperation failed because of the discrepancy between the capability but the unwillingness of the Americans to take the leadership in international monetary cooperation and the willingness but the lack of capability of the British to provide such leadership.[17] This would contrast with the situation during the Second World during which the US proved to be both able and willing to take such leadership.[18]

More recent scholarship has questioned this view. One strand of the literature stresses that if international monetary cooperation eventually failed, it was not for the lack of initiatives but for a lack of political will. The proponents of this view insist on the need for a wider perspective which includes the divergences between the three main political and economic power: the US, France and Britain.[19] Complementary to this view is the one that highlights the extent to which the interwar period was not marked by a lack of international cooperation in monetary matters but rather by a lack of formalized cooperation through credible institutions.[20] Finally, a last strand of the literature prefers to stress the discrepancy between the ideas expressed by experts and central bankers and the reluctance of politicians to accept them as possible solutions as one of the reasons explaining the failures of restoring international monetary cooperation in the interwar period.[21]

This chapter will argue, however, that these views overlook the extent to which the different actors involved in international financial diplomacy such as businessmen and central bankers found it difficult to design a new negotiating framework for international monetary cooperation. Indeed, during the interwar period, different frameworks were tried.

The first framework was adopted for the International Economic Conference in Brussels in 1920. It consisted of experts, not mandated by their respective governments. The conference, though convened by the League of Nations, came as a result of the work of financial experts and economists sometimes referred to as the 'Memorialists'.[22] The second framework was the one of Genoa in 1922 of experts and politicians mandated by their own governments but without much preliminary preparation. As a result, the Genoa conference got entangled in political and security issues.[23] The third framework, in 1927, at the Geneva International Economic Conference, the League of Nations consisted of gathering of delegates from different fields of the social and economic life, not acting as representatives of their respective governments while devoting more than a year for its preparation.[24]

In 1933, the International Monetary and Economic Conference held in London reflected a mixture of the three frameworks, consisting of delegates mandated by their respective governments while preparatory work was carried out by experts. Nevertheless, this combination also failed to deliver a positive outcome. This does not mean that the failure of such conferences was only due to the different negotiating frameworks.[25]

For certain, these different frameworks certainly reflected the fundamental difficulty of negotiating in a multilateral setting while respecting the principle of equality between countries at least on paper if not in reality.

In other words, the path to formal cooperation proved to be a long and difficult one. The problem lied in the difficulty to break with the practices inherited from interwar period that reflected different arrangements, all called by different sponsoring bodies and leading to a series of *ad hoc* arrangements without real continuity of policies.[26] This would be particularly visible in the first discussions on the postwar monetary order that took place in London in 1942 and 1943. Although these discussions have been somewhat overlooked in the literature on the history of the Bretton Woods agreements, they seem important to us for at least two reasons: First, because they reflect the endurance of an ethos of negotiating monetary arrangements as inherited from the interwar period; and second, as they would reveal the difficulty for the actors to embrace the concept of multilateralism as opposed to bilateral cooperation.

Gutt's View on Postwar International Economic Cooperation

There is no doubt that Gutt paid a lot of attention to the issue of the postwar international cooperation. Nevertheless, as he always prided himself on being a pragmatist and not a theoretician, one should not expect to find long theoretical memos exposing his views on the issue. Indeed, his interwar experience taught him that if winning the war was difficult, winning the peace might reveal to be even more challenging. The reason for this view was to be found in the situation most Belgians found themselves in after the First World War. This perspective was based on the belief that even if the war was won, victory became quickly bitter sweet owing to the lack of preparedness to address postwar reconstruction. This is why, for example, Gutt, as early as 1942, decided to prepare a monetary reform for liberated Belgium. It is, however, worth noticing that the only real statement of Gutt about his view of postwar international economic cooperation can be found in his comments on the van Zeeland report on postwar European economic reconstruction submitted in August 1943 to the European governments-in-exile in London.

We have seen before the extent to which the relationship between Gutt and van Zeeland had been affected by the experience of 1935 (see Chapter1). During the Second World War, the former Belgian prime minister relentlessly put pressure to be included in the Belgian government in exile. On the one hand, if some ministers such as Spaak were open to the idea, Gutt stood very firmly against it. On the other, to keep van Zeeland as a free electron was not seen as a good option either. In this context, when, at the end of 1940, the idea emerged of creating a special committee in charge of studying the postwar situation of Belgium, Gutt quickly realized that this would provide him with the best solution to sideline van Zeeland by appointing him as its chair. In this context and during his trip to the US in April–May 1941, Gutt offered van Zeeland the position of chair of a new committee in charge of studying postwar problems known under its French acronym of CEPAG.[27] This commission was only given a consultative role and was quickly nicknamed by Gutt the 'Commission of Illusions' in reference to the mountain of papers mostly dealing with theoretical ideas.[28]

Van Zeeland himself realized that this appointment constituted a bit of a trap but nevertheless used it to connect with a lot of important figures in Britain and in the US. In London, the former Belgian prime minister consulted with the other representatives of the Allied governments based in the English capital. The objective was clear. It consisted of the small European nations taking initiatives in terms of postwar cooperation. This would, in turn, avoid the postwar agenda being dictated by the Americans and the British. In addition, the smaller European nations would be able to demonstrate that they were able to cooperate contrary to the experience of the interwar period when they proved incapable of doing so.[29]

In view of this, van Zeeland met in London in October 1942 with the London- based committee made of the foreign ministers of the Belgian, Czechoslovak, Dutch, Greek, Luxembourger, Norwegian, Polish, and Yugoslavian governments-in-exile.[30] This committee was placed under the chairmanship of the Greek diplomat, Thanassis Aghnides, an old acquaintance of van Zeeland's dating back to his first mission in 1938 when Aghnides had held the function of assistant secretary general of the League of Nations. A month later, in November 1942, Spaak sent van Zeeland a letter inviting him to explore on behalf of the respective governments' foreign ministers the utility of appointing a special committee in charge of studying the issue of European postwar reconstruction. The idea was to assess the possibility of creating a European committee able to provide a regional view on postwar reconstruction.[31] In August 1943, van Zeeland eventually submitted his report.

When Gutt received a copy of the draft report, he looked at it very carefully and not without suspicion. His comments confined to a draft letter give us an idea of his views on postwar international economic cooperation.[32] Before discussing Gutt's views, it is first important to examine the van Zeeland report itself.

The van Zeeland report consisted of two parts. The first part contained a series of suggestions dealing with improving the cooperation between the existing international committees in charge of postwar planning. In the second part, the former Belgian prime minister presented his own views on postwar economic cooperation. Van Zeeland's approach was dual, political and economic. As far as political cooperation was concerned, van Zeeland suggested they base international cooperation on three different layers: the global level under the aegis of the future United Nations Organization; the regional level under the aegis of regional integration; and finally the national level. According to van Zeeland, the different levels had to be organized in compliance with the principle of equality between states. As far as economic cooperation was concerned, he proposed two organizing principles: the principle of free trade and the coordination of economic policies in order to foster economic development. In terms of trade policy, the regional level would be most conducive to trade liberalization. In terms of economic development, van Zeeland suggested a policy of international planning based on an ambitious programme of public works to be carried out at the level of the regional groupings through a concerted policy related to public finances and social policy.[33]

Finally, in terms of monetary policy, van Zeeland highlighted the need to promote cooperation including within the field of credit. This could be achieved by the creation of regional systems of credit inspired by the Federal Reserve System to be coordinated under the aegis of the BIS. This last idea was directly inspired by his report of 1938.[34]

The van Zeeland report was not without contradictions. For example, the former Belgian prime minister never explained how to reconcile his free trade principles with economic planning based on government intervention. In this respect, Keynes's approach was more coherent as it addressed the external aspects of full employment through his plans for an International Clearing Union (hereafter ICU). Van Zeeland also evaded the question of federalism by maintaining sovereign states as fundamental units of his system. At the same time, he suggested the possibility of transnational cooperation of different technical fields such as monetary policy or financial policy. In this respect, van Zeeland's approach is reminiscent of the functionalist agenda defended by David Mitrany.[35]

In London, Gutt found that the van Zeeland report looked like a copy of the report of 1938. In general, Gutt agreed with most of van Zeeland's ideas but found them still too vague and general. As far as van Zeeland's views on economic cooperation were concerned, Gutt held much in common with the former Belgian minister but with one important exception: his view on international planning. Gutt's objections to international planning were motivated both on ideological grounds and also on the basis of his own experience as Belgian finance minister. First, he strongly believed that such international planning would undermine the spirit of entrepreneurship that had, according to him, been at the root of the tremendous development of the Belgian economy since the middle of the nineteenth century. Until 1914, Belgium had ranked as one of the top industrial nations. Belgian banks, such the Société Générale de Belgique, were major financial players not only in the Belgian Congo, but also in Central and Eastern Europe and in China.[36] In this respect, Gutt was convinced that any control or channelling of investments would kill what he called the '*Belgian miracle*'. Gutt's objections were also based on the results that he considered as negative of the van Zeeland experience between 1935 and 1937 in Belgium that consisted of an attempt at emulating Roosevelt's New Deal in order to relaunch the Belgian economy (see Chapter 1).[37]

In New York, when Theunis learned about the mission offered to van Zeeland, he made no secret of his scepticism. After reading the report, Theunis also considered that it was nothing more than a copy of the 1938 report.[38] More fundamentally, Theunis's scepticism lay in his knowledge of the lack of credibility van Zeeland enjoyed *vis-à-vis* the American authorities and particularly at the State Department. In January 1943, he was told that Herbert Feis had not given a great deal of credit to the van Zeeland report. This would be later confirmed in March by the Belgian ambassador in Washington. Not only, according to the diplomat, the State Department did not pay too much attention to the van Zeeland mission, but he also received reports confirming how little credibility the former Belgian prime minister enjoyed in Washington.[39]

Finally, when van Zeeland submitted his conclusions to Aghnides in August 1943, he received confirmation that there was no will on the part of the Allied governments to set up a European Committee undoubtedly owing to the reluctance of the British to contemplate such an idea. On their part, the Americans devoted so much of their attention to their plan leading to creation of new international organizations that they barely took notice of the report.[40] As for Gutt's views on international economic cooperation, they appear certainly much closer to the views of the classical economists opposed to state intervention in the economy and in favour of free trade (see below).

The International Clearing Union and Inter-Allied Discussions in London (1942–3)

In London, discussions over postwar international monetary cooperation began in earnest in 1942. However, at the international level, other initiatives had also been taken. In the early 1942, the foreign ministers of the American countries convened in Rio and adopted some first proposals put forward by Harry Dexter White calling for the creation of an international stabilization fund.[41] If these resolutions made a great impression on Boel, Gutt did not consider them of great importance. According to him, the Rio resolutions were 'nothing more than empty promises that would soon vanish in smoke as it had been the case in the preceding twenty years'.[42]

In London, the main subject of discussions became the plan presented by Keynes calling for the creation of an ICU. The history of the genesis of the ICU project is today well known. When, in July 1940, Keynes came back to the Treasury, he was only given an unpaid part-time advising position to the chancellor of the Exchequer. However, as Skidelsky (his most recent biographer) emphasized, Keynes's influence was based on personal authority rather than on his official position.[43]

In November 1940, Keynes started thinking about postwar international monetary cooperation at the request of Harold Nicholson, parliamentary secretary to the Ministry of Information, who asked him to refute the arguments put forward by Dr Walther Funk on the extension of the Schachtian bilateral clearing system into a payment system managed by a central clearing office in Berlin. In such a system, exchange rates were fixed and free trade was to be established on the basis of a clearing system encompassing all European countries under German occupation and control. The irony was that Keynes actually subscribed to most of Funk's ideas to the great surprise of Nicholson himself. Indeed, Keynes was concerned with the negative effects of a restoration of a free trade regime between an impoverished Europe and the US that had accumulated most of the monetary reserves. In this light, the idea of a clearing system would make monetary issues and relations between debtor and creditor of secondary importance.[44]

At first Keynes thought of a possible extension of the sterling area to willing countries such as Belgium and the Netherlands. This system would allow the different countries to deal with their reconstruction needs without constraints on their balance of payments. Within that extended sterling area, exchange rates were to be fixed on a bilateral basis.[45]

Keynes's system, however, still lacked a crucial element: namely, a multilateral credit mechanism. To overcome this problem, some of Keynes's ideas already designed in the early 1930s – exposed in *A Treatise of Money* published in 1930

– calling for the creation of an international organization proved useful. In April 1941, Keynes proposed the creation of an ICU, the detailed plan of which was discussed with the British Treaury and Bank of England later in the autumn. As such the ICU was based on a new currency, called Bancor whose value was fixed in gold and which was to be accepted as means of payment. The system was based on multilateral clearing between central banks that would be able to settle their account between one another. Any remaining outstanding balances were to be settled by the ICU through cooperation between creditor and debtor countries. The ICU also provided for monetary stability but opened the scope for depreciation of deficit countries and appreciation for surplus countries. It was revolutionary in many ways. First, it broke away with the old paradigms of the gold standard while preserving the equilibrium of balance of payments. During the interwar period, the hoarding of reserves had led to widespread deflation and unemployment, especially in the deficit countries that remained faithful to the gold standard. Secondly, Keynes's system put pressure both on the creditor countries and on the debtors. The creditor countries were also concerned with ICU adjustments and not only the debtor countries as had been the case in the interwar period. Finally, the plan for an ICU reconciled both the need for international cooperation and for automatic adjustments in order to guarantee high rates of employment at the domestic level.[46]

As revolutionary as they may have been, Keynes's ideas were also shaped by Britain's experience during the interwar period. Indeed, after the failure of the World Economic Conference of 1933, British monetary policy turned towards prioritizing its domestic and imperial concerns rather than the needs of the international economy. In this context, the legacy of the 1920s combined with the effects of the 1930s justified a more domestic orientation reflected both in the formation of the sterling area and of the preferential trade regime established by the Ottawa system in the early 1930s.[47] In this respect, the multilateral aspects of Keynes's plan were limited to British interests centred on the future of the bilateral relationship with the US and the rest of the British Empire.[48]

On 12 February 1941, Keynes confided in Gutt his initital ideas during a dinner. He mentioned to the Belgian minister what he saw as the main challenges of the postwar monetary order.[49] The question was to avoid an excessive accumulation of gold in the US. According to Keynes, it was also utopian to think that the US would offer their reserves to the Europeans. Then he put forward his idea for an extension of the sterling area to Western European countries. This enlarged sterling area would be able to deal with the US on a more equal basis. It would therefore only buy American products against exports to the US market, i.e. what Keynes would later refer as 'trading goods against goods'.[50] These views anticipated by a few weeks a letter written on 25 April 1941 by Keynes to Frank Ashton-Gwatkin of the Foreign Office and in which he presented his initial observations on postwar monetary cooperation.[51]

However, Gutt was not convinced that this system suited Belgium's best interests. Indeed, Belgium had remained faithful to the gold standard and the question was how to ensure for the country to avoid painful adjustments in order to maintain its gold reserves while the others, that had severed their monetary links with gold, would not have the same constraints. In any case, the conversation of February 1941 would be important, especially in the context of Gutt's plans for regional integration as embodied in the Benelux project.[52]

The first inter-Allied discussions on the postwar monetary order started in April 1942 under the aegis of the Leith-Ross Committee. If the main object of the Inter-Allied Committee on Post-War Requirements chaired by Leith-Ross and set up in 1941 was to deal with the question of postwar relief, it also included a section dealing with monetary issues.[53] In the same month, William Frazer, on behalf of the Treasury, asked the Allied ministers to send him their first thoughts regarding their postwar monetary policies. For the British, these two initiatives had to fulfil a simple objective. It consisted only in gathering information in order to lay the basis for future cooperation in monetary policy.[54] On behalf of the Belgian government, Gutt sent a very short note just mentioning the different aspects that any future monetary policy would involve both in terms of inflation, resulting from the German occupation and of the need to freeze part of monetary circulation in postwar Belgium with measures dealing with exchange control and external trade. As Gutt stated in this note: 'I'm just giving you the headlines which at present summarize our main concerns'.[55]

Contrary to the Belgians, the French decided to seize the opportunity to expose their own project of future monetary organization. What would be known thereafter as the French plan was written by Hervé Alphand, director of economic affairs within the National Committee of Liberation headed by General de Gaulle in London. The French plan was essentially based on the provisions of the Anglo-French financial and monetary agreement concluded by Paul Reynaud and John Simon on 13 December 1939.[56] This agreement, on top of guaranteeing exchange stability, provided for a bilateral cooperation between the British and the French equalization funds in order to guarantee the provision of means of payment for purchases in both markets. On these premises, Alphand suggested the expansion of bilateral agreements to other European countries. These agreements were being superseded by an International Clearing Office that would supervise the exchange currencies between all the participants in the scheme through a clearing system. In cases of balances of payments' disequilibrium during the period of reconstruction, the French plan also provided for two additional correcting mechanisms dealing respectively with the so-called 'accidental disequilibrium' and 'permanent disequilibrium'. The first were to be corrected by transfers of gold whilst the second by more structural measures such as a change in exchange parity or the conclusion of special trade agreements.

If the French plan was very similar to Keynes's ideas for an ICU, it nevertheless presented three main differences. First, it failed to make the leap into genuine multilateralism as it was essentially based on the pre-1940 bilateral agreements. Secondly, it was not as revolutionary with respect to the role of gold which remained very much central to the scheme. Finally, the French plan was much more limited in scope as it was meant only to deal with the period of reconstruction in order to lay the basis for a return to the gold standard.[57]

After receiving the proposals from the Allied governments in London, the Treasury decided to convene a meeting of the Allied finance ministers in London. There was, nevertheless, still no question that the British would divulge their own plan. The first meeting took place on 24 July 1942 under the chairmanship of Captain Crosshanks. As he was still recovering from surgery Gutt did not attend it and instead sent Ansiaux and Boël to represent him. As soon as the meeting started, the British stressed the nature of the meeting. It had to be considered a purely informal, private and no communiqué would be issued to the press. According to its chairman: 'this is, I am sure I have your agreement – a purely private meeting ... there is no question of any communiqué or issue to the Press'.[58]

Not all the governments took the trouble to send a representative; the Soviet Union, for example, did not bother, while the US only sent an observer, Dr Penrose, and the Dutch only an expert Jan Beyen. As for the French, a special arrangement allowed them to take part as 'Free French' represented by René Pleven and Alphand.[59] At the meeting, the discussions actually focused on a declaration on the transfer of funds in occupied territories. Only the Dutch representative Beyen expressed his views on postwar monetary cooperation and his support for the French plan.[60] At the end, the only concrete decision was to delegate the study of the questions relating to postwar monetary questions to a sub-committee of experts. This sub-committee would meet in the autumn of 1942. On 18 November, the experts representing the Allied governments in Europe issued a protest against the British–American decision to set the exchange rates for the French franc in liberated North Africa.

The ministerial meeting, convened on 26 February 1943, proved to be much more important with respect to postwar international monetary cooperation. This time, Gutt attended the meeting alongside his counterparts of the allied governments-in-exile in London. It was then that Keynes decided to submit his project for an ICU. The release of the first copies of the White plan for a Stabilization Fund (see Chapter 4) to the British, the Russians and the Chinese had indeed led the Treasury to rush to convene the meeting in order to submit their own proposals.[61]

At the meeting, the speeches were arranged in alphabetical order of the nations represented. As a result, Gutt was the first to intervene. Not expecting this arrangement, he had to improvise – something that he always tried to avoid when speaking in English. Gutt's speech started by making a clear reference to the failures of international monetary cooperation during the interwar period and to the London conference of 1933:

> We all remember of course the most resounding of those failures because it took place just ten years ago in this very town, happily not in this building, but funnily enough in a Museum of Antiques. I hope today we are going to open a new age and turn our back to antiques.[62]

After mentioning his interest in the French plan as 'one of the most useful contributions to our work',[63] Gutt then dealt with the question of postwar international monetary cooperation and the dilemma between monetary and economic policy:

> This inability to settle the two subjects simultaneously makes me think of poor Alice in Wonderland. I suppose you remember when she was big enough to reach the key leading to the garden on the bid table, she was too big to pass through the door, but when she had grown enough to pass through the door, she was too small to reach the key on the big table.[64]

In any case, Gutt made clear that he would privilege the need to provide a stable international monetary system and this was for two main reasons. First was the need for every liberated country to build its postwar reconstruction on a sound monetary basis. Second, monetary policy was directly linked to the question of supplies. In this respect, Gutt confirmed his interest in the French plan. When Keynes's turn came, he called the ministers to study carefully his plans for an ICU as well as the American plan which had just been made known.[65]

In reality, Gutt as well as Theunis were quite sceptical of the project for an ICU. According to Gutt, Keynes's plan still appeared far too theoretical. Nevertheless, he acknowledged that the project presented the advantage of tackling postwar economic reconstruction from the monetary angle. What worried Gutt the most was the lack of limits put on the overdrafts from the ICU and, consequently, the risk that it would soon run out of liquid assets. His criticisms echoed very much the ones voiced by the Bank of England. As a response, Keynes argued that his system had to be seen as a closed system in which any increase in bank's liabilities (credits) would be matched by any increase in assets (debits).[66]

Finally, Gutt realized that with the publication of the American plan, there was little chance for Keynes's plan to succeed (see Chapter 5). As he confided to Theunis: 'I have the impression that Keynes's plan will be buried without the flowers'.[67] More fundamentally, Gutt's scepticism on grand schemes of international cooperation inherited from his own interwar experience resurfaced in the context of these discussions. Instead, he favoured a more gradual approach from country to country at the regional level as reflected in the Benelux projects (see Chapter 4). Gutt then wrote to Theunis: 'to my mind, a universal machine as this one [the Keynes plan] or the White plan will never work because of its universal character. This brings me back to my Dutch-Belgian agreement, British-Dutch-Belgian and then Atlantic'.[68]

Gutt and Keynes: An Appraisal

Appraising the views of Gutt alongside those of Keynes is certainly not easy. Such appraisal has to take account of biographical elements, archival evidence and then divergences or convergences of views. First, Gutt does not feature as a central character in Keynes's biographies. All of them only mention Keynes's allusion to Gutt in the context of the Savannah conference and Gutt's appointment as the first managing director of the International Monetary Fund.[69] Nevertheless, there is no doubt that the two men had known each other for a long time and at least since the Paris conference of 1919. At the end of the war, Keynes referred to Gutt as 'an old and trusted friend'.[70] As Gutt stated when intervening at the meeting of inter-Allied finance ministers of February 1943 with respect to Keynes: 'I would only say, as other people have said, that I have listened to each of his exposés for the last, I should think, the last twenty-five years'.[71]

During the war, Gutt and Keynes met at several occasions in London among which four may be singled out. The first one was in February 1941 when they met for dinner at Gutt's invitation. The second time was in June 1942 when Gutt invited Keynes at a dinner alongside a number of his collaborators. The third time was in February 1943 when Gutt with his Dutch counterpart, van den Broeck, gave Keynes a copy of the Belgo-Dutch Monetary agreement (see Chapter 4). And the fourth time was in November 1943 when Keynes told Gutt about the progress made in the discussions between the British and American Treasuries with respect to their different plans on postwar international monetary institutions (see Chapter 5).

In one particular case Keynes even gave a considerable push to Gutt's positions in the context of the discussions over the postwar exchange rates for Belgian currency. Gutt, who argued for a limited devaluation had to fight hard, especially against van Zeeland who favoured a stronger one. At the beginning of December 1942, Keynes, via Waley, had circulated his views on postwar monetary reforms among Allied governments in which he defended the position that wage levels constituted a better basis for the fixation of the postwar exchange rates than the volume of money in circulation or the price levels. In this respect, Keynes's position was very close to Gutt's and certainly helped the Belgian finance minister to win his battle against van Zeeland and other Belgian personalities in London (See Chapter 5).[72]

That being said, there was little that Gutt and Keynes shared in common as far as their respective background was concerned. Keynes appeared as an intellectual, a philosopher and an idealist in international relations.[73] Gutt was a pragmatic businessman, a lawyer by training who adopted a harsh realist stand. For example, and as far as postwar Germany was concerned, Gutt favoured the establishment of the country's postwar borders on the Rhine, 'by exchange of populations, if needed' and the neutralization the Ruhr industrial region.[74] As for Keynes, he would repeat during the war his views on the need to help reconstruct the German economy for the sake of European postwar prosperity.[75] Nevertheless, both shared the idea that economic issues had been neglected in the aftermath of the First World War, even though they diverged as to the best way to deal with them.

Conversely, the question of whether Gutt could be considered as a kind of anti-Keynesian is even more difficult. It can be approached from at least two angles. The first one concerns the scope of the spread of Keynesianism in Europe and particularly in the French-speaking world. The second relates more to Gutt's personal views.

Before the Second World War, Europe had not yet been 'converted' to the new paradigm in economic policy even though some of the principles, such as advocating public spending to bring about full employment, were already floating in the air since the middle of the 1930s. In reality, one should perhaps not overestimate the power of economic ideas on government policies during the 1930s. Indeed, most of the policies were essentially empirically applied without too much reference to economic theoretical approaches. For example, the economic policies that were led in countries such as Sweden, France and the US, not mentioning Italy and Germany, were often defined as 'proto-Keynesianism' as they relied on non-Keynesian spending measures.[76]

In other words, if the Keynesian revolution in terms of policy principles was already underway with variable results, Keynes himself defined its theoretical underpinning by the publication, in 1936, of his *The General Theory*.

In this book, Keynes explained that the rate of interest did not automatically equilibrate at full employment level. In this context, an action on interest rates would undermine the preference for liquidity to the profit of investment. In other words, Keynes argued for the possibility of counter-cyclical policies and prioritized the fight against unemployment over monetary stability.[77]

In the US, there is little doubt that the new ideas of *The General Theory* had reached a number of high profile people, including important figures at Harvard and at the Federal Reserve. In Europe, such influence is more difficult to assess. Paradoxically, what James Meade called the 'Keynesian

revolution' hit the Treasury and the Bank of England only in small propor-
tion.[78] On the Continent and in the French-speaking countries in particular,
Keynes's *The General Theory* was still largely unknown until the beginning
of the Second World War. The French translation by Jean Rioust de Largentaye was published only in February 1939.[79] Consequently, Keynes was
much better known on the Continent and in Belgium in particular for his
pamphlets against the Versailles Treaty or against the return of the pound to
the gold standard.[80]

In Belgium especially, the views on monetary policy were very much influenced by the Swedish economist Cassel and his theory of purchasing power
parity. In 1935, the economists at Leuven University had used it to calculate the
scope of the devaluation of the Belgian franc.[81] In other academic and business
circles, the name of Keynes was mentioned only sporadically.[82]

Finally, the Belgian personality on whom Keynes produced the greatest
impression during the Second World War was Jeff Rens, a trade unionist and
close adviser of Spaak in London.[83] In other words, if the new ideas of the *The
General Theory* had already spread to the US, in Europe they were not yet widely
known and discussed. More specifically, in Belgium the strong position of the
Austrian neo-classical school considerably hampered the penetration of Keynesian ideas in both academic and political circles. [84] In this respect, to define Gutt
as anti-Keynesian would amount to a historical anachronism.

As for Gutt and with respect to monetary policy, there is no doubt that he
remained faithful to the exchange stability and the gold standard. As seen above,
when finance minister in 1934–5 and again in 1939–40, Gutt rejected firmly
any currency devaluation without mentioning giving up the gold exchange
standard. His arguments against monetary depreciation were based on moral-
ity and economics. First, any devaluation had to be considered as a breach of
contract between the governments and their investors by imposing on them a
change in the value of their assets. Secondly, the advantages, if any, of a monetary devaluation would be at best short-lived. According to Gutt, devaluation
would only lead to an even worse situation when the effects of the devaluation
on the price levels would feed a new inflationary spiral, requiring even harsher
deflationary policies. Such views were very similar to the ones defended by
the proponents of a return to the gold standard in Britain during the 1920s.[85]
Already in 1934, Gutt made his position clear in his opposition to abandon-
ing the gold standard, when joining an appeal by the International Chamber of
Commerce, alongside Theunis and other prominent business leaders including
the economist Theodore Gregory – a former member of the MacMillan Committee reporting on financial problems in summer 1931[86] – supporting the gold
standard as a basis of the international monetary system.[87] In other words, Gutt
appeared to have fully adhered to the 'gold standard ideology'[88] that proved to

be so resilient in the interwar period despite the pressing economic realities suggesting an alternative course of action.[89] In this context, one may argue that he was much closer to the neo-classical economists faithful to the old paradigms of the gold standard such as Ludwig Mises and Friedrich Hayek.[90] Mises and Hayek had repeatedly argued against discretion in monetary policy while advocating free trade and the primacy of exchange rates stability.[91]

Finally, it was not so much by the *The General Theory* that Gutt was mostly impressed, but rather by the economic principles defended by Keynes in *How to Pay for the War* (1940).[92] Keynes first presented his views on war finance in a series of articles published in *The Times* in November 1939. In his articles, he warned about the inflationary risks of the British war financial policy. Indeed, according to Keynes, the new additional taxes would not suffice to offset the increase in purchasing power expected from the renewed industrial activities generated by the country's preparation for the war. In this respect, he suggested limiting the inflationary impact of an increase of real earning by establishing a system of compulsory savings or as they would be later called, postwar credits. This system had the additional advantage of mobilizing resources that would be returned to the workers once the war was over, thus avoiding a postwar slump. Eventually, these proposals were partially included in the 1941 British budget by Kingsley Wood, the new chancellor of the Exchequer.[93]

These principles, in fact, were very similar to Gutt's financial policy during the phoney-war (see above). As for Hayek, Gutt fully endorsed them.[94] In a letter to Theunis in March 1943, Gutt confirmed his admiration for Keynes and his views on war finance:

> To come back to Keynes, I blamed him in the past for being too much a theoretician but he has changed a lot in this respect. It is him, you remember, who, just before the War launched the drive against inflation and his views on voluntary and involuntary savings which has been implemented with the success which you know.[95]

Conclusion

This chapter has addressed the positions of Gutt on postwar monetary reconstruction and more specifically the Keynes plan for an ICU. In doing so, an initial idea of Gutt's views on postwar economic and monetary reconstruction have been presented. These views show the extent to which Gutt was still prisoner of his personal experience of the failures of interwar attempts at laying down the basis for a stable system of monetary and economic cooperation.

First, in the light of his views on postwar monetary cooperation, it is striking to notice that someone like Gutt did not question the fundamentals of the pre-First World War monetary policy. Indeed, his views were still very much shaped by the idea of a possible return to a situation whose very basis had been definitely shattered by the First World War. Gutt's rejection of van Zeeland's ideas may be explained on two levels. The first is the personal level of the real incompatibility between the two. The second is more fundamental and concerns Gutt's belief in the possibility of returning to the pre-war situation while van Zeeland embraced the new ideas developed in the 1930s, especially those deriving from the New Deal experience in the US.

This chapter has also dealt with the genesis of Keynes's ideas for an ICU and the first discussions on the postwar monetary order between the Allied governments in London. At a general level, these discussions were very much reminiscent of the interwar monetary diplomacy in the use of informal discussions between experts behind closed doors. At a more specific level, they show the extent to which such experts on the Continent, including Gutt, were still trying to restore the gold standard and found it difficult to adhere to Keynes's ideas. It would take another negotiating method to induce them to adopt the ideas of multilateral cooperation.

Finally, this chapter has addressed the positions of Gutt on Keynesian economics. It has showed the extent to which one should not overstate the spread of Keynesian economics, in particular on the Continent. Despite a good personal relationship, this chapter indicates that Gutt was reluctant to adhere to the new economic paradigms of the Keynesian revolution. Instead, Gutt appeared as a defender of the gold standard, much closer to the neo-classical views on monetary affairs defended by Hayek and Mises than the new views proposed by Keynes.

4 EXTENDING THE BENELUX AGREEMENTS: REGIONAL INTEGRATION AS AN ALTERNATIVE TO THE ANGLO-AMERICAN PLANS

This chapter explores the role played by Gutt in the negotiations that led to the conclusion of the Benelux monetary and trade agreements between Belgium, the Netherlands and Luxembourg, also known as the Benelux agreements. These agreements are important for several reasons: First, because they reflect the importance of financial and economic diplomacy in shaping the postwar order; and secondly, because they encapsulate most of the questions that would dominate the debates in the history of European integration such as the place of Britain and the future of French economic policy.

This chapter argues that the discussions that led to the first monetary and trade agreements concluded by the three Benelux nations. However, these agreements posed some political challenges for the Belgians in exile despite their potential benefits for the development of the country's external trade. These challenges would lie both in preserving the country's national sovereignty and in convincing its partners to adhere to the principles of trade openness. Conversely, the Benelux agreements also show the extent to which the ideas for such cooperation were in fact nothing new and had to be put in the context of the failed attempts of Belgium in the interwar period to build some kind of a Western European bloc. Finally, these plans have to be considered in their wider context as an alternative to the Anglo-American plans for the postwar monetary order. Indeed, for Gutt, the Benelux agreements would be fulfilling the objective of providing another approach, gradual and regional, confined to Western Europe. These aspects, especially the latter, have been somewhat overlooked in the existing literature on the Benelux agreements (see below).[1]

This chapter is divided into three parts. The first part will deal with the discussions among Belgians in exile in relation to postwar international cooperation in connection to the challenges they posed from the point of view of a small power eager to maintain its national sovereignty. The second will focus on the genesis of the idea of a customs union between Belgium and the Netherlands.

The third will address the failure of the Belgians to extend their agreement to Britain and France.

Small Powers and the Defence of Sovereignty: The Case of Belgium

The negotiations that took place during the two first years of the conflict on the Belgian contribution to the British war effort made a complete rethinking of Belgium's foreign policy increasingly necessary. This process, however, proved to be long and difficult for most of Belgian politicians in exile who were unable to formulate credible alternatives. The lack of vision was at best reflected in the discussions that took place among Belgians in exile on the future of Belgium's sovereignty, especially in the context of the federalist views developed in the Free World and aiming at the disappearance of the smaller European nations such as Belgium. Among them, the actions deployed by the tireless European federalist Richard Coudenhove-Kalergi and his committee reconstituted in New York should be mentioned. This committee included a number of high-profile personalities such as the Norwegian Carl J. Hambro and van Zeeland (see below).[2]

In March 1942, the Belgian diplomat de Gruben published an article defending the idea for a federal organization of Europe in which Belgium would lose her sovereignty. A month later, in April, Franz van Cauwelaert, a former Belgian minister in exile in New York replied to this article refuting vehemently de Gruben's ideas. Instead of a European federation, Franz van Cauwelaert, advocated the idea of an Atlantic Community including both Britain and the US. Such a Community or Union could transform the Atlantic in a kind of new *Mare Nostrum*.[3]

On the publication of this article, de Gruben felt like answering van Cauwelaert but was prevented from doing so by his minister, Spaak. For the Belgian foreign minister, these discussions could not continue because they would only show how unprepared the Belgian government was when dealing with such questions. Both Theunis and Gutt became concerned by the lack of clear guidelines produced by the Belgian foreign affairs minister. In March 1943, their anxiety increased when they learned that van Zeeland had joined the Coudenhove-Kalergi Committee. According to Theunis, the Austrian–Czech–French aristocrat had to be considered as: 'a dangerous fool in so far as all his plans for a European federation are against the interests of the small powers'.[4]

Finally, in January 1943, Spaak sent some official guidelines to Belgian diplomats on the issue of Belgium's postwar foreign policy in relation to the projects for European unification. These guidelines were largely drawn from a speech the Belgian foreign affairs minister delivered in Oxford on 11 January at the invitation of the National Peace Council. If in both his speeches and guidelines Spaak expressed a lot of reservations towards the idea of a European federation, he nevertheless refused to commit himself too much either way. According to him: 'In conclusion, it seems to me thus that a European federation would be impossible in the aftermath of the War, but that the federal idea is a just one'.[5]

In reality, in refusing to settle the matter, Spaak, as a skillful politician, was certainly still waiting to see where the wind would blow before committing himself too much. There is, however, no doubt that in the absence of clear guidelines, Belgian diplomacy was stuck in its old principles dating back to the policy *of independence* based on both a refusal to commit the country too much to any postwar scheme and a strict defence of Belgian sovereignty.

If someone like Gutt certainly shared the second aspect of these positions, he vehemently objected to the first one. Again his obsession with the need to lay down the basis for postwar reconstruction made him believe strongly in the need to take initiatives that would both help Belgium's postwar economic reconstruction while preserving her sovereignty. These principles constituted the backbone of his idea of both a monetary and customs union agreement between Belgium, the Netherlands and Luxembourg, best known under the acronym of Benelux.

Project for a Customs Union between the Benelux Countries (1941–3)

The idea of a customs agreement between Belgium and the Netherlands was anything but original. The Belgian economy and the economy of Luxembourg had already been merged as a consequence of the 1921 Belgian–Luxembourg Economic Union.[6] As a result, the countries formed the same economic unit and used the same currency, the rate of which was decided by the Belgian central bank. In the 1930s, in the context of growing economic fragmentation, the small European nations such as Belgium tried to unlock the trade restrictions at the level of the Continent while providing for exchange rates stability. The adoption of the Import Duties Act in 1931 was seen as a real threat to the Belgian economy. Belgium, however, remained committed to free trade and tried to find a solution in regional economic agreements.[7]

On 7 February 1932, Belgium became a member of the Oslo Convention that consisted of a commitment to a tariff truce between its contracting parties (Belgium, Denmark, Luxembourg, the Netherlands, Norway and Sweden). A few months later, on 19 July, the Belgians, Luxembourgers and the Dutch agreed on the Ouchy Convention aimed at reducing existing tariffs between the two economic units. For its proponents, the Ouchy agreements had a more ambitious objective. The latter was aimed at providing a basis for a Western European economic bloc with British, French and possible German participation. Finally, however, the whole project failed. In 1932, with the Ottawa agreements, Britain opted for the empire and trade protectionism. As for France, the project was received with much reluctance. Economically, it ran against pressure from within the country for greater protectionism. In reality, the Belgians quickly understood that their trade policy was very different from that of the French, which was still attached to trade protection. Politically, such rapprochement between Belgium and the Netherlands also raised the spectre in Paris of opening the way for an Anschluss between Austria and Germany. As for Germany, the progressive closure of its economy made such a project impossible to contemplate.

To conclude, the Ouchy agreements never achieved their overall objective and represented a second best for Belgium. With respect to exchange rates, the Belgians and the French shared the same commitments to monetary stability and the gold standard. In the shadow of the London International Conference of 1933, the two countries as well as the Netherlands negotiated a loose monetary bloc based on gold, and named the Gold Bloc, that was to be extended to other European countries such as Switzerland, Poland and Italy. This monetary bloc, however, which contained some clauses of financial cooperation between their respective central banks did not resist the successive Belgian, French, Dutch and Swiss devaluations in 1935 and 1936. It is worth mentioning that Gutt, alongside Francqui, had been involved in the negotiation of the Gold Bloc.[8]

Therefore, in the first year of the war, the idea of an economic agreement between Belgium and the Netherlands was not a completely new idea. It nevertheless encountered a number of obstacles. If both governments-in-exile were on good terms in London, they were far from adopting the same policies. The Dutch pursued a quite individualist approach with respect to their support of the war effort. This contrasted with the Belgian attitude of lending their gold to the British, albeit with some conditions. It is also true that both governments enjoyed a very different position in London. In the Dutch case, the presence of the Queen and of the ministers in the Free World was a huge advantage. As for the Belgians, their government only consisted of a handful of ministers without the backing of the King who had decided to remain in occupied Belgium (see Chapter 2). Therefore, if for the Belgians the need for recognition was essential, this was not the case for the Dutch.[9]

The literature on the history of the Benelux agreements often mentions the meeting, in April 1941, between Gutt and his Dutch counterpart, Johannes van den Broek, an old acquaintance of Gutt's dating back to the tin cartel.[10] While this meeting was important, it can only be understood in the context of an earlier meeting between Gutt and Keynes that had taken place a few weeks before. Perhaps this meeting proved to be much more crucial than another one with Keynes that took place in 1942 between Keynes and some Belgian personalities which is also mentioned in the historiography on the Benelux agreements.[11] The latter had, indeed a much larger scope and consisted mostly of the Belgians discussing postwar issues in very general terms (see Chapter 3).

Two Important Meetings: Gutt–Keynes (February 1941) and Gutt–van den Broek (April 1941)

On 11 February 1941, Gutt invited Keynes to dinner. Keynes seized the opportunity to explain his ideas on the postwar economic order with Gutt.[12] As we have seen, these ideas were based on a sterling bloc between Britain and a number of European countries (see Chapter 3). Gutt quickly saw the British interest in such a project. What about Belgium's interests? In contrast to Britain, the country had kept the link between its currency and gold. In this situation, the Belgians would be forced to maintain deflationary policies to defend the value of their currency while their likely trading partners in such a scheme would not be subject to the same financial constraints. In Gutt's mind, there was therefore a compelling need for the Belgians to take an initiative in this respect that could potentially be presented as an alternative to Keynes's ideas. In the conclusion of his notes about the meeting sent to Tennis, Gutt wrote:

> I left Keynes around midnight. It is 9 o'clock and I indicate this quickly so my letter can leave with the plane: this is to tell you that I am asking myself questions without having the time to answer them nor to think about them sufficiently.[13]

Two months after this meeting, in April 1941, Gutt set off for his first wartime trip to New York. There he had lunch with the Dutch businessman, van den Broek, who was working for the Dutch Purchasing Commission. The two men knew each other quite well. Indeed, they had met in the 1930s when they both had taken part in the discussions leading to constitution of the tin cartel (see Chapter 1). No traces remain of this discussion apart from Gutt's own account of the meeting in his war memoirs. When discussing postwar reconstruction, the two men agreed on the need to start discussing a possible customs union between Belgium, the Netherlands and Luxembourg. The need to start the negotiations and not to wait for the liberation was also motivated by their willingness to avoid facing their different national economic constituencies eager to protect their own interests. Gutt and van den Broeck parted with the promise of submitting these ideas to their respective governments.[14]

Submission of the Idea to the Belgian Government (June 1941)

A few weeks later, in June, Gutt communicated these ideas to Spaak, the Belgian foreign affairs minister. This note also vanished from the records, but Spaak published it in his own memoirs. In it, Gutt explained the numerous advantages that a customs union with the Netherlands would present for postwar Belgium without, however, concealing the pending problems. Among them, Gutt mentioned two difficulties. The first was to do with the possible British reactions towards such an idea. The second concerned the existing trade agreements concluded by Belgium that included the most-favoured-nation clause.[15] In his reply, the Belgian foreign minister made no secret of his opposition to the whole idea. Indeed, meanwhile, Spaak had been exchanging correspondence with the Belgian ambassador to the Dutch government who informed him of the Dutch reluctance to contemplate the possibility of a customs union with Belgium and its willingness to keep all options open for the future.[16] Despite this letter, Gutt decided nevertheless, on 26 June 1941, to present his idea to his colleagues of the Belgian government. Not surprisingly, he met their opposition, and in particular Spaak's, who declared that such a project was too premature. Two reasons may explain the Belgian foreign affairs minister's opposition. The first one lay in his reservations on changing completely the principles of Belgian foreign policy of independence. The second is more strategic and resided in Spaak's insistence on the need to negotiate a comprehensive agreement with the British. In a recent speech, Eden had declared that his government intended to discuss postwar economic relations with their European allies.[17] For Gutt, this last argument was seen as even more compelling for the Belgians to take initiative in this respect. As Gutt wrote in his war memoirs:

> Usually, when it is question of economic and financial matters, my colleagues trusted me. That time, the answer I received was unexpected; my proposal was rejected unanimously by my three colleagues: Pierlot, Spaak, De Vleeschauwer! ... I then wrote to van den Broek and told him I had failed. Though, I did not consider myself beaten and I would try again.[18]

The final burial of the idea would come from a report drafted in July by Spaak's close advisor, van Langenhove. If according to the Belgian diplomat, an idea of a customs union presented some advantages, these did not outweigh a number of difficulties. From the political point of view, Belgium would have to negotiate an agreement with a country of more or less equal size. This would reflect a sea change for Belgian diplomacy which was used to controlling, at least economically, a tiny neighbour such as Luxembourg. As for the potential benefits of a customs union with the Netherlands, the Belgian diplomat highlighted the divergence in terms of interests in some important sectors in both national economies. Finally, van Langenhove advocated that the two countries first negotiate fiscal if not a monetary union before thinking of a customs union.[19]

1943: The Turning Point

In the beginning of 1943, a series of events contributed to reviving the project of a customs union between Belgium and the Netherlands. The evolution of the war with the news of the first defeats of the German army in Russia opened for the first time a window of hope for a near end to the conflict. At the end of 1942, van den Broek's appointment as new Dutch finance minister had also constituted an important element. Before leaving New York for London, van den Broeck had told Sengier, one of his Belgian business acquaintances, about his willingness to work closely with Gutt in regard with their idea of a closer economic cooperation between their respective countries.[20] In January 1943, another ex-Belgian minister, August de Schryver, who had just arrived in London from France declared himself in support of the idea of a closer economic union between the two countries. In New York, de Schryver met also with van den Broek and the two men agreed on a method to push the idea forward. At first, contacts were to be limited to experts of the two countries. Then the questions were to be handled by the two countries' diplomats and foreign affairs ministers. Van den Broeck and de Schryver also agreed on the need to emphasize the economic aspects of such a customs union over the political ones. [21]

As for Gutt, he shared with van den Broek the idea that an economic agreement between Belgium and the Netherlands first required the conclusion of a monetary agreement between the two countries. As soon as March 1943, the first Belgian–Dutch discussions started. They proceeded in two parallel directions. The two finance ministers would create a positive atmosphere while the political aspects of such an agreement would be handled by the two countries' foreign affairs ministers.

Not surprisingly, between the two Belgian and Dutch finance ministers there was complete agreement on the means as well as on the objectives of a customs union. In their minds, this project was aimed at showing the Anglo-Americans that the small European nations were ready to take concrete initiatives for economic and monetary rapprochement. It was also seen as particularly useful for political reasons, especially with respect to the public opinions in both occupied countries. Finally, this initiative would indeed demonstrate the readiness of the two governments-in-exile to address the issue of their postwar reconstruction. The only remaining divergences between the two ministers concerned the determination of the new exchange rates between the Dutch and the Belgian currencies (see Chapter 5).

The climate was very different between the two foreign ministers, the Belgian Spaak and the Dutch Nicolaas van Kleffens. On 3 March 1943, the two ministers had a tête-à-tête meeting to discuss postwar issues. According to Spaak, his Dutch counterpart told him that his government was not yet ready to make any commitment regarding the postwar period. A few days later, the Belgian diplomat, van Langenhove, submitted another note expressing great reservations on the possibility of concluding such an economic agreement without consulting the Belgians in occupied Belgium.[22]

On 26 March, the progress made by the two finance ministers bore its first fruit and the two governments agreed on a meeting which included their two foreign affairs ministers. The amiable atmosphere took the two foreign affairs ministers by surprise as they realized the work done by their respective experts. The meeting led to an agreement on a project for a Belgian–Dutch draft monetary agreement. The draft agreement was prepared by Boël and Ansiaux, the Belgian experts, and by Crena de Jongh and Jan Beyen on the Dutch side. Its provisions were certainly not entirely original. They were indeed very similar to the Reynaud–Simon financial and monetary agreement concluded between France and Britain on 13 December 1939 (see Chapter 3). In short, the Belgian–Dutch financial agreement contained two main provisions. The first related to fixation of monetary parity in order to avoid all non-concerted devaluation. As Gutt mentioned to his colleagues in the Belgian government: 'What we want to avoid are the monetary manipulations of one of the two countries' currency by the other'.[23] The second provision concerned the opening of reciprocal credit lines for a maximum amount of 1 billion francs. In case of an overdraft, the agreement could be either cancelled or the debt accumulated would be converted into the creditor's currency.[24]

When presented to the Belgian government in May 1943, the Belgian–Dutch monetary agreement was easily accepted. There were, however, some remaining technical and political questions to address. The first derived from the fact that the postwar parity of both the Belgian and the Dutch currencies was still unknown. On Gutt's suggestion, the existing parity would be first inserted in the agreement with the understanding that it would have to be changed as soon as the new parities were agreed upon. A second question concerned the status of Luxembourg. As mentioned, Belgium and Luxembourg shared, in effect, the same currency – the Belgian franc – through the Belgian–Luxembourger Economic Union. In this respect, on Spaak's suggestion, the ministers agreed to include Luxembourg in the agreements. When discussed by the Dutch government, the monetary agreement was received with much less enthusiasm. Their minister of economic affairs, Piet Kerstens, was indeed concerned with the possible negative impact of the proposed agreement on the Keynes–White projects relating to the postwar monetary order. At a later meeting between Spaak and van Kleffens, however, the two ministers agreed on the possibility of extending the agreement to other countries and proposed the possibility for a joint membership to the planned international monetary agreement still under discussion between the British and the Americans. Finally, the agreement was signed on 21 October 1943 by the finance and foreign affairs ministers of Belgium, Luxembourg and the Netherlands. In their joint *communiqué*, Gutt and van den Broek were eager to emphasize the idea that the agreement was perfectly compatible with the Keynes–White plans still under discussion in Washington DC.[25]

As far as the Belgians in exile were concerned, Gutt had already explained the main provisions of the agreement to van Zeeland in May–June 1943. The former Belgian prime minister, while supporting the project, still expressed some criticisms especially with respect to the danger of binding the Belgian economy too much to the Dutch. In view of the negotiations of the Western European Union, van Zeeland also warned Gutt of the fact that the Dutch were known as tough negotiators.[26] Gutt replied that the agreement presented two clear advantages. On the one hand, it set the example for international cooperation. On the other hand, it would allow the Belgian economy to take advantage of the bigger Dutch market. Finally, there was no danger with respect to future negotiations on the Western European Union as the idea was equally strongly supported by the Dutch themselves.[27]

Once the financial and monetary agreement was concluded, Gutt thought it timely to re-launch the discussions on a possible customs union agreement. In this field, however, the hurdles proved to be even greater. Experts of both countries raised a series of objections, ranging from diverging economic interests to the political reluctance of the French-speaking Belgians. Both sides agreed on the need to consult not only their own industrialists and experts both in exile and in their occupied countries but also their British–American allies. This proved to be a difficult and long process which delayed the negotiations considerably. Nevertheless, while both governments received a number of responses towards the project of a customs union, they felt confident that on the whole they had gathered a large amount of support.[28]

Another problem came from the difference in terms of the trade nomenclature between the Dutch and the Belgians. Belgian tariffs were based of the League of Nations nomenclature and were established on the volume of goods. The Dutch had opted instead for tariffs based on the value of the goods or *ad valorem*. To make things easier, Gutt convinced Spaak that the planned trade agreement should be based on the Dutch system. So, negotiations at different levels took place in 1943 and 1944. They led, in May 1944, to the drafting of the agreement and its submission to both governments. Meanwhile, the Belgians felt the need to consult their American allies who gave their support to it. The agreement was signed on 5 September 1944. Concretely, it provided for the elimination of all exiting tariff barriers between the three countries – Belgium, Luxembourg and the Netherlands – as well as the establishment of a common external customs tariff. The agreement also contained provisions relating to the creation of common institutions in charge of dealing with the technical trade aspects of its implementation. Finally, as a long-term objective, it also mentioned the possibility of establishing an economic union between the three countries. In reality, this economic union only took place in 1958 with the conclusion of the Treaty for an Economic Union between the Benelux countries.[29]

Expanding the Benelux Agreements to Britain and France

From the start of the negotiations between the Belgians and the Dutch, Gutt was aware of the fact that they attracted a lot of interest from the British authorities, within the Bank of England, the Treasury and even Keynes. He wrote to Theunis, in March 1943: 'Keynes, the Treasury and the Bank of England follow all this very closely'.[30] The British interest in an agreement between small European nations was nothing new. In March 1942, Sir Lancelot Oliphant, the British ambassador to the Belgian government-in-exile, confided to Spaak of Eden's interest in the matter.[31] In October 1943, Gutt and van den Broek gave Keynes a copy of the Belgian–Dutch monetary agreement which he considered as an important first step towards exchange-rate stability. In the meantime, Keynes expressed his doubts as to the possibility of extending such an agreement to a larger country. An extension, according to him, would require more rigid rules than the ones included in bilateral agreements. This, of course, in Keynes's mind, would only be feasible in the context of his own projects. In a note by Waley to Phillips, the first reported Keynes's comments on the Belgian–Dutch agreement: 'Once you spread the net wider more rigid rules become appropriate. Thus you are back to the C.U [Clearing Union] and the S.F. [Stabilization Fund]'.[32]

On the American side, reactions to the Belgian–Dutch agreement were rare. This lack of interest of the American administration could be attributed to two main reasons. The first was due to the fact that the Americans wanted to concentrate exclusively on their own plans. The second was explained by the reluctance of the US administration to make any commitments for the future.[33]

In concrete terms, the impact of the two agreements was limited. The monetary agreement concluded in 1943 was never ratified while the customs agreement would only be ratified in 1947. It is true to say that the first agreement which had as its primary purpose the stabilization of currencies became redundant in the context of the Bretton Woods agreements.

Benelux and Britain: The First Best Option

On 26 October 1943, just a few days after the Belgian–Dutch monetary agreement had been signed, Gutt brought a copy to the chancellor of the Exchequer, Sir John Anderson.[34] The latter would praise the agreement the day after at the Commons as a 'practical proof of the effective and close cooperation between Allied Governments'.[35] Nevertheless, when replying to a question raise by the member of Parliament, Mander, about the likelihood of Britain joining such an agreement, the chancellor remained particularly non-committal.[36] The possibility was also discussed in other circles in Britain, especially within the Bank of England and the Treasury. For the British, the Belgian–Dutch agreement looked very similar to their own agreements concluded in the context of the sterling area. The Belgian–Dutch agreement, however, went further in terms of financial and monetary cooperation. More importantly, it provided for the settlement of outstanding balances in hard currencies or in gold. Such provision was seen as unacceptable to the British financial authorities. In a secret memo, unidentified officials of the Bank of England stated:

> So far, our own agreements have survived a period of increasing accumulation of ster-ling by the Special Account countries ... which have led the primary goods producing countries to sell for Special Account of Sterling rather than not to sell at all. In their case, there is always the hope of eventual conversion of their sterling into goods or at the worst the repayment of their outstanding capital liabilities. Such possibilities, however, will not be available in the case of the new Agreement.[37]

Despite these statements, the Belgians remained hopeful of a possible British decision to enter their financial and monetary agreement. Towards the end of 1943 and the beginning of 1944, a series of signals coming from the Brit-ish authorities justified this hope. In November 1943, a speech given by general Smuts mentioned the idea of an *entente* between the Western European coun-tries under British leadership. In May 1944, Belgians, Americans and British agreed on the establishment of a tripartite committee called the Economic Liaison Group in charge of supervising discussions for postwar problems. The same month, Spaak mentioned to his colleagues the possibility of the Belgians concluding a wider agreement with the British that would allow them to be fully associated with the British policy in terms of full employment.[38]

This enthusiasm, however, was cut short following another meeting between Gutt and Anderson on 6 April 1944. During the meeting, Gutt expressed the Belgian misgivings at the lack of initiatives taken by the British in terms of regional agreements. The chancellor replied that the Treasury's attention was exclusively occupied by the negotiations relating to the postwar monetary coop-eration. Yet, Gutt tried a last time to convince the chancellor that the Belgian plans were in no way incompatible with the ones discussed between to the British and the Americans. On the contrary, in Gutt's mind they would consti-tute a possible alternative should the big Allies fail to reach a compromise. The chancellor, however, remained oblivious to such arguments and told his Belgian counterpart that nothing could be envisaged before the coming elections.[39] At the political level, in June 1944, Spaak made a last attempt to convince the Brit-ish in a meeting with Eden. The two ministers then started some preliminary discussions on the question of a Union of Western Europe, the result of which would only be visible following the conclusion of the Brussels Pact of 1948.[40] Finally, the Belgians concluded a monetary agreement with the British on 5 October 1945. This agreement only dealt with the settlement of the sterling balances and provided for the opening of credit lines up to 5 million pounds. It also led to the Belgian Congo leaving the sterling area.[41]

Extending the Benelux to France: The Second Best Option

If most of the Belgian hopes lay in attracting Britain to the Belgian schemes, it was the French option that would progressively impose itself. This, however, would raise a number of problems. On the personal level, the relations between the Belgian ministers and the Free French were very good. In November 1940, Gutt met General Charles de Gaulle for the first time in London. The leader of the Free French made quite an impression on him. As he wrote to Theunis: 'He [De Gaulle] is a lucid man, master of himself, not losing time in words, seeing clearly the main lines of politics'.[42]

This good impression was mutual, so much so that Gutt became a regular visitor of the General's mansion in Colombey-les-Deux Eglises after the war.[43] In October 1941, the Belgian government-in-exile was prompt to recognize the French National Committee even if this recognition was largely inspired by the British government.[44]

In 1943, after the confusion surrounding the Allied landing in North Africa and the assassination of François Darlan, de Gaulle was able to strengthen his position among the new Committee for the French Liberation constituted in Algiers to the satisfaction of the Belgians in general and of Gutt in particular.[45] This committee included some important figures such as Pierre Mendès France as finance minister, René Massigli as foreign affairs minister, André Dietlhem as minister of the economy and Monnet as minister for the armed forces and relief.[46]

In this light, the problems between the Free French and the Belgians in exile lied elsewhere than in personal divergences. First, there was the question of the Belgian gold seized by the French authorities in Senegal. Since 1939, the Belgians had transferred an amount equivalent to more than 5 billion Belgian francs to the Bank of France. In June 1940, the British had put a ship at Belgian disposal for carrying the precious reserves to Britain. Meanwhile, the French kept the Belgians in a state of ignorance about their plans. Secretly, they had shipped the Belgian gold, alongside the Polish gold to Kayes, North of Dakar. With the French Armistice of June 1940 and the conclusion of the Wiesbaden agreement with the Nazis, the Vichy regime decided to send the Belgian gold to the Reichsbank's chest in Berlin. Then, the Belgian gold was shipped to Berlin via North Africa and Marseilles. In reality, it would be deposited in foreign banks in Switzerland and Romania, including in the account of the German embassy in Bucharest.[47]

In the Free World, the Belgians in exile learned about the Wiesbaden convention with dismay. The immediate reaction of Theunis was to start legal proceedings against the Bank of France before the New York State's Supreme Court, which, in its first ruling, decided to freeze the French gold reserves in the US. The trial became quickly embedded in an endless legal battle between the two parties and their attorneys, Dulles of Cromwell & Sullivan representing Belgian interests and the law firm Coudert Brothers & Cos the French ones. A major obstacle to the resolution of the case came from the refusal of the Free French, not only to be made responsible for Vichy's actions but even to condemn them. In short, the question of the Belgian gold was still pending when Belgians and French started negotiating a possible extension of the Benelux agreement to France. The question would only be definitely settled in October 1944 and the gold was finally restored to the Belgians in December.[48]

A second problem, this time more of a political nature, lay in the uncertainties regarding postwar French economic and monetary policy. On 4 November 1942, the landing of the Anglo-American forces in North Africa raised a number of questions among the European governments-in-exile in London. From a political point of view, the American support to Darlan and then to General Henri-Honoré Giraud was met with reprobation by the European allied ministers in London. The consequent decision to impose a new exchange rate for the metropolitan franc to 300 for a dollar and 75 for a pound without consulting the Free French in London was seen as a dangerous precedent. As Belgian finance minister, Gutt reacted quickly to these events. According to him, there was no doubt that the determination of par values was a matter of sovereign decisions to be made by the relevant national authorities.[49] The counter-attack of the Allied governments in London took different forms. On 18 November 1942, the Free French seized the opportunity of a meeting of the under-committee of experts in charge of discussing postwar monetary issues to emphasize the need for consulting the legal national authorities for the determination of the par values in liberated territories.[50] The importance of the issue led the Belgians, and Gutt in particular, to initiate a number of meetings with French and British officials both at the Treasury and at the Bank of England (see Chapter 5).[51]

On 20 November, John Stewart Lithiby of the Bank of England informed Boël of the readiness of the British authorities to support a joint statement on behalf of the Belgian, Dutch, French and Norwegian governments.[52] This proposal looked strange to Gutt who realized that the exchange rate imposed in North Africa had been the result of a concerted action between the Americans and the British in the first place. Eager, however, to find more information about the British position, Gutt asked to meet with Waley and Frazer at the Treasury. During the meeting, Waley explained to Gutt the reasons that led the British and Americans to impose such an exchange rate, namely that the decision was above all decided by the Americans who controlled most of the military operations on the ground. At this moment, Gutt took full measure of the danger of giving too much power to the military when deciding on economic and monetary issues.[53] For the Belgians, the new exchange rate of the metropolitan franc was also considered harmful to the interest of the Belgian Congo whose currency was exchanged at the rate of 176 for a pound. In other words, the new exchange rate presented the risk for the Belgian colony to find it harder to export to the French colonies while making it easier for the French colonies to penetrate the Congolese market.[54]

It is in this context that the Belgians and Gutt in particular entered in discussions with the Free French with respect to fostering cooperation in the monetary field. Alas, the first contacts proved to be disappointing. Indeed, the French had to confess that they had not yet decided about the postwar par value of their currency towards the sterling and the dollar.[55] To make things more difficult, the Belgians had to deal with a double division within the French Committee of National Liberation established in June 1943.

Until Giraud's resignation, most of the financial and economic policy was put in the hands of men closer to Algiers than to London. In March 1943, René Mayer, frustrated by de Gaulle's silence regarding his offers of service, decided to rally Algiers where he was given the portfolio of Communications. This example was followed by Maurice Couve de Murville who was offered the Finance portfolio. Finally, Monnet also decided to go to Algiers but on a mission given by the Roosevelt administration in order to supervise Allied supplies. In London, de Gaulle could count on the support of his close collaborators such as René Massigli, René Pleven and André Dielthem.[56] On this first division, i.e. London versus Algiers, an additional one regarding the future of French economy policy and postwar European cooperation emerged. A first group, consisting of Alphand and Monnet, saw some form of European integration of the Western European economies as the best way to force the opening of the French economy as well as to provide for its modernization. Conversely, de Gaulle remained attached to a more traditionalist view that was based on both aims of asserting French power in Western Europe and its supremacy over Germany. A third view, supported by Mendès France and his close collaborator Georges Boris, was in favour of concluding bilateral monetary and economic agreements with France's neighbours. These agreements were seen as the best way to secure a rigorous monetary policy that was considered a prerequisite of structural reforms of the French economy, in other words, of economic planning.[57]

At the end of 1943, the Alphand–Monnet camp experienced a first defeat following the report written by L. Blum-Picard discarding the option of a European economic union. According to the high-profile French civil servants, such an economic union was seen as both politically as well as economically too complicated and ambitious to achieve.[58]

It was, therefore, in this context that the Belgians approached the French about the possibility of enlarging their monetary agreement concluded with the Dutch. In a meeting in July 1943 Spaak confided to his French counterpart, Massigli, about the Belgian willingness to extend their monetary agreement to France. The meeting, however, led to no results.[59] Later, in November, Monnet and Alphand intended to take advantage of the United Nations Relief and Rehabilitation Administration (hereafter UNRRA) Conference convened in Atlantic City to approach this time the Belgians, namely Spaak and Boël. If Monnet did not know Spaak very well, he was well acquainted with Boël whom he had worked with in the context of Anglo-French Purchasing Committee in London. In Atlantic City, Monnet put forward to the Spaak and Boël his ideas for a pooling of postwar relief between France, the Netherlands and Belgium. If these ideas were welcomed with scepticism by the Belgians, Alphand who also attended the meeting, submitted on behalf of the French Committee for National Liberation, a proposal to settle the question of the Belgian gold seized by Vichy.[60] For Gutt and Theunis, this proposal, which fell too short of Belgian demands, had to be rejected. As a result, it was officially turned down on 18 November 1943 by the Belgian government-in-exile.[61]

During the same year, the French negotiated their own monetary agreement with Britain. The negotiation of the agreement reflected yet another line of division between the French, especially with respect to their postwar exchange rates. On one side, those in favour of a rigorous monetary policy such as Mendès France and Boris were advocating the smallest possible devaluation of the French franc at the liberation and a freeze of wages. On the other, the camp of the supporters of a more lax monetary policy that included Pleven and to some extent Monnet considered this option untenable both for political and economic reasons and favoured instead a greater postwar devaluation followed by wage increases.[62] As for de Gaulle, he decided not to intervene in these discussions and to postpone his judgement.[63]

The conclusion in November 1943 of the Anglo-French monetary agreement marked the victory of the first camp over the second one. In the agreement, the Free French agreed to put the par value of the French franc towards the sterling to 200 francs instead of the 176 mentioned in the previous agreement concluded in December 1939. In reality, however, in choosing this par value which was the current one of the French franc in the French Empire, the Free French avoided settling the question of their postwar monetary policy. In any case, their refusal to agree on a further devaluation was seen as an encouraging sign even if the Belgians in exile were still unconvinced about the French decisions with respect to their postwar monetary policy.[64] In further meetings later in December in Washington fears of a further devaluation regained momentum. Different figures were put forward. A range between 225 and 275 was mentioned by André Istel.

Another proposal, this time mentioned by Alphand and Monnet, set the value of the French franc between 200 and 300 towards the sterling.[65]

In this context, Gutt took the initiative of convening two meetings between Belgian, British, Dutch, and French officials to discuss their postwar monetary policy at the US Treasury: the first, on 5 January 1944; and the second, on 13 January. At the first meeting, it seemed that from the statements of the French officials, Istel and Monnet, the French par value would be between 225 and 250 if not 250. As concluding remarks, Monnet stressed the importance of consultation amongst the European governments-in-exile before determining their respective par values. This point was strongly supported by Gutt and Waley.[66] At the second meeting, the French and Monnet in particular appeared reluctant to commit themselves to the future parity of their currency. For the Belgians, Theunis stressed the difficulty for the European allies to discuss their postwar par values while not knowing about the future par value between the sterling and the dollar. In conclusion and as far as the Belgians were concerned, Monnet's lack of clarity reflected both the fragility of his personal position within the Free French and the great uncertainty still reigning among the French in exile regarding the future of their monetary and economic policy.[67]

The publication of the Anglo-French monetary agreement, on 9 February 1944, confirmed the rate of 200 franc for a pound. This rate was, however, considered only provisional. In reality, the debates among the French even intensified in the spring of 1944 leading Mendès France to threaten to resign owing to the lack of support from de Gaulle. Nevertheless, the General still refused to take position in these discussions. Only in February 1945 would de Gaulle finally choose his camp in favour of a more lax financial policy by replacing Mendès France with Pleven.[68]

When informed about the Anglo-French monetary agreement, Boël was struck by its similitude with the 1942 Belgian–Dutch agreement. For him as well as for Spaak, that similitude should lead to the two countries signing an economic agreement. In London, Gutt was quick to react and to try to temper Spaak's enthusiasm. The objections of the Belgians in London towards the conclusion of a Belgian–French agreement were threefold. First, the priority should be given to the conclusion of the Anglo-Belgian agreement considered as the most important issue. In other words, negotiating an agreement with the French would divert their attention from their main objective. Secondly, the great uncertainty as to France's postwar economic policy was considered as an additional reason for caution. Finally, any French–Belgian agreement had to be preceded by the settlement of the Belgian gold.[69] The Belgian government-in-exile's refusal to accept the offer made by Alphand with respect to the Belgian gold made this third condition rather impossible to fulfil.

Finally, the announcement in late 1943 of Spaak's departure from Washington back to London was seen by the French as a sign of lack of interest on the part of the Belgians towards a Belgian–French agreement.[70] In January 1944, Gutt decided nevertheless to pursue his discussion with the French and with Monnet in particular on the future of Europe. There is no doubt that Gutt held a high opinion of Monnet. He wrote to Spaak: 'I have witnessed his cleverness for twenty years. I know about the position he secured towards the British, then towards the Americans. At the same time, I believe he is loyal.'[71]

In these discussions with Monnet, Gutt made no secret of his belief that Britain would be ready to accept to participate in a European organization. As to the possibility of Britain joining a customs union between the Benelux and France and other countries such as Italy, Gutt stressed that the key to such a question lay in the future of French economic policy towards trade liberalization. This, for Gutt, meant that the French had to break with their interwar protectionist stance and accept to open their market to foreign trade. As a result, Gutt considered that the French were still undecided on the future direction of the economic and financial policy. He also made Gutt aware of the difficult position of Monet among the Free French.[72] However, if he was happy to learn that Monnet was able to consolidate his position, he remained inflexible with respect to the issue of the Belgian gold.[73]

Finally, in July 1944 at Bretton Woods, Gutt had a last long discussion with Mendès France about the possibility of a Belgian–French agreement. Gutt stressed to his French counterpart once more the need for the French to change their interwar trade policy towards liberalization. Without denying the importance of the issue, Mendès France replied to Gutt that both countries would have to adjust their postwar economic policy to each other and that future negotiations would show whether such an agreement could be possible.[74] With respect to the Belgian gold a breakthrough was finally achieved in August 1944 thanks to a new French proposal. The question would finally be settled by an agreement on 10 October 1944. This opened the way for the conclusion of the French–Belgian payment agreement signed on 23 February 1945.[75]

Conclusion

This chapter has shown that the importance of the Benelux agreements concluded during the war should not be exaggerated. Rather, these agreements were very much in line with the failed attempts of Belgium during the interwar period to open trade relations with its European neighbours. As such, the monetary agreement signed in 1943 provided for exchange rate stability and was inspired by the Reynaud–Simon agreement of December 1939. For Gutt and the Belgians, it represented another big advantage. Indeed, the Benelux monetary agreement made it possible for the Belgians to enter an international cooperation without encroaching on their sovereignty as it was based on the idea of full reciprocity. In other words, this agreement provided a concrete answer to the discussions that divided the Belgians in exile on the future of Belgium's sovereignty.

Nevertheless, the Benelux agreements were important for different reasons. First, they reflected the extent to which for the Belgians in exile, and Gutt in particular, international cooperation on the Continent had to be restricted to its Western dimension. Secondly, the Belgian attempts to convince the British to join them confirmed the priority given to their relations with Britain. The extension of the same agreements to France reflected a more complex situation. Indeed, it highlighted the failure of the Belgians and of Gutt in particular to convince the French to abide by the principles of sound monetary policy and trade openness.

Finally, the Benelux agreements are also to be understood as a possible alternative to the failures of the discussions underway on the British and American plans for a postwar international monetary cooperation. In this respect, Gutt's first meeting with Keynes proved to be crucial. Indeed, it convinced the Belgian minister to design a possible counter-plan to Keynes's project that was seen as harmful to Belgium's interests, especially with respect to its future commitment to the gold standard. As for the American plans, Gutt was not more convinced about the chances of a universal international monetary cooperation. Instead the Belgian minister favoured a gradualist approach with countries presenting similar levels of economic development. Ironically enough, with the success of the Bretton Woods conference and the establishment of the IMF and of the World Bank, these aims quickly lost their pertinence. What was left was the only concrete example of economic cooperation between the European allies concluded during the Second World War.

5 THE BIRTH OF A MONETARY SYSTEM: CAMILLE GUTT AND BRETTON WOODS (1943–4)

When the US administration decided to release their plans for the postwar monetary order to the Allies' governments, Gutt was still not very optimistic as to the prospects of establishing universal monetary institutions. It is true that the Belgians, and Gutt in particular, did not play a central role in the negotiating process that led to Bretton Woods conference of July 1944. Nevertheless, they had to take a position on the Anglo-American plans for a Stabilization Fund and an International Bank.

This chapter proposes to address Gutt's views on the American ideas for postwar monetary order as presented by Harry Dexter White. It will emphasize not only Gutt's assessment of these ideas but also his participation in their discussions. The main argument will be that the Belgian minister's positions were very specific. In short, while agreeing with White's plans as far as their basic principles were concerned, Gutt nevertheless opposed their institutional features, preferring instead the ones included in Keynes's project for an ICU. This position was not only the result of some personal feelings but had also to be understood in the context of the challenges these plans posed for Belgium in terms of international economic cooperation. In other words, such schemes presented Gutt and the Belgians with the challenge of reconciling international cooperation and the safeguard of Belgium's sovereignty over monetary policy.

This chapter will be divided into four main parts. The first part will revisit the historiography of the process that led from White's plan to the Bretton Woods conference of July 1944. The second will address Gutt's view on White's plans and then on the Anglo-American plans. The third will deal with the international dimensions of the discussions on the Belgian franc postwar parity while the fourth will revisit the Bretton Woods conference itself, not only from the point of view of Gutt's own assessment of it but also in terms of his contribution to it.

From White's Plan to Bretton Woods

The historiography on the process that led from the release of White's plan to the Bretton Woods conference of July 1944 has given rise to a rich literature. This contrasts with the preceding period (see Chapter 2) when discussions were held in London. However, the historiography on this phase is marked by a paradox. Indeed, while the literature has been prone to address the importance of the American phase during which discussions were held in Washington, it has mostly focused on the role played by Keynes at the expense of White.[1]

The second aspect of the literature on the birth of the Bretton Woods institutions is the emphasis on the notion of a convergence of views among Allies economists and officials in terms of their main principles and objectives. This has led authors to refer to the idea of the formation of an epistemic community as the main explanation for the success of the Bretton Woods conference.[2] Such an ideational approach that emphasizes the importance of consensus-building around ideas and principles can be found in Kenen's edited volume of the fifty years of the Bretton Woods institutions, in James's recent history of the IMF and Woods's book on globalization.[3] Other authors such as Odell have, however, considered this approach insufficient in explaining the success of Bretton Woods as compared with the failure of the 1933 London International Economic Conference. Instead, Odell argued that the ideational approach has to be included into a wider perspective addressing the bargaining strategies of all the main players.[4] Other views suggest that the establishment of the Bretton Woods system has to be addressed in the context of the division between bankers active in international financial diplomacy in the 1920s and economists defending new views based on the experience of capital and exchange controls as adopted since 1931 across the Western world.[5]

Some further historical accounts such as van Dormael's history of the Bretton Woods conference or Horsefield's official history of the IMF have underscored the numerous divergences existing among the main actors, especially but not only between the Americans and the British.[6] But these accounts are very much based on American sources and have paid little attention to the positions of the other countries and in particular of the European countries.

All these views, however, share one element in common: the emphasis on principles relating to economic policy in the discussions leading to the Bretton Woods conference at the expense of the institutional features of the proposed new international organizations. Indeed, the discussions on the Bretton Woods institutions raised some important issues in terms of limitation of sovereignty for its members and powers given to them. For Gutt, as a representative of a small nation, these questions were of fundamental significance. The challenge was not only how to preserve some forms of national sovereignty without impeding on international cooperation in the monetary field but also how to make sure that countries would comply with the new rules of the game. These questions were at the heart of Gutt's experiences of interwar financial diplomacy when he had to face the inability of the Western powers to ensure compliance, especially with respect to the payment of the German reparations.

That being said, to locate the role of Gutt in these discussions is far from an easy task. Certainly, Gutt and the Belgians did not play a critical part in the discussions that took place mostly between the American and the British Treasuries. Nevertheless, Gutt's position towards the American plan was interesting as it reflected the extent to which the institutional features of the proposed new international monetary organization were seen as equally important as the discussions over economic policy. In other words, as representatives of a small nation, Gutt and the other Belgians were indeed more interested in the legal features of the proposed international institutions than in economic policy as such.

Gutt on the White Plan for a Stabilization Fund and for an International Bank for Reconstruction and Development

When Gutt learned about White's plans for postwar international monetary cooperation, he was no less optimistic than about Keynes's plans. Nevertheless, he was convinced that the British ideas would be quickly buried by the Americans (see Chapter 3). The White plans consisted of the creation of two new international financial institutions, a Stabilization Fund and an International Bank for Reconstruction. If they stemmed from the same premises as Keynes's, they nevertheless presented four major differences.

In White's plan, the new Stabilization Fund was to play an active role in terms of purchasing and selling of currencies and gold, whereas the UCI was to see its role confined only to the purchasing of gold. In terms of quotas, the White plan proposed to calculate them on the basis of different aspects such as the members' gold reserves, and other parameters while Keynes essentially based the quotas of the ICU on its members' levels of trade. With respect to capital flows, White's plan suggested scrapping them except for the ones approved by the Fund while Keynes put forward the idea of a more comprehensive control.[7] Finally, if the two plans proposed to deal with balance of payments disequilibrium, Keynes's plan emphasized the need for flexibility and the preservation of national monetary sovereignty, whereas White underlined the need for more rigidity and the possibility for the Fund to intervene in its members' monetary policy.[8]

When Gutt read White's plan for a Stabilization Fund, he was first struck by its differences in terms of form with Keynes's project. He wrote in a note addressed to Theunis:

the first is written by a poet, the second by a American lawyer. In other words, Keynes's plan is thought through with all the art, the refinement and the clarity of an old civilization, the White plan with the lack of experience, of nuances and sense of relativitism that one can find in the young nations as well as in young individuals. The White plan looks complicated, by its presentation, when it is brutally simple.[9]

On his part, Gutt was very prone to highlight what he considered as the main difference between the two plans, namely: the fact that, contrary to Keynes's plan, the White's plan put some limit to its members' contributions and liability. In other words, this constituted a clear departure from the principles of unlimited liability on which Keynes's plan was based.[10]

In New York, Theunis was more concerned with the divergences between the British and American plans that made him fear a repetition of the disaster of the 1933 London Conference (see below). He also discussed these plans with van Zeeland. According to the former Belgian minister, the future monetary institution's role should be limited to exchange rates issues. All the other economic issues should be dealt with by the proposed international bank or even by the BIS itself. The mention of the BIS made Theunis believe that van Zeeland was also thinking of his own brother, Marcel van Zeeland, who was working for the Basel-based international financial institution.[11]

In April and May 1943, Gutt presented the Keynes and the White plans to his colleagues in the Belgian government. In his presentations, he underlined again the flexibility of the first compared with the rigidity of the second plan. The Belgian minister also emphasized the extent to which the White plan would give way not only to American preponderance in international monetary affairs but would also represent a danger of a possible interference in other countries' conduct of domestic monetary policy.[12] Nevertheless, in his conclusion, Gutt repeated his scepticism towards the chances of success of either of the two plans. Only Spaak, the Belgian foreign affairs minister, intervened in the discussions and raised three main objections to the White plan. The first concerned its supranational aspects. If Spaak did not reject them outright, he nevertheless considered that there should be equality in the limitation of national sovereignty and that no single nation should be in a position to control the new international economic institutions. The second related to the fact that these discussions were taking place only among experts and did not leave enough room for politicians to engage in the debate. The third concerned the risk of the exclusion of the Soviet Union. In response, Gutt only insisted that in terms of limitation of sovereignty, it should be made proportional. In other words, the Belgian finance minister rejected all ideas of a hegemonic domination of any single nation over the planned international monetary institutions. But he refused to draw any conclusions on the two plans, as the negotiations were still in their preliminary stage.[13]

When the Americans released their plan, they made clear that the discussions should only take place in Washington and not in London. They also designed a new method for these discussions. Instead of plenary sessions as was the case in London, bilateral exchanges of views with the experts of the Allied nations was chosen in Washington DC.[14] In June 1943, Gutt seized the opportunity of his visit to the US to discuss the postwar monetary plans with White.[15] The meeting between the two men took place on 3 June. Gutt told White what he saw as the three main weaknesses of his plan. The first concerned the question of compliance of the Fund's members to his decisions. What if a country just decided to refuse to accept the Fund's decision and chose to leave it? Linked to this question were the soft-law aspects of the Fund's powers, especially with respect to the publication of a report as a means to incite its members to revert their monetary policy. The second concerned the need to establish different international institutions in order to take care of other economic problems such as relief and international investments. The third related to the universal aspect of the Fund. According to Gutt, this would entail the extension of membership to countries whose lack of economic development might prove to be more of a liability than an asset for the new organization.

In reply to Gutt's points, White said that he was convinced that the publication of a report by the Fund would have a considerable impact on the concerned countries' public opinions and would, therefore, influence governments' policies. White explained that the still vague aspects of some of his plan's provisions were justified by the need to ensure a successful approval at the US Congress. Gutt wrote in his note about the meeting that this did not surprise him as he was told by Keynes that the latter considered the White plan as excellent but with one major flaw: that it would never be approved by the US Congress contrary to his own plan that had all the chances of being approved.[16]

Finally, regarding the establishment of other international agencies, White replied that if he did not feel very concerned with the question of relief, he had also the plan of proposing the creation of an international bank to deal with the question of international investments. But he confessed that he had been prevented from presenting it at the same time as his plan for the Stabilization Fund as the question was considered to be too sensitive.[17]

From his stay in the US, Gutt drew the main conclusion that if there was still large opposition between the Americans and the British on their plans for postwar monetary cooperation, this opposition was mostly political and not technical. In other words, from a technical point of view, the two plans looked very similar. At the same time, the Belgian finance minister excluded the idea of a Belgian mediation between the two Allied Treasuries as had been suggested to Boël by some Canadian officials. As a shrewd negotiator, Gutt preferred to leave the Americans and the British to settle their differences. Only then could the Belgians intervene and try to take advantage of their state of exhaustion. As he wrote to the Belgian prime minister: 'The day when their antagonism shows itself, when the struggle takes place, when the adversaries exhaust themselves, then we will be able to intervene'.[18]

After Gutt's departure for London, the discussions continued with Boël and de Gruben as Belgian representatives. When, on 13 October, the British and Americans finally published their joint statement, Boël was told by Edward Bernstein that the divergences between Keynes and White were still important, especially on the point of whether or not the Fund should pursue an activist role as proposed by White or just a passive role as proposed by Keynes. But Boël was particularly worried about another issue, which was the one of the possible liquidation of the Fund.[19]

In November, Gutt had another meeting with Keynes who explained to him the way he had been working with the Americans. Gutt was told that both Treasuries had agreed up to 75 per cent and that they would now propose new sets of principles that would be then released to the Allied governments. This took form in the publication, on 21 April 1944, of the joint statement. On the same day, Roosevelt accepted Morgenthau's proposal to convene an Economic and Monetary Conference to take place in Bretton Woods. This conference was to be preceded by a meeting in Atlantic City at the end of June. The conference at Bretton Woods was scheduled to start on 1 July.[20]

Meanwhile, the Americans had also sent their project for the establishment of the Bank for Reconstruction and Development in November 1943. The Bank was aimed at dealing with international investments, especially in the context of postwar economic reconstruction. It was also designed to complement the actions of the Fund. The latter would only provide short-term assistance towards balance of payments disequilibrium while ensuring exchange stability. The Bank would provide long-term financial assistance for reconstruction and development. The capital of the Bank was to be of 10 billion dollars and its loans would mostly be levied by private bankers with the bank's guarantee.[21]

In November 1943, when taking part in the UNRRA conference, Gutt officially received the American proposal for the establishment of the Bank for Reconstruction and Development. On 7 January 1944, a Belgian delegation composed of Gutt, Theunis, Boël and Ansiaux was invited to a meeting with White and Bernstein to discuss the Bank project. In this respect, the Belgians told their American counterparts the extent to which their project looked very similar to a Belgian institution set up in the aftermath of the First World War and named the Société Nationale de Crédit à l'Industrie. The latter institution had been established in order to finance the reconstruction of the country by offering long-term credit facilities and was funded by Belgian private banks up to 40 per cent of its capital.[22] However, if the Belgians were sympathetic to the American project, they nevertheless raised a number of questions. The first related to the possibility of a member of the bank to use loans to finance the purchase of subsidized goods or goods whose prices had been depreciated as a result of a monetary devaluation. This question went to the heart of the issue of the relationship between the Fund and the Bank. White replied that if the Fund was deprived of any powers to sanction, it had to be understood that only countries on good terms with the Fund could have access to the Bank's credit facilities. The second question concerned the reciprocal use of credit facilities, in other words: the possibility for a lending country to use its borrowings for the defence of its own interests. In his reply, White emphasized the truly multilateral aspect of his schemes that dictated that loans would be solely granted for the sake of their beneficial impact on world trade. This last point was particularly supported by Theunis who then declared: 'Belgium's primary interest is the overall level of world trade'.[23]

The Determination of the Postwar Belgian Monetary Parity: International Dimensions

The determination of the Belgian franc par value included both a Belgian and an international dimension. At the level of the Belgian government-in-exile, some ministers, and particularly Spaak, were reluctant to take such a decision in London. But the prime minister settled the question in putting forward the need to include a new parity in the Belgian–Dutch financial and monetary agreement. Perhaps a more compelling reason for the Belgian government in exile to come up with a decision with respect to its monetary parity was the precedent created by the landing of the Anglo-Americans in North Africa and the way they dictated their own parity for the French franc.[24] On 18 November 1942, the Allied governments' experts in London had already issued a declaration which considered the determination of postwar parities as a matter of national sovereignty while accepting the need to consult with the British and American Treasuries (see Chapter 4). At the end of November, Gutt circulated a memorandum to the British and the American Treasuries emphasizing that the determination of postwar monetary parities was a matter of national sovereignty even if this did not preclude a close cooperation with Belgium's allies.[25]

For the Belgians in exile, the discussions over the new parity of their currency re-opened the debates over interwar monetary policy.[26] On the one side, van Zeeland was advocating a Belgian franc-parity at 300. In other words, the former Belgian minister considered the need to restart the economy more important than the preservation of the Belgian population's purchasing power at the end of the war. Conversely, Gutt favoured a limited devaluation to 161 that would present in his mind the advantage of not only defending the purchasing power of the population but of creating room for further flexibility. In his colourful language, Gutt would often refer to the fact that 'no human force will ever be able to cut a leg of a legless man'.[27] In New York, Theunis was more hesitant about the question. According to him, a further devaluation of the Belgian currency presented the advantage of alleviating the burden of the debts accumulated as a result of the German occupation of Belgium. But he nevertheless agreed with Gutt on the need to limit any depreciation of the Belgian franc in the immediate postwar period.[28]

Different elements would make the balance tip in favor of Gutt's approach. First, in London, Gutt's position was supported by Otto Niemeyer and Georges Bolton of the Bank of England. However, the decisive support came from Keynes himself. Indeed, already at the end of 1942, Keynes argued for the need to take account of the purchasing power of wages on the level of prices as a key element for the determination of postwar par values.[29] From occupied Belgium, Gutt also received valuable information from some key Belgian business and economic figures who put forward a series of figures from 123, (i.e. no devaluation), 150 or 170 but no more as the new parity for the Belgian francs towards the sterling.[30] Finally, Gutt accepted that his and van Zeeland's theses be tested in the light of the available statistics. In reality, both showed rather similar results in terms of the increase in the cost of living in occupied Belgium within a range of 46–50 per cent. In conclusion, Gutt thought that a rate around 170 would be an option but preferred to opt for 161 as this would give him additional room for manoeuvre.[31]

As soon as July 1943, Gutt sent a memorandum to the British and American Treasuries proposing the parity for the Belgian postwar currency at 161 for a pound and 41 for a dollar. During a meeting with the chancellor in October, the Belgian finance minister was told that this rate was considered rather unrealistic as opposed to 176 seen as a more acceptable option.[32] Later in December, Gutt discussed the Belgian franc parity with White. Before the meeting, he was told by Waley that the US Treasury considered 176 as too low and proposed instead a parity of 200 for a pound and 50 for a dollar. This would be confirmed following Gutt's meeting with White who confided to the Belgian minister his scepticism about the proposed rate. Much of White's reluctance to endorse the Belgian proposed parity lied in his assumption that it did not take enough account of the devaluation that occurred in occupied Belgium as a result of the war.[33]

Faced with such reluctance, Gutt became strongly convinced that unless he found a possible agreement on the postwar Belgian franc's parity, such a decision would be taken by the British and Americans. Hence the Belgian finance minister took the initiative to convene meetings with the other Allies' Treasury representatives when in Washington in January 1944. In these meetings with the French, British and Dutch representatives at the US Treasury, he finally reached an agreement on the parity for the Belgian currency at 176,625 for a pound and 43,827 for a dollar.[34]

This solution presented the additional advantage of being the existing parity of the Congolese currency. In the middle of April 1944, Gutt forwarded to the Allied Treasuries the new parity for the Belgian franc. However, he accompanied this decision with the reservation that such a parity could be reconsidered in view of the circumstances on the ground after the liberation of the country from the German occupation.[35] For the time being, the Belgian minister had fulfilled his main objectives. First, he had succeeded to impose the decision on the future parity of the Belgian currency as a sovereign decision. And secondly, he had showed the other Treasuries that such a sovereign decision could also be made on the basis of a close cooperation with them.

The Ghosts of London: Gutt, Theunis and the Bretton Woods Conference (1944)

When he returned to London in February 1944, Gutt kept at some distance from the discussions that were taking part in Washington. Indeed, he did not lack important issues to be resolved, such as the completion of the Benelux agreements and the final preparation of a monetary reform to be undertaken after the liberation of Belgium. But this did not prevent Gutt from keeping himself informed about the progress of the Anglo-American discussions.

In April 1944, the publication of the joint statement gave rise to much discussion, in the press and among Allied ministers. On 23 May, Keynes gave an important speech on the subject before the House of Lords, refuting all the possible objections to the project for a Stabilization Fund. In his speech, Keynes went as far as to argue that the scheme would not affect British wartime provisions while preventing a return to the interwar gold standard. [36] If the speech seemed not to have caught Gutt's attention, Theunis reacted immediately and saw in it a first sign of a possible failure of the Bretton Woods conference (see below).

In June 1944, Gutt finally presented the British–American plans for a Stabilization Fund and a Bank for Reconstruction and Development to his colleagues in the Belgian government. Once again, Spaak intervened and expressed a number of misgivings at the British–American plans. The Belgian foreign affairs minister was especially concerned with their impact on his plans for Western European cooperation under British leadership (see Chapter 4). However, Gutt was eager to temper Spaak's reluctance by saying that there was no question at this stage for the Belgian government to enter the two planned institutions as the discussions were far from being completed. In addition, the Belgian minister also put forward the possible advantages that the Fund might bring to Belgium.

Its creation would bring a number of years of stability and protect Belgium against any future competitive monetary devaluations while giving more credibility to the adopted parities. Nevertheless, he also highlighted his scepticism about the scheme and more particularly about the possibility of the scarce currency clause that he thought no one would dare use.[37]

In New York, Theunis was especially concerned with the rising opposition to the Keynes–White plans in the context of the campaign leading to the new presidential election of November 1944. The Republican camp was indeed deeply divided on these plans between an isolationist faction led by Senator Robert Taft and a more interventionist faction composed of Thomas Dewey and Dulles. The latter tried to present an alternative plan based on the Reconstruction Finance Corporation that had been set up by Hoover in 1932.[38]

New York bankers were also extremely critical of the Keynes–White projects. Private banks such the National City Bank of New York, the Chase Manhattan Bank and J. P. Morgan feared that the newly created institutions would either limit or compete with their own investment activities in the world. This was especially the case with the project for a Bank for Reconstruction and Development to which their opposition was even stronger.[39] Instead, some New York bankers favoured either a loan to Britain alongside a stabilization agreement between the dollar and the sterling or even, a return to the pre-war gold standard.[40]

The combination of Keynes's speech to the House of Lords and the objections raised in the US towards the Keynes–White plans made Theunis fear a repetition of the disastrous failure of the 1933 London Monetary and Economic Conference. But this time, according to the Belgian diplomat, the bombshell would not come from the Americans but from the British who would prefer the resolution of their own financial problems over international cooperation.

> There is a striking resemblance between the arguments presented recently by Keynes and the arguments made by President Roosevelt during the London conference in 1933. At that time, in the message that fell as a bomb on the conference, the President declared that a healthy economic system is more important for the well-being of a country than the value of its currency compared to the other currencies. The future conference will have to answer the following question very clearly: do we really believe in stable currencies and stable exchange rates or will we have to go back to the situation of 1933, after the bomb dropped by Roosevelt?[41]

At the end of June 1944, Gutt left London for the US in order to attend the Bretton Woods conference. However, his trip to the US was delayed due to problems relating to communications between Allied governments (see Chapter 2). Before going to Bretton Woods, Gutt decided to stop in New York where he met with Theunis. There, he also had a meeting with van Zeeland who told him that the planned conference was a step, however small, in the right direction and that Belgium should support it.[42]

As a preliminary task, Gutt also had to think about the composition of the Belgian delegation to the planned conference. Already in the spring of 1943, when the first rumours spread about the possibility of a future monetary conference, Gutt and Theunis had already exchanged some ideas about the likely people to select. According to them, two possibilities had to be retained. If the conference was to include experts only, then the delegation would be led by Theunis and van Zeeland. If, on the other hand, the conference was to include political personalities, then the agreement was to include the Belgian delegation to experts such as de Gruben, Ansiaux, Boël and the diplomat Van Langenhove.[43] In 1944, when the Belgians learned that the Dutch were thinking of sending a high-profile delegation, Theunis considered that the Belgians should do the same as well. Amongst his own collaborators, Theunis suggested Joseph Nisot, a lawyer who had taken part in the legal case of the Belgian Central Bank against the Bank of France and who had already assumed with success the function of Secretary of the Belgian delegation to the International Labor Organization in April 1944. In New York, Theunis also mentioned to Gutt the presence of a number of bankers and other specialists on financial questions who might be of interest.[44] In London, Gutt favoured a small team consisting of his closest advisors but with the difficulty that two of them, Ansiaux and Baudewijns, were busy with the negotiations of the monetary agreements with Britain and France and would therefore be staying in London. Finally, Gutt and Theunis agreed that the Belgian delegation would consist of the following personalities: Gutt, Theunis, de Gruben, Boël as delegates, the Belgian economist who found refuge in New York, Boris-Serge Chlepner and Nisot as advisers while de Selliers was appointed as secretary (see Table 5.1).

In the organization of the conference, the Belgians were given important positions. On 3 July, Gutt was elected as one of the four vice-presidents of the conference alongside the Brazilian Eduardo da Souza, the Australian, Leslie G. Melville and the Soviet Michael Stepanov. As a result, Gutt became a member of the steering committee chaired by the US Treasury secretary Morgenthau that included Mendès France, Louis Raminski to name the most important ones. As for Theunis, he was appointed as the reporting delegate of Commission II discussing the International Bank for Reconstruction and Development and chaired by Keynes (see Table 5.2).

The information relating to the contribution of the Belgian delegates to the conference is rather scarce. During the whole conference, Gutt only had the time to write three letters to the Belgian prime minister and to send a few telegrams. The main reason for his silence, Gutt confessed to Pierlot, was that not only had his time been fully occupied by the conference but that most of the motions discussed had been of such technical nature that there was no need to mention them at all. Overall and despite the numerous divergences that arose during the conference, Gutt remained relatively optimistic as to its outcome. There was nothing euphoric in his mind, just the realization that the British and the Americans would do anything they could in order to have a final act approved by all parties.[45]

Table 5.1: Task repartition of the Belgian delegation to the Bretton Woods conference (July 1944).

Belgian delegation:
Chairman: Camille Gutt
Georges Theunis
René Boël
Baron Hervé de Gruben
Advisers: Joseph Nisot, Boris-Serge Chlepner
Secretary: Ernest de Selliers de Moranville
Bretton Woods Conference
Steering Committee:
Henry Morgenthau Jr (US)
Camille Gutt (Belgium)
J. L. Isley (Canada)
Hsiang-His K'ung (China)
Carlos Lelras Restrepo (Colombia)
Pierre Mendès France (French delegation)
Abol Hassan Ebtehaj (Iran)
M. S. Stepanov (USSR)
Lord Keynes (UK)
Commission I: International Monetary Fund
Chairman: Harry Dexter White
Committee I (General Objectives and Capital): René Boël
Committee II (Operation): Georges Theunis
Committee III (Organization and Management): Camille Gutt
Committee IV (Form and Status of the Fund): Joseph Nisot
Commission II: International Bank for Reconstruction and Development
Chairman: Lord Keynes
Reporting delegate: Georges Theunis
Chairman Belgian delegation: Camille Gutt
Committee I: René Boël
Committee II: Georges Theunis
Committee III: Boris-Serge Chelpner and Joseph Nisot
Commission III: Other Means of International Financial Cooperation
President: Eduardo Suarez
Belgian delegate: Hervé de Gruben

There was indeed a great deal of contentious issues under discussion at Bretton Woods. First, the Americans had to please the Soviets and agreed to raise their quota. The British, led by Keynes, tried to resist American attempts to locate the Fund's headquarters in Washington instead of New York. At the same time, Keynes was lobbying for an independent monetary institution consisting of experts not linked to their own national administrations.[46] The French were particularly angry at the size of their allocated quotas. This reaction was part of the wider issue of the unequal balance between the American bloc and the European bloc in terms of voting shares in the new monetary organization (see Table 5.2). The opposition of Mendès France on this matter was especially strong and the French finance minister even threatened to leave the conference altogether.[47] However, the French finance minister failed to mobilize the other Europeans behind him apart from the Belgians. According to Theunis, Gutt himself translated Mendès France's speech on the issue and supported his position. However, the other European countries that had first promised to back the French demands remained silent.[48]

In general, the Belgian delegates were satisfied with their contribution to the Bretton Woods discussions. They had succeeded in presenting themselves as trustworthy intermediaries between the Americans and the British while keeping on good terms with the French, Dutch and Canadians in particular. On a more personal level, Theunis's contribution to the conference had also been important. As reporting delegate of the Commission II on the project for the International Bank for Reconstruction and Development, he had to deal with Keynes's attitude that had been a constant source of irritation for some, not least for the Americans themselves.[49] At the end, Theunis and Keynes closed the discussions in good spirit. Keynes also reminded Theunis of their trip in 1919 through devastated Belgium behind the German lines.[50]

In his final report to the delegates, Theunis also highlighted a number of issues that had, according to him, appeared to have been a source of problems during the discussion. The first one of these was the impression that the Bank project had been somewhat neglected in the discussions during the preceding months to the profit of the Fund. He concluded his report by alluding to the 1927 International Economic conference that he had had the privilege of chairing and reminded his audience of all the recommendations that had been then adopted but never implemented. This time, however, Theunis saw some ground for optimism as recommendations had given way to action.[51]

Despite all the speeches of satisfaction, Bretton Woods left a number of important issues unresolved. Questions such as the future location of the new institutions, the role of the executive directors and of the managing director, not to mention an array of more technical aspects, were still to be settled. The final Act of the conference had also to be ratified by the national parliaments of its members. To Gutt, the conference had a hopeless taste of déjà vu of interwar financial diplomacy. As he reported to the Belgian Consultative Committee:

> This conference was the exact reproduction, with respect to its main aspects, its framework, and its end, of dozens of conferences that I attended from 1920 to 1944: the same trend to reach an agreement on a text, ambiguous enough, so everyone would be able to bring it back home as a success on the basis of each person's interpretation ... the same interventions of the great powers, negotiating back-door deals and imposing them on all ... the same coalitions of particular interests ... the same appeals to the general interest in the speeches[52]

In this context, Gutt showed only a limited enthusiasm regarding the future of the two new organizations. As for Theunis, he was much more concerned with the political dimensions of the discussions and underscored the American manoeuvring in order to accommodate the South American countries' demands. With respect to the Soviet delegation, Theunis also experienced their contrived way of negotiating:

> Twice, I chatted with one of them [the Soviets] and twice he quickly stopped short the conservation, fearing to get compromised. Everyone had the same experience. At times, it is another Russian who comes to pull the arm of the delegate in danger.[53]

Back in London, Gutt presented the results of the conference to the Consultative Committee. In his assessment, Belgium had fulfilled its main objectives. As far as the Council of the Executive Directors was concerned, the Benelux countries were ensured to have one seat on it. As far as the Bank was concerned, the Belgians and the Dutch succeeded in convincing the other members to reduce its lending capacity to 100 per cent and not to 300 per cent as first suggested. Finally, the Belgians and the Dutch secured a seat at the Committee of Directors of the Bank.[54]

Table 5.2: Repartition of quotas and number of votes within the Fund as decided at the Bretton Woods conference (July 1944).[55]

Countries	Quotas (million USD)	Number of votes
US	2,750	27,750
American bloc total	3,539	40,615
Britain	1,300	13,250
France	450	4,750
The Netherlands	275	3,000
Belgium	225	2,500
Luxembourg	10	350
Other Europeans	403	5,510
Total Europe (Minus Britain)	1,363	13,410
USSR	1,200	12,250
Other countries	1,399	19,475
Total	8,800	99,000

Conclusion

This chapter has presented Gutt's views on the White plans for a Stabilization Fund and an International Bank as well as with his participation in the Bretton Woods conference. As far as the White plans were concerned, Gutt and the other Belgians in exile felt certainly more sympathetic to its basic economic principles and especially the limits imposed on the Stabilization Fund's liability. However, Gutt was more reserved with regard to its institutional features and its possible encroachment on national sovereignty. Here again, Gutt and the other Belgians in exile were caught in their main dilemma as representatives of a small power with respect to international economic cooperation. On the one hand, Belgium badly needed such cooperation for its economic survival, as it would guarantee stable exchange rates and the prospect of open trade. On the other hand, the country had to be ready to pay the price for such cooperation in terms of the limitation of its sovereignty. In this respect, Gutt's interwar experience also played an important role in shaping his positions. First, Gutt refused the play the role of possible mediator between the US and the British. Instead, he considered that it would be better for the Belgians to wait for the two Treasuries to tire themselves in their discussions and then to seize the opportunity. In many respects, this was reminiscent of the Belgian strategy in the negotiations of the German reparations during the 1920s. Secondly, in his discussions with White, Gutt was particularly sceptical of the biting effect of the soft-law mechanisms proposed by the Americans in their project for a Stabilization Fund. Once again, as Belgian negotiator during the 1920s, he experienced the difficulty of any international cooperation mechanism to ensure the implementation of its decisions. On the whole, however, he certainly favoured Keynes's plan in so far as it provided for a more passive fund and greater automatic arrangements with respect to monetary policy.

In any case, both Gutt and Theunis were still profoundly sceptical as to the chances of a successful conference. In New York, Theunis was haunted by the memory of the failure of the 1933 London conference. Theunis's fears found their origins in the combination of Keynes's May speech before the House of Lords and the objections raised by some financial and political circles in New York towards the White–Keynes plans. Interestingly, Theunis's suspicion was based on a repetition of a break-up of the conference, not because of the Americans, but this time because of the British who might decide to privilege the resolution of their specific economic problems at the expense of international monetary cooperation. In London, Gutt appeared to defend the White-Keynes plans but with little conviction.

If the Belgians did not play an important role at the forefront of the discussions that took place in Bretton Woods, they were nevertheless satisfied by their participation. Both Gutt and Theunis imposed themselves as important figures during the conference. There is no doubt that they succeeded in presenting themselves as important intermediaries between the most important delegations without antagonizing anyone of them. Such a position will certainly contribute to explain, at least in part, the choice made to appoint Gutt as first managing director of the IMF in Savannah (see Chapter 6). This, however, did not prevent Gutt and Theunis from being struck by the importance of political issues over technical ones in the discussions at the Bretton Woods conference.

6 CAMILLE GUTT, FIRST MANAGING DIRECTOR OF THE INTERNATIONAL MONETARY FUND (1946–51)

The road that led to Gutt's appointment, in May 1946, as the first managing director of the IMF was certainly an unexpected one. In February 1945, when the Pierlot government fell, there was no doubt that Gutt thought of retiring. Nevertheless, there were still some issues that needed to be resolved. The first was the negotiation of the end of the Lend-Lease agreement between Belgium and the US. The second was the implementation of the Bretton Woods agreements. In the first case, Gutt's wartime experience made him almost a natural choice for conducting the negotiations. In the second case, Gutt's presence in the Belgian delegation in Savannah came as a result of the good relationship forged by the former Belgian finance minister with both the British and the American Treasuries during the War.

Once appointed as the first managing director of the IMF, Gutt had to face the challenge of making the new international organization work. More difficult proved to be the relationship between the IMF on the one hand and the US on the other, as well as between the IMF and Western Europe in the context of the rising Cold War. These issues were first reflected in the questions of the dollar scarcity and of the French devaluation of 1948. Then, the question of economic and monetary cooperation in Europe revealed to be another challenge for the IMF, raising the question of its relevance. Finally, the 1949 sterling devaluation and its handling by the fund would reopen the discussions about the nature of its powers.

In all these questions, the existing literature has not been very charitable towards the action of the IMF during its first five years of existence (see below). Strangely enough, however, very little research on the activities of the IMF during this period was done. This chapter will try to propose a more balanced assessment of the activities of the IMF under Gutt's management. Its main contribution will lie in the combined use of IMF's archives with Gutt's personal archives for the period. It will argue that the nascent Cold War revealed the extent to which the new international monetary institutions were poorly equipped to address the challenges of the new system of international relations that emerged from the Cold War.

Camille Gutt and the Postwar Order: Lend-Lease Agreements and the Savannah Conference (1945–6)

Gutt's resignation in February 1945 with the rest of government did not mean the end of his public activities. Indeed, two important questions were still left unresolved. The first concerned the ending of the Lend-Lease agreement between Belgium and the US. The second concerned the establishment of the Bretton Woods institutions, and more particularly the nomination of their management teams. In both cases, Gutt's experience during the Second World War proved very useful for the Belgian authorities who did not hesitate to call on his services.

Negotiating the End of the Lend-Lease Agreements (1945)

As soon as the new Belgian government was constituted, Gutt warned his successor, Gaston Eyskens, of the urgent need to send a delegation to Washington DC to negotiate the settlement of the Lend-Lease agreements. For Gutt, the sense of urgency was justified on two accounts. First, the Belgians were still left in the dark as to the compensations they would be entitled to in return for their contribution to the US war effort that was increasing by 12 million dollars on a monthly basis. The second is more political. In January, Boël tried to start the discussions with the Americans but failed. Meanwhile, the French and Monnet in particular, succeeded in being the first to negotiate such an agreement with the Foreign Economic Administration (hereafter FEA). According to Gutt, the priority given by the Americans to the French could be easily explained by Monnet's influence on the US administration (see Chapter 4). But it also revealed the extent to which Belgium had lost most of its importance for the US administration. In this context, Gutt was appointed on 23 February as head of the Belgian Economic Mission which also included Boël in charge of negotiating the end of the Lend-Lease agreements with the Americans.[1]

When he arrived in Washington DC, Gutt took notice of the changing mood in American political circles marked by the rising of isolationism in Congress. In the Senate, the isolationists led by Senator Taft almost succeeded in rejecting the British–American Loan Agreement. Eventually, it would be approved by both Houses in July 1945. In addition, the Roosevelt administration was poised by a growing rivalry between agencies, each defending their own agenda. On the one hand, the Treasury had always been critical towards the Lend-Lease and tried its best to limit its scope. On the other, the FEA was waiting for the opportunity to take advantage of the Lend-Lease as a means of expanding trade relations between the US and Europe.[2] Lastly, the death of Roosevelt on 12 April 1945 raised questions about the foreign policy of his successor, Harry S. Truman. As Gutt stated in his memo on the Lend-Lease negotiations: 'The electoral position of the new President seems to suggest that he would be less European than his illustrious predecessor'.[3]

The negotiations meant to settle the Lend-Lease agreement with Belgium may look technical, but the stakes were nonetheless important. Contrary to a number of countries, Belgium presented the characteristic of being creditor of the US under the Lend-Lease for an amount of about 123 million dollars (see Table 6.1).

The Lend-Lease agreements did not contain a precise provision with respect to their final settlement. Only article 5 provided that at the end of the hostilities, the amounts of aid provided by both sides were to be determined in a way that would take account of the reciprocal interests of the contracting parties. Under the master agreement, two categories of supplies were defined. The first category, or schedule one, included all the supplies in goods and equipments provided until the end of the Lend-Lease. The difference was to be transformed in a thirty year credit bearing a 2.8 per cent rate of interest. The second category, or schedule two, covered the same supplies as the first one but consisted of a credit involving an upfront payment of 20 per cent.[4]

On 17 April 1945, after some lengthy and difficult negotiations, the Belgians and Americans reached a first agreement. Contrary to the other Europeans and the French especially, Gutt succeeded in including all the American supplies in schedule 1. But at the same time, the US decided to decrease the total amount of the Belgian credit line from 575 million to 322 million dollars. With respect to the future trade relations with the US, the Belgians also failed to be granted most-favoured nation status. A final aspect of the negotiations concerned the reimbursement by the Americans of the Belgian bills supplied to the American and British troops in Belgium. As a result, Gutt came back from Washington with an immediate reimbursement of 13 million dollars.[5]

In August 1945, the Belgians, as the other allies, were dismayed at Truman's announcement of putting an end to the Lend-Lease altogether. Belgian foreign affairs minister Spaak shared his surprise with Dean Acheson, the new US secretary of state but with no result.[6] For the Belgians, the situation was made even more difficult as they had advanced, as mentioned, more than 120 million dollars to the US. The importance of the Belgian credits towards the Americans could be explained by two main factors. First, due to the German counter-attack in the Ardennes in the autumn of 1944, the American troops stayed on Belgian territory much longer than expected. Secondly, as the Belgian army had been incorporated in the British forces, it had received very little supplies from the US.[7]

Table 6.1: Lend-Lease and Reverse Lend-Lease between Belgium and the US.[8]

Lend-Lease	Amounts (in USD)
US Lend-Lease to Belgium	50 million
US Lend-Lease to Congo	5 million
Lend-Lease	178 million
Belgian Reverse Lend-Lease to the US	
Difference	123 million

The final settlement was finally negotiated in Washington in September 1945. Once more Gutt was included in the Belgian delegation that consisted of Spaak (Belgian foreign minister), Paul Kronaker (Belgian minister of agriculture) and Boël as adviser of the government. For the Belgians, the objective was clear. It consisted of getting from the Americans as much compensation as possible for Belgium's remaining surplus in order to provide for the postwar economic reconstruction needs. To this purpose, two options were possible: either to include a number of American supplies in the Lend-Lease or to diminish Belgian's contributions to the Lend-Lease. On the American side, the situation was more complicated. The decision to put an end to the Lend-Lease made the first Belgian option impossible to contemplate. In addition, in view of the planned convening of the United Nations Conference of Trade and Employment, the US administration was reluctant to take any measures that would undermine trade liberalization. Finally, the negotiations almost entirely focused on ways of reducing the American deficit towards Belgium. The Belgians then succeeded in getting some 115 million dollars of additional supplies. The difference of 8 million was to be covered by American stocks already stored in Belgium.[9]

The last aspect of these negotiations consisted of the conclusion of a loan contracted by Belgium from the Eximbank. The use of the bank first created to fund American exports was made possible thanks to the changes made by the Truman administration. The changes included the suppression of the provisions of the Johnson Act that prohibited financial assistance to countries in default towards the US. The Belgians then secured, in October 1945, a loan of 35 million dollars to be paid by 31 December 1950.[10]

In all these negotiations, Gutt was able to get a sense of the change of mood in Washington. Even if he could rely on his good relationship with the US Treasury and with Morgenthau in particular – quickly replaced by Fred Vinson – the tide was turning. With the end of the war, the American foreign economic policy would drift more and more away from its first economic priorities to increasingly integrate new political dimensions. Within the US administration this shift led to the gradual weakening of the Treasury in favour of the State Department. If this change became visible in 1947 with the launch of the Marshall Plan, the first signs were already showing in 1945.

Appointing the Managing Director to the IMF: The Savannah Conference (1946)

According to the provision of the Bretton Woods agreement, the ratification procedure provided for the member governments to present their ratification instruments by 31 December 1945 at the latest. If at this moment, more than 65 per cent of the capital had been subscribed, the agreement would then come into force and a first meeting of the Governors – national representatives of the IMF's members – could be convened as soon as after 1 January 1946.[11]

In Belgium, the ratification of the Bretton Woods agreement proved to be a mere formality. On 20 December 1945, the Belgian Parliament unanimously approved the new monetary organization.[12] This unanimity reflected a clear contrast with the difficult ratifications in the UK, France and the US itself.[13]

At the beginning of 1946, White and Keynes started planning for the first meeting of the IMF governors. The meeting was to be held in Wilmington, a small town near Savannah in the state of Georgia in March 1946. A number of important items were put on the agenda as the meeting was meant to implement the Bretton Woods agreement. These items related to issues such as the location of the head office for the Bretton Woods twins, the appointment of their executive directors, including the managing director and their status.

In the discussions prior to the meeting, a number of divergences between the Americans and British had already emerged. The first concerned the status of the executive directors. The British, and Keynes in particular, were in favour of giving the management of the two institutions to representatives of each government who would act as technicians in constant contact with their own Treasury administrations. In this perspective, the managing director would be in charge of the technical supervision of the IMF. In Keynes's mind, the choice of a strong personality for this position was important. As Keynes stated in conversation with White: 'Unless the Fund has a real good manager it will not make very much difference whether the executive directors are good or just mediocre'.[14]

The Americans had a very different view on the matter. They wanted the position of executive directors to be a full-time one. Such a provision was seen as the safest guarantee for the independence of executive directors vis-à-vis their respective governments and as the best protection from political pressure. But the British, who had concluded, after laborious negotiations, the loan agreement with the US were not in a position of strength to fight for their arguments.[15]

In January 1946, Gutt was informed by Waley during a stay in London about the British positions. He then confided to Gaston Eyskens, his successor as Belgian finance minister, that he was more in favour of the British views than of the American ones. At the same time, Gutt was of the opinion that there was very little chance that the British views would prevail. According to him, the only hope resided in a strong community of views between the Belgians, British and Dutch. The new Belgian minister of finance also asked Gutt whether he would be interested in the position of Belgian executive director. To this demand, Gutt replied that he would only accept if it did not imply a full-time position.[16] This seemed to confirm the extent to which Gutt shared the British views on the management of the future international monetary organization. The demand made by the Belgian minister was also motivated by the strong desire made known by the Americans of seeing Gutt in Savannah. Indeed, a few days earlier, White had contacted the new Belgian ambassador in Washington, Robert Silvercruys, to tell him how much he expected Gutt to be present.[17]

Finally, the Belgian delegation consisted of the Belgian finance minister, Franz De Voghel as governor of the Bank and Gutt as governor of the IMF with Maurice Frère as alternate. Former wartime collaborators, of Gutt such as Ansiaux and Boël, complemented the delegation as advisers with the addition of the Belgian diplomat de Gruben and, Guillaume Rolin-Jacquemyns, a young economist freshly graduated from Harvard as secretary.

The Savannah conference opened on 8 March 1946. It ended on 18 March. The conference, on top of appointing the IMF's management, had to deal with two questions of importance which had been left unresolved since Bretton Woods. The first dealt with the location of the Bretton Woods's institutions' head office. The second concerned the powers of the executive directors.

According to the Bretton Woods agreements, the headquarters of the newly created institutions had to be in the country having the greatest quota – the US. But Keynes was eager to see the head office located in New York and not in Washington DC and this for two reasons. First, it was normal for the Bretton Woods twins to be close to the newly created United Nations' headquarters. Secondly, to base the Bretton Woods in New York constituted the best protection from possible pressures exercised by the US administration. Not surprisingly, the Americans were defending the opposite view. To locate the Bretton Woods institutions in Washington DC would give easier access to its members to access their respective diplomatic representations and would enable their staff to escape from the pressures of the financial community based in New York. Despite French support on this point, the British proved to be unable to convince the Americans. As a result, the decision was made to choose Washington as the location of the Bretton Woods institutions' headquarters. The second point of contention concerned the remuneration of the executive directors. But here again Keynes had to cave in and to accept the American point of view of having full-time executive directors based permanently in Washington.[18]

The more practical aspect of the Savannah conference consisted in the election and the appointment of the IMF's main officials, i.e. the executive directors. According to the agreement reached at Savannah, the number of executive directors was limited to twelve. Apart from the executive directors representing the five countries with the largest quotas, five others had to be elected. The election procedure was not simple and turned quickly into a farce. In order to be elected, every candidate had to get at least 19 per cent of the votes. At the first round, three candidates, the Canadian Louis Raminski, the Dutch G. W. Bruins and the Czechoslovak Jan Mladek met the threshold and were elected. After a third unsuccessful round, Fred Vinson, the US Treasury secretary had to design a new procedure in order to enable the two other candidates, Gutt and the Egyptian Ahmed Zaki Saad, to fill the two positions of executive director.[19]

In the aftermath of the Savannah conference, two points remained on the agenda of the new monetary organization. The first was the appointment of the managing director of the IMF. For the position, the appointment of White looked almost natural and was eagerly supported by Keynes. But at the last minute, White's application was pulled back by Vinson. Officially, the decision was explained by the willingness of the US administration to secure the chairmanship of the Bank for one of their own. In reality, White's application was withdrawn when his name was mentioned on an FBI list of people suspected of having transmitted secret information to the Soviet Union.[20] With White out, the choice for managing director was more open. For their part, the British and Keynes were in favour of a strong personality able to compensate for the possible weakness of the executive directors. At first, the Americans thought of proposing the position to Graham Towers, governor of the Bank of Canada. Towers, however, declined the offer on the ground that he was opposed to the choice of Washington DC as the headquarters of the IMF. The Dutch tried to push one of their own, Beyen, but the British rejected because he was seen as not a strong enough personality for the job. Desperate to find a suitable candidate, the British turned then to Gutt who was supported by the Canadians, Dutch and French. After a discussion with Keynes, Gutt finally accepted the offer.[21] As the Americans did not have any objections, Gutt was appointed on 6 May 1946 after a meeting behind closed doors in Washington as the first managing director of the IMF. He was replaced by his former wartime adviser, Ansiaux, as Belgian executive director while de Selliers de Moranville was appointed as his alternate.[22] A few weeks later, he signed his contract for a mandate of five years while obtaining the permission of keeping the position of Board member of Ford Motor Cy (Belgium) in a non-executive capacity.[23] The appointment of Gutt as managing director of the IMF came a bit as a surprise for the American media even of most their attention was attracted by high remuneration of the position, about 30,000 dollars a year.[24]

The second point concerned the first revision of the quotas following the Soviet decision to leave the Bretton Woods institutions. The French who had vehemently complained about the small size of their quota in Bretton Woods were finally rewarded and the decision was made, in October 1946, to increase it from 450 million dollars to 525 million dollars. As a result, the French quota became the third in importance and on par with China's, but far smaller than the quotas of Britain and of the US.[25]

Camille Gutt, the IMF, and the Reconstruction of Western Europe (1945–51)

In many respects, the first years of the existence of the IMF were its most challenging ones. Apart from the issues linked to the setting of the new international organization, the challenges posed by the postwar economic reconstruction of Europe tested the limits of the new international economic regime created at the end of the Second World War. This part will focus on these challenges rather than on Gutt's actions with respect to the management and staff issues relating to its mandate as managing director of the IMF as these have already been addressed in the literature.[26]

In this respect, both economists and economic historians have not been very charitable towards the IMF's role. As early as 1951, Kindleberger gave a very critical assessment of the relevance of the Bretton Woods institutions and even raised the question of a possible liquidation of the IMF.[27] According to the American economist, the Bretton Woods were considered 'irrelevant' and 'inadequate' when referring to their roles with respect to postwar economic reconstruction.[28]

This negative view can also be found in more recent literature on the postwar European reconstruction and the Marshall Plan. In his book on *The Reconstruction of Western Europe*, Milward is not less clear when he wrote: 'In fact the Bretton Woods agreements proved so unsatisfactory an international basis for reconstruction that they had little force or influence on European reconstruction once the international payment crisis made their inadequacy evident'.[29]

For Eichengreen, 'the role of the IMF should not be exaggerated with respect to postwar reconstruction', and the institution only became meaningful after 1958.[30] A similar point can also be found in H. James's history of the IMF where he reached similar conclusions when opposing the unsuitability of the Bretton Woods institutions in dealing with postwar European economic problems and the effectiveness of the Marshall Plan and of the European Payment Union (hereafter EPU).[31] More recently, however, another view has emerged. Indeed, in a recent contribution Skidelsky argued that it was the Cold War and resulting American political and financial commitment to European economic reconstruction that eventually rescued the Bretton Woods institutions and contributed to ensuring their survival.[32]

This part will propose to assess the IMF's policies towards the reconstruction of the Western European economies during Gutt's mandate as managing director of the IMF. It will argue that the personal views of Gutt on Europe and European reconstruction are critical in order to understand the possible shortcomings of the IMF when dealing with the reconstruction of Western Europe. One the one hand, it will suggest that Gutt's views, which were so much shaped by his interwar and war experiences, failed to capture the emerging new nature of international relations as generated by the nascent Cold War. On the other hand, it will be argued that, ironically enough, the turn of events would confirm some of Gutt's early scepticism about the possibility of a universal approach to postwar economic reconstruction.

This part will proceed in three steps: The first will deal with the issues of dollar scarcity and the discussions around the par values of the major European currencies; the second will address the impact of the Marshall Plan on the IMF; and the third will deal with the relations between the IMF and the EPU.

The IMF and European Reconstruction: Dollar Scarcity and Par Values

The origins of the scarce currency provision in the Bretton Woods agreements can be traced back to the American plan for a Stabilization Fund of December 1942. By this provision, the IMF was empowered to ration a currency in case of excess demand for that currency. In practical terms, it meant the possibility for countries to restrict their imports from the country whose currency was deemed to be scarce. This provision was particularly welcomed by the British who saw in it the first sign that the Americans would be ready to accept their full share of responsibility in case of fundamental trade disequilibrium. This optimism, though, was not shared by Keynes who considered this provision as 'unworkable'.[33].

According to the scarcity clause provisions, the IMF had the right to declare a currency as scarce when facing a shortage of supply in this currency. In August 1948, the IMF's Executive Board started discussing whether the dollar shortage justified a declaration of scarce currency.[34] Officially, the IMF's own Research Department explained the dollar shortage as a result of a production gap in Western Europe. In other words, it was not due to the failure of the US to import European goods but rather to the abnormal level of American exports.[35] However, another document in the IMF archives tells a different story, one less favourable to the US. This document highlights the consequences of the lifting of price controls by the Truman administration.[36] This decision was part of a new economic policy aimed at promoting private enterprise and reducing the tax burden.[37] The policy had two important consequences for Western Europe. The first was a decrease in the purchasing power of the loans, grants and credits from the US. The second was the risk of a knock-on inflationary effect which would undermine the financial stabilization policies carried by most Western European governments. Therefore, the IMF pointed out that even if the Americans were not responsible for the dollar shortage, they were nevertheless responsible for the intensification of the dollar scarcity.[38] One solution would be to devalue the dollar in order to alleviate the Europeans' financial predicament. But this solution would meet major obstacles. The first of these was the difficulty of convincing the public in the US that their currency had lost part of its value. No less troublesome was the second difficulty of contemplating dollar devaluation, given that the link between gold and the dollar was paramount in the Bretton Woods agreement. Thirdly, it confirmed what White had already written in January 1945 – that the US authorities would be reluctant to accept an adjustment of the dollar to promote exchange stability but rather expected their partners to adjust to the changing American economic policy.[39]

The second important issue that the IMF had to deal with concerned the determination of the par values or the exchange rates for the currency for its members. With respect to Western European countries, the problem presented itself under two main aspects. On the one hand, overvalued parities would allow the European countries mainly to increase their purchasing power of goods needed for their reconstruction. On the other hand, undervalued parities would help stimulate their exports. The IMF decided in favour of the first option, believing that the priority lay in the possibility for its European members to increase their imports. In other words, the IMF accepted existing parities as agreed at the end of the war.[40] Problems started to arise, however, when the French decided to change their parity and to devalue their currency by more than 44 per cent towards the dollar.

This change in the French par value was part of an economic package prepared by Robert Schuman, France's finance minister during the spring of 1947 in order to balance the national public finances.[41] During a trip to Paris a few months later, in August, Gutt was informed about the French projects in meetings with Prime Minister Ramadier and Schuman as well as with officials from the Finance ministry and the Bank of France. Before his French interlocutors, Gutt supported the idea of devaluation but on the condition that it should be linked to a tight control of French public finances. But, at a meeting with Guillaume Guindey, Gutt also learned that the French had the intention to restore a currency market albeit limited to some currencies. In other words, the French were made unable to guarantee their cross rates with other currencies such as the sterling and this would, in effect, lead to the establishment of multiple exchange rates. Gutt told the French in response that if the IMF agreed to the French devaluation it would certainly object to their plans for multiple exchange rates.[42]

In the autumn, the French also contacted the British about their projects and met with strong opposition. According to the British, measures such as the multiple exchange rates would not only undermine the very spirit of the Bretton Woods agreements but would also expose the sterling in accentuating the pressure for its devaluation.[43] Even more worrying for the British was the possibility for such a system of multiple exchange practices to divert British exports from the US to France which would result in an accumulation of unconvertible French francs in Britain.[44]

In December 1947, the French sent a high-profile delegation to Washington led by the former finance minister, Mendès France. The American administration was divided on the French plan. The Department of State supported it, knowing that the future of Schuman's government was at stake.[45] A failure would lead to new elections and the possibility of the return of the Communists to power in France. The Treasury Department was more reluctant to accept what was considered an infringement to the Bretton Woods agreements. More importantly, the Treasury was worried that the multiple exchange rates would accentuate the pressures on the devaluation of the sterling.[46]

In January, the IMF started debating the French projects. On 19 January, Jean Rioust de Largentaye presented the French plans to the Board of executive directors in the following terms:

> The French government wants to collaborate fully in the spirit of the Fund agreement and is convinced that the proposals would cause no real or appreciable damage for other Fund members. Above all the plan should be considered as an attempt to achieve a realistic and adequate solution to the present French exchange problems. It is a move in the right direction and should be accepted.[47]

The IMF's executive directors were rather reserved with respect to the French plan. In order to avoid a crisis, Gutt made a last proposal in his discussions with Mendès France for a larger devaluation of the French currency and for the restoration of a free exchange system restricted to transactions regarding invisible goods. The French, however, refused to budge and opposed the rate proposed by Gutt. Even Bolton, one of the British executive directors suggested postponing the IMF's decision for six months before being instructed by the British Treasury to drop the idea.[48]

On 23 January, Gutt made a last unsuccessful attempt to convince Schuman, who had succeeded to Paul Ramadier as prime minister in November 1947.[49] On 25 January, the executive directors had no other choice than to consider the French regime of multiple exchange rates as 'inconsistent with the purpose of the Bretton Woods agreements' and declared that France ineligible to use IMF resources.[50] The day after, the French communicated the new parity for their currency at 214 to the IMF. Consequently, the new parity of French franc was not recognized by the IMF and France lost possible access to the IMF's resources for some 135 million dollars on a yearly basis until 1954.[51] In reality, the punishment inflicted on France quickly lost its significance, especially in the context of the Marshall Plan (see below).

The severity of the IMF decision surprised the Europeans and shocked the French. Good friends of Gutt, such as Ansiaux, rejected the IMF decision, believing that the IMF had ignored the economic problems of Western Europe. Ansiaux wrote to Gutt: 'The general feeling is that the IMF has acted more like a Court of last resort, relying on rigid principles rather than like a financial expert who would offer reasonable and humane solutions'.[52]

In answering these criticisms, Gutt explained the four main reasons for the IMF's decision. First, the decision was the logical consequence of the Bretton Woods' agreement provisions. For the IMF to allow multiple exchange rates would be to risk the collapse of the Bretton Woods' regime based on fixed-exchange rates. Worse, according to Gutt, this could potentially have led to a new period of monetary instability reminiscent of the competitive devaluations of the 1930s. Secondly, there was the position of the French government. In reality, Gutt was in favour of an even greater devaluation of the French franc. However, the credibility of the IMF was at stake in the context of the early discussions about its participation in the Marshall Plan. Finally, there were the likely consequences for the sterling. There was no doubt that the new cross-rate sterling/dollar would have revealed the extent to which the pound was overvalued towards the dollar. As former minister of finance in the Belgian government – in exile during the Second World War and witness of the cost of the conflict for the British, Gutt was not ready to precipitate the collapse of the pound. As he wrote to Ansiaux:

> The world has long lived on the solidity of three key currencies. Before the First World War [there was] the French Franc, the Pound Sterling and, a bit less solidly, the Dollar. After the Great War, the Dollar and, a little less solidly, the Pound Sterling and the French Franc. At the moment, the French Franc is out of the picture. The Dollar has maintained its primacy. In the Land of the Blind, the one-eyed man is king, and the Pound, if you will, is playing the role of one-eyed man (in the sense that the pound has been shaken but remains, to a certain degree, a world currency). Is it in our interest to precipitate its collapse? Personally, I think not.[53]

With regard to the French, the IMF's decision reinforced their hostility to the Bretton Woods agreements. It reinforced their belief in a European solution to their monetary and financial problems without involving the IMF. The search for this European solution would be supported by the US Department of State within the framework of the Marshall Plan, in which France would occupy a central position. Indeed, France would not only become the main recipient of the Marshall Plan aid but, following the IMF's decision to exclude the countries benefiting from the Marshall Plan aid from having access to IMF's support, her exclusion quickly lost its singularity (see below).[54]

The IMF and the Marshall Plan

In 1947, the changing political conditions in Europe, the deadlock on the future of Germany and the assessment of the economic challenges of reconstruction led the Truman administration to launch a new aid programme known as the Marshall Plan or European Recovery Program (hereafter ERP).[55] The ERP consisted of two main aspects. On the one hand, the Americans committed themselves to supporting the rehabilitation of the European economies through the allocation of credits, grants and gifts for a period of four years. On the other hand, the benefit of this financial support was made conditional on the ability of the European countries concerned to coordinate their reconstruction needs. In doing so, the Marshall Plan was serving the political objective of fostering economic and political cooperation in Europe.

Although the Marshall Plan did not reveal a profound change in US foreign economic policy, it did constitute a departure from its postwar basis. Economic foreign policy became now linked with short-term political and security objectives. Now, the main objective became the unification of Western Europe instead of the fulfilment of the Bretton Woods objectives. In other words, a new reality set in, the one of the looming Cold War, changing the bases of the postwar order settlement negotiated in 1944.

Within the Truman administration this change of priorities translated into a growing overlap between the State Department, the newly created Economic Co-operation Administration (hereafter ECA) and the Treasury Department.[56] As for its more concrete aims, the Marshall Plan was designed to boost industrial and agricultural production as well as monetary stabilization and trade liberalization in Western Europe.[57]

Personal, public and official support from Gutt for the Marshall Plan was immediate. In a public lecture at The Hague, the managing director stated: '[The European countries] are aware that the ERP gives them a unique opportunity to modernize their economies'.[58] He nevertheless confessed to Spaak, Belgium's minister of foreign affairs: 'Unfortunately, I remain skeptical of the ability of Western Europe to agree on a common economic plan'.[59]

According to Gutt, the main obstacle would come from the French and their lack of commitment to a new liberal trade policy. In this respect, the IMF managing director made no secret of his support for Monnet.[60] At the same time, he considered that, thanks to the prestige of his position as president of the First

United Nations General Assembly, Spaak was the best person to take charge of the future of European cooperation.[61]

In January 1948, the IMF was confronted with the question of whether countries taking part in the Marshall Plan should be allowed to draw on IMF resources. The Executive Board decided that they should not. The main reason was that, according to the IMF Research Department, European countries would still have a deficit towards the US at the end of the Marshall Plan in 1952.[62] Therefore, it would be prudent for them to keep their reserves for that period. But the US executive directors declared that the IMF was not to be involved in the Marshall Plan as its main objectives concerned reconstruction needs rather than short-term financial aid.[63] In April 1948, the IMF released its ERP decision stating that purchases of US dollars from the IMF would be allowed only in 'exceptional and unforeseen circumstances'.[64]

As far as IMF and the ECA relations were concerned, the Board of the executive directors recognized the need to maintain a close relationship between the two organizations. In this respect, the US Executive Director, Andrew Overby, stated that the ECA would not interfere in IMF activities. Nevertheless, he added that the cooperation between the two organizations should remain informal.[65]

At the personal level, Gutt, as a former businessman, enjoyed good relations with the ECA staff, dominated by fellow businessmen: Paul Hoffman, head of the ECA; Averell Harriman, ECA special representative in Europe; Richard Bissel, executive secretary and William Clayton, former undersecretary of state who served on the ECA investment panel. During a European trip in the summer of 1948, Gutt and Edward Bernstein met the ECA officials in Paris. From these discussions, the IMF's managing director remained optimistic about the prospect of close cooperation with the ECA. Gutt told the executive directors: 'When in France we had a meeting with Mr Hoffman and Mr Harriman. The people there were manifestly struck by the close liaison and understanding existing between the two organizations, and I may say that it increased their respect for the IMF.'[66]

The IMF and the 1949 Sterling Devaluation

In 1949, the economic situation of Western Europe, despite the assistance from the Marshall Plan showed only little signs of improvement. If the dollar gap had been reduced, it remained substantial. On the political level, the creation of the Federal Republic of Germany only resolved the German question from a political point of view but not from an economic one. On a monetary level, the situation of the sterling was considered as a major impediment to the liberalization of payments. To make matters worse, in the first semester of 1949, the American economy was showing the first sign of a recession that would be short-lived. [67]

In this context, the ECA was still determined to achieve its two main objectives: to end the existing trade discriminations in Europe and to provide for the economic recovery of Western Europe. One solution envisaged was to proceed to general exchange rates realignment. The devaluation of the sterling, remained, however, a sensitive issue. One solution for the US administration was to give the IMF the initiative in this respect. This would allow a less direct approach to the issue.[68] So, at the end of March 1949, the US executive directors, Frank Southard, took advantage of a discussion on the exchange rates situation in Europe to ask Gutt to examine the possibility of a general realignment of European exchange rates including the sterling.[69] The British remained adamantly against such an operation. For Stafford Cripps, the chancellor of the Exchequer, such a devaluation was to be considered as an action relevant not only to British domestic policy but to foreign policy as well. In other words, the chancellor of the Exchequer was only ready to contemplate it if put in the wider discussion including the British–American economic relationship, the future of the sterling area and the issue of commodities. In addition, a general election was convened for the next year with a looming prospect of a Labour washout raising the spectre of their 1931 defeat in the aftermath of the devaluation of the sterling.[70]

However, when the pound was once again attacked by speculators in April 1949, these plans were quickly shattered. Between April and June 1949, the British reserves melted by more than 150 million dollars. If in public Cripps denied all rumours of devaluation, in private the first contacts with the Americans started. Even Prime Minister Clement Attlee, wrote directly to a convalescent Cripps to press him on the devaluation. On 18 September 1949, in the midst of the annual meeting of the IMF governors, the British government announced its decision to devalue its currency by 30 per cent.[71] This devaluation be followed by the devaluations of the French franc (22 per cent) and of the Belgian currency (by 12 per cent).[72]

There is no doubt that such an exclusion of the IMF from the discussions by the Americans and the British contrasted greatly with the numerous contacts that had surrounded the devaluation of the French franc of 1948. Gutt himself was well aware of the situation. In a letter to Spaak he wrote: 'the methods that are used are not the ones one would wish for'.[73] According to Gutt, this attitude, however, was logical as it reflected the British views on the nature of the IMF (see above) that Gutt had been supporting since Savannah.[74] Nevertheless, he objected to the British handling of the whole issue: 'Even with this conception, the British could have acted differently'.[75]

From an economic point of view, the scope of the sterling devaluation was considered excessive. The French in particular did not hesitate to use the term 'trade war'.[76] But Gutt supported the operation. According to him, it would enable the British economy to cope with international competition without imposing too much sacrifice on the British themselves.[77]

On a more general level, the contribution of the devaluations of 1949 to European recovery is difficult to establish. According to the economist Jacques Pollack who succeeded Bernstein at the head of the IMF Research Department, the key to the European recovery was to be found in the growth of the American economy boosted by the new rearmament policy decided following the adoption of the National Security Council Report 68.[78] The document, which was not exempt of economic considerations, laid down the ground for the adoption of the Mutual Assistance Programme (hereafter MAP) of 1952. This MAP would ensure, though on the different basis, the continued supply of dollars to the Western European economies beyond the Marshall Plan that was to end in 1952. But at the same time, this policy would completely undermine the very foundations of the Bretton Woods institutions in resuming inflationary and expansionist budgetary policies. It would also relegate the economic imperatives of the restoration of multilateralism to a secondary priority compared with new strategic objectives justified by the Cold War.[79]

The IMF and the EPU

One of the main issues of interest to the IMF was the question of payment and trade liberalization in Western Europe. Following the Marshall Speech of June 1947, Europeans decided to set up a pan-European organization, the Committee for European Economic Co-operation – later renamed the Organization for European Economic Co-operation (hereafter OEEC) – designed to administer the ERP. During the conference convened in Paris in early July and gathering the sixteen nations taking part in the ERP, the Belgian Ansiaux presented a plan aimed at creating a system of compensations among European countries.[80] The plan introduced the concept of transferability of the European currencies, aimed at paving the way for their convertibility in gold and in dollars. The Europeans also agreed to use part of the US aid to finance the system until full convertibility was achieved. Finally, the CEEC decided to create a special committee in charge of payment problems, the Committee on Payments Agreements, under the Ansiaux's chairmanship.[81] One the first resolutions of the Committee was to express the wish to see the IMF playing a role in advising its members on measures aiming at the liberalization of inter-European payments.[82]

In September, the Payment Committee decided to convene a technical conference in London. During the conference, the British decided not to take part in the Ansiaux scheme preferring the option of bilateral agreements. As a result, the conference led to a possible payment agreement between the three Benelux countries, Italy and France. In November, the agreement was signed between the five countries in Paris. Among its provisions, it gave the BIS the function of clearing agent. This provision was decided in London in the absence of IMF representatives.[83]

More than one year later, Gutt explained the absence of the IMF as the result of a 'genuine misunderstanding'.[84] However, this decision would have far-reaching political and economic consequences. First, and against Gutt's wishes, the IMF found itself excluded from a discussion of issues directly related to its mission, such as currency convertibility and payment liberalization. Secondly, this decision resurrected the BIS, created in 1929, whose liquidation had not been agreed by the delegates at the Savannah conference.[85] In this perspective, such a decision revealed the preference of the Western European central bankers to rely on old networks of cooperation embodied in the BIS rather than the ones embodied in the IMF.[86]

Ironically enough, this view was strongly defended by the president of the BIS, the Belgian Maurice Frère who was an old acquaintance of Gutt dating back to the negotiations on German reparations. In 1944, Frère was appointed by Gutt as the new governor of the Belgian Central Bank in replacement of Theunis. There is no doubt that the European character of the BIS made it a more appropriate framework, especially for the French, to deal with European issues.[87] Finally, as Gutt acknowledged, the IMF staff were reluctant to contemplate a clearing agreement that would have allowed countries to exchange non-essential goods between each other.[88]

At first, the use of the BIS did not impress Gutt. Even if he did not support the idea of its liquidation, Gutt believed that the BIS had become irrelevant in the new monetary order. In addition, the role of the BIS in the EPU was purely one of book-keeper. Finally, Gutt was confident that the US Treasury was supportive of the IMF. In 1949, the appointment of Overby as deputy managing director was seen as a sign of the strengthening of the support to the IMF. As Gutt wrote to Ansiaux: 'If there is one organization that has the backing of the American Treasury, it is not the International Bank [but rather] it is the Monetary Fund, via Overby'.[89]

At the same time, Gutt remained involved with the ECA in the discussions leading to the creation of conditional aid and offshore accounts for ERP countries. However, he failed to convince the IMF's Board of executive directors to remain committed to European problems. In November 1948, Gutt pleaded for an IMF commitment to the OEEC projects. He stated to the executive directors: 'the OEEC represents the first – and if it failed, it might be the last attempt at inter-European cooperation'.[90]

According to Gutt, there was an even more compelling argument for IMF involvement:

The Paris plan is much concerned with multilateralization, i.e. convertibility ... the Fund agreement is an attempt at convertibility ... therefore nothing of what passes in Paris can leave us indifferent ... our two fields are too near to each other, have too many connections with each other.[91]

In December 1949, the ECA decided to commit itself to the European payments problem by drawing up a blueprint for a European Currency Union, later renamed the EPU. The EPU blueprint was mostly inspired by the Ansiaux plan and was aimed at creating a system of compensations in multilateralizing the bilateral European payment agreements. However, although the system sought to end discrimination within Europe, it actually contributed to maintaining a discriminatory regime against the US. The EPU also infringed the Bretton Woods rules by allowing exchange controls and discriminatory practices.[92]

Nevertheless, the IMF was particularly interested in two issues related to the EPU: its relations with EPU and the IMF involvement in the EPU's institutional framework. With respect to the relations between the IMF and Europe, the EPU plan was a retreat from the Ansiaux Plan which still had offered a possibility for the IMF to be involved in European payments.[93]

The acceptance of the IMF in the EPU framework, however, posed some institutional difficulties. On the one hand, countries such as France, Greece and Austria were unable to draw on IMF resources. On the other hand, ERP countries such as the new Federal Republic of Germany, Portugal, Sweden and Switzerland were not yet members of the IMF.[94] The second difficulty came from the question of whether the EPU should have a strong managing board, with IMF participation, even though the French and British were opposed to such an idea, each for their own reasons. For the French, the IMF's involvement was unthinkable after their rebuff of January 1948, while for the British, the creation of a strong managing board was seen as a threat to their economic sovereignty. In addition, as far as the sterling was concerned, the desire of the British to keep it as an international currency – as a currency used by other countries in settlement of international transactions and as a monetary reserve – and the existing bilateral monetary agreements of Britain were the main obstacles for their participation in the European Payments system. In respect to these problems, the EPU provided that there would be an option for net creditors to elect to hold the sterling instead of claims expressed in the unit of account and for net debtors to use the sterling balances whether accumulated before or after the EPU.[95]

In January 1950, Gutt tried to re-launch the issue of an IMF involvement in the EPU. This time, the Belgian executive director, de Selliers de Moranville, raised some objections based on what he called the negative attitude of the IMF towards Europe,[96] and stated that an IMF initiative would be counter-productive at that stage. In September 1950, the signing of the EPU agreement confirmed the expulsion of the IMF from Europe in favour of the BIS as clearing agent of the new organization.[97] In January 1951, Gutt held a meeting with Overby, Mladek as well as Irving Friedmann, director of the Department of Change Restrictions and Georges Weyer, director of the Department of Latin America. The subject of the meeting was the relations between the IMF and Europe.[98] Overby then stated that he considered the question of relations between the IMF and the EPU as secondary. In his mind, priority ought to be given to the IMF members' problems.

In 1951, Gutt acknowledged in his last address to the meeting of the Board of executive directors the failure of the IMF with regard to the EPU and pleaded for a 'policy of presence' for the IMF instead of a 'policy of absence' which, according to him, prevailed with respect to Europe.[99]

It is in this context that Gutt announced his intention to resign only a few weeks before a possible renewing of his mandate. Officially, Gutt's decision was motivated by personal reasons.[100] In reality, the proposals of the Executive Board only to offer him a three-year contract was considered by him a form of disavowal even if he was finally relieved to learn that a similar offer was finally made to Trygve Lie by the United Nations.[101] In any case, his decision was revealing of the growing tension between the IMF and the US in a changing geopolitical context which affected the mechanism of multilateral economic cooperation.[102]

After his resignation from the IMF, Gutt went back to Brussels. Upon his return, he was approached by his former wartime adviser, Boël, who asked him to become the new president of the Free University of Brussels, Gutt's *alma mater*. However, the project failed and Gutt joined the board members of the revamped Banque Lambert, an old private Belgian bank that worked as the agent of the Rothschilds in the nineteenth century. In the board, Gutt was reunited with another former adviser and IMF's former Belgian executive director, de Selliers de Moranville. In November 1952, Gutt led a UN mission to Iran to assist the new prime minister, Mohammad Mossadegh, to reorganize the domestic economy of the country. In 1953, Gutt was appointed as president of the International Chamber of Commerce that he left in 1955. From 1964 onwards, Gutt retired progressively from his business activities as the one of chairman of the board of the Ford Motor Cy (Belgium). He died in Brussels on 7 June 1971.

Conclusion

In the direct aftermath of the war, when negotiating the settlement of the Belgian war contribution to the Allied war effort, Gutt already witnessed the first signs of changes linked to the coming to power of the new US administration and the looming Cold War. Gutt's appointment as the first managing director of the IMF may be explained by two elements. There is no doubt that he quickly became, for political reasons, one of the very few possible candidates. On the one hand, Gutt's position on the functioning of the IMF was closer to the British views than to the American views. On the other hand, Gutt had also been able to secure a good relationship with the US Treasury. As a result, the Americans were eager to see Gutt take part in the conference in Savannah.

The five years that Gutt spent at the head of new international monetary organization were not without challenges. But the question of whether he deserves the negative assessment within the literature on the period should be balanced by two main factors. First, there is the personal factor, linked to Gutt's interwar and war experiences. Gutt's views were still dominated by the importance of legal commitments made by the IMF's members and the political imperative not to precipitate the collapse of the sterling. Ironically, these two positions would prove to be untenable. In view of the decision towards the French, it certainly created an irreparable gap between the IMF and Europe. With respect to the sterling, Gutt's willingness to preserve the British currency could not avoid the 1949 devaluation from which the IMF was completely sidelined. The second factor is linked with the looming Cold War. In this respect, Gutt seems to have failed to grasp the political transformations of the second half of the 1940s that led unavoidably to a redefinition of the plans made during the war for postwar reconstruction. These transformations undermined considerably the universal character of the newly founded Bretton Woods institutions. Ironically enough, during the war, Gutt had been highly sceptical as to this dimension. But as the managing director of the IMF, he was confronted with an increasingly unilateral US economic policy. The decision not to declare the US dollar a scarce currency, if explained by economic reasons also reflected that the US had no intention of accepting the burden of adjustment that would only lie on other IMF members. The ERP's decision not only reflected the recognition of the need for a more ambitious initiative to support the rehabilitation of the Western European economies but also the recognition of the growing overlapping within the US policy between long-term economic objectives as the ones set in the Bretton Woods agreements and short-term political imperatives linked to the Marshall Plan. Nevertheless, Gutt still wanted to believe in the sustainability of the newly founded universal institutions. The 1948 ERP decision was taken with the aim of a possible association of the IMF with European reconstruction. But this association proved impossible as a result of the French antagonism, the new American unilateralism and the reluctance of the European central bankers to embrace a new system of financial cooperation as shown in their decisions to reactivate the BIS within the EPU agreement. Certainly, the combination of these factors may explain the failure of the IMF to assert itself with respect to the reconstruction of the Western European economies. In other words, the Cold

War imposed a new relationship between economics and politics for which the Bretton Woods institutions were not designed. If anything, the Cold War enabled the coexistence of two different routes towards convertibility and trade liberalization, i.e. the universal one embodied in the Bretton Woods regime and the regional one embodied in the nascent European integration process. Ironically enough, Gutt, who was a partisan of the regional route during the Second World War, had to deal with its effects on an international organization such as the IMF over which he presided.

CONCLUSION

Postwar international finance was the result of the interactions between states-men and experts, each having their own particular views and interests at stake. These views and interests may not be fully understood unless put in the context of past experiences not only individual but also collective. Gutt played a role as both a witness and an actor in this process. However, his role has not attracted significant attention of historians so far. This book suggests that Gutt's career has to be approached in the wider perspective of the emergence of an international financial diplomacy whose practices proved enduring in the context of the Second World War.

The first question that was raised in this book concerns the involvement of private businessmen in public policy, and their role in shaping financial policy, either in its domestic or its international dimensions. The case of Gutt gives an interesting insight into such questions. It showed that the involvement of big business interests in Belgian financial policy came to an end neither with the Great Depression nor the Second World War. Such an involvement took different forms. From the end of the First World War until the middle of the 1930s, Belgium presented the case of an almost complete takeover of Belgian domestic and external financial policy by big business. The second period started with the Great Depression and ended with the downfall of the 'government of bankers' in 1935. Its immediate effect was to lead to a retreat of big business from the forefront of Belgian politics. That period also reflected some larger divisions on the future of monetary and financial policy, especially with respect to the management of the domestic economy. On the one hand, business leaders such as Gutt supported the financial discipline imposed by the gold standard. On the other hand, the new generation of professional economists that emerged in the late 1920s was more inclined to revive domestic demand and Belgium's competitiveness by relying on the devaluation of the Belgian currency.

The opposition between Gutt and van Zeeland has to be understood in the light of these diverging views, and it would resurface in the context of the Second World War. Finally, the third period started with Gutt returning as finance minister in 1939. This period showed a more complex dynamic between business interests and financial policy. Indeed, Belgian business objected to Gutt's war finance and fiscal policy on the ground that they sought to benefit from Belgium's self imposed neutrality. The other dimension of Gutt's interwar career certainly lay in his involvement with international financial policy. The case of Belgium showed that despite growing divergences between big business and economic experts with respect to domestic monetary policy, big business representatives remained very much in control of international issues such as the negotiation of German reparations and other international monetary questions. As for Gutt, his constant journeys between private and public positions reflect the high fluidity between business and politics in interwar Belgium. The last aspect of Gutt's interwar career relates to the genuine transnational aspects of his activities. However, instead of nurturing a new form of idealism about international cooperation, these transnational experiences strengthened his scepticism as to the possibility of such cooperation. In other words, Gutt's experience of transnationalism taught him both the limitations but also the opportunities available to a small power like Belgium in the exercise of diplomacy.

The second question raised in the introduction relates to the influence of private interests in shaping foreign policy choices. In many respects, the situation of the Belgian government-in-exile was rather specific and stemmed from the confusion and the unexpected turn of events between May and June 1940. In effect, the English capital brought together most of the transnational elites that had been active during the interwar period both at governmental and business levels. This considerably helped Gutt in his dealings with British officials in London.

In general, the discussions over the Belgian contribution to the war effort showed the impact left by the First World War and its aftermath on Gutt and the rest of the Belgians in exile. The insistence on the priority of the defence of Belgian interests in these negotiations can be understood by their concern not to repeat the experience of the First World War when postwar issues had been overlooked in the discussions over the war effort. During the Second World War, the negotiations of Belgian participation in the Allied war effort, first with the British and then with the Americans, revealed the complexity of the relationship between private and national interests in the conduct of financial diplomacy.

In the case of the negotiations over the Belgian participation in the British war effort, private interests were less visible as they were included in a more general agreement of consolidating the economic relationship between Belgium and Britain in the postwar period. The only dissenting voice would come from the Belgian colonial business community eager to keep its hands free when dealing with Britain and the US. There is no doubt that Gutt played a central role in these negotiations owing to the fact that the Belgian contribution was more of a financial nature than that of a military one. However, his views on postwar cooperation were not that different from the rest of the Belgians in exile. Perhaps, the only difference was his ability to design a coherent approach to these negotiations. With respect to the US, the same template of the legacy of the First World War and its aftermath applied but with even more important consequences. The Belgian political neglect of the US found its origins in the fear of postwar debts and the lack of renewal of the existing networks that had been forged during the 1920s. The combination of the two laid down the ground for a privatization of the Belgian–American relations. If anything, this privatization showed that business interests alone are often unable to generate a political vision that goes beyond their immediate gains. Such a privatization was reflected in the handling by the Belgian government-in-exile of the negotiations over the Belgian assets frozen in the US, over the Lend-Lease agreements and finally over the Belgian uranium. In the last case, the past experience of Gutt as businessman proved to be crucial and contributed to salvage them from complete failure.

The third question that this book has raised concerns the construction of the post-War monetary order: to what extent were the discussions on the postwar monetary order more concerned with the problems inherited from the interwar period rather than with laying down the basis for a *new* departure? The discussions that took place in London over the future international monetary cooperation gave a clear idea of Gutt's views on postwar international finance. There is no doubt that Gutt was still prisoner of his interwar experience, individual but also collective, that led to the failure of laying down the basis for a stable system of monetary and economic cooperation. These discussions also showed the inability of most of the European elites to design a new negotiating framework and their reliance on an old methodology that had already demonstrated its shortcomings during the 1930s. More specifically, they also revealed the extent to which Gutt and other transnational elites, were far from subscribing to Keynes's views on postwar international monetary cooperation. Indeed, Gutt appeared to have paid little attention to the doctrinal developments in economics and remained very much influenced by the gold standard legacy.

More importantly, he rejected the universal approach defended by Keynes and was in favour of a regional approach as the one embodied in his projects for an economic union between the three Benelux countries: Belgium, the Netherlands and Luxembourg. In doing so, Gutt was just taking over some old ideas that had been developed in the 1930s. These ideas were based on the need to open market access for Belgian exports and to secure some kind of monetary stability in the context of the growing monetary and economic fragmentation of the Continent. If, however, the impact of these agreements remained marginal, they also served some more concrete purposes. In Gutt's mind they unlocked for Belgium the dilemma between the defence of national sovereignty, on the one hand, and international cooperation, on the other. In a nutshell, the reciprocal basis on which these agreements were based ensured that they did not encroach on Belgian national sovereignty. In such a way, Gutt was providing an answer to the debates that emerged on the future of Belgian sovereignty and international cooperation. Finally, these Benelux agreements were to be extended to Britain and France. In doing so, they would provide for an alternative if the universal plans defended by the British and the Americans were to fail. However, the failure of securing an agreement of the same type with Britain revealed the extent to which the British were giving priority to their transatlantic relationship with the US. The difficulty in securing an agreement with France found its main reasons in the great uncertainties relating to postwar French economic policy both in terms of monetary and financial policy.

The negotiations that led to the Bretton Woods conference would confirm Gutt's views on international monetary and financial cooperation. As such, his positions on Keynes's and then the White's plans were quite original. Indeed, if Gutt appreciated the fact that Keynes's plan did not encroach too much on national sovereignty, he was certainly closer to the principles defended by White, especially in terms of limited liability for the planned new monetary organization. Once again, Gutt defended the view of the assertion of national sovereignty as a pre-condition for international cooperation as shown in the discussions over the fixation of Belgian postwar monetary parities. Nevertheless, if this position would have made of Gutt an ideal go-between for the British and the Americans, his interwar experience taught him not do so and to wait for the best moment to intervene. It is true that the Belgian contribution in general and Gutt's in particular to the discussions were limited. However, they would reflect a different narrative of postwar reconstruction in emphasizing the aversion to political intervention in monetary policy and the belief in the regional approach over the universal one.

The last period of Gutt's career covered by this book concerned Gutt's mandate as IMF managing director from 1946 to 1951. During this period Gutt was confronted with the gradual transformation of international cooperation that resulted from the nascent Cold War. In a way, such a transformation signalled the end of an era. For Gutt, the new era would confirm some of the views that he had expressed during the Second World War in favour of a regional approach to postwar international economic cooperation. On the one hand, the challenges posed by the economic reconstruction of Western Europe demonstrated the importance of the regional approach over the global one. On the other hand, the nascent Cold War strengthened the economic unilateralism, especially on the part of the US, at the expense of genuine multilateral cooperation. To some respect, Gutt foresaw these developments during the Second World War. Ironically enough, he was the first one to suffer from their consequences.

GLOSSARY OF NAMES

Acheson, Dean (1883–1971): American lawyer, Democrat. Undersecretary of the US Treasury 1933; undersecretary of state 1941–5; 1945–7; secretary of state 1949–53.

Aghnides, Thanassis (1875–1934): Greek diplomat; Greek ambassador to Britain 1942–7.

Albert I (1875–1934): King of the Belgians (1909–34), who died accidentally on 17 February 1934 from a fall while climbing a rock in Belgium; succeeded by his son, King Leopold III.

Aldrich, Winthrop (1885–1974): American lawyer and banker. President of Chase 1930–40; unofficial emissary of Roosevelt to Britain and chairman of the National War Fund during the Second World War.

Alphand, Hervé (1907–94): French civil servant and minister; entered the Finance Mnistry in 1923. Financial Attaché at the French embassy in Washington in 1940; commissioner for Economy, Finance and Colony within the French National Committee 1941–3; director for Economic Affairs within the French Committee of National Liberation 1943–4.

Anderson, Sir John (1882–1958): British civil servant and minister. Lord President of the Council 1940–3; chancellor of the Exchequer 1943–5; co-director of the British nuclear research programme during the Second World War.

Ansiaux, Hubert (1908–87): Official at the Belgian Central Bank. Director of the National Bank of Belgium 1941–54; deputy-governor 1954–7; governor 1957–71; Belgian executive director to the IMF 1946–8.

Ashton-Gwatkin, Frank (1889–1976): British diplomat. Assistant undersecretary at the Foreign Office 1940–4; senior inspector of HM diplomatic missions with the rank of minister 1944–7.

Attlee, Clement (1883–1967): British politician. Prime minister 1945–51.

Baudewijns, Adolphe (1887–1964): Belgian official at the NBB. Secretary 1936–7; director 1937–44.

Beatty, Sir Alfred Chester (1875–1968): American-born and naturalized British subject mining magnate. Founding shareholder of the Société Internationale Forestière et Minière or Forminière in 1906; served during World Word II on government committees dealing with diamonds and non-ferrous metals.

Bemelmans, Arthur (1881–1952): Belgian businessman. Belgian deputy-delegate to the Reparation Commission 1919–22; member of the Board of directors of the Banque d'Outremer 1922–39; member of the Board of directors of the Société Générale de Belgique.

Berle, Adolf (1895–1971): American lawyer; assistant secretary of state 1938–44.

Bernstein, Edward (1904–96): American economist; assistant director of Monetary Research at the US Treasury 1941–6; assistant to the secretary of the Treasury 1946; director of Research at the IMF 1946–58.

Beyen, Johan (1897–1976): Dutch financier and banker. President of the Bank for International Settlement 1936–9; financial adviser of the Dutch government 1940–52; executive director to the IMF 1948–52; Dutch minister of foreign affairs 1952–6.

Bissel, Richard (1909–94): American economist and civil servant. MIT assistant professor of economics 1948–52; assistant administrator, Economic Cooperation Agency 1948–51; acting administrator in 1951; special assistant to the director of the CIA 1954–9.

Blaise, Gaston (1880–1964): Belgian businessman. Adviser of the Belgian Prime Minister de Brocqueville during the First World War; entered the non-ferrous activities of the Societé Générale de Belgique and vice-governor 1944–51.

Boël, René (1899–1990): Belgian industrialist. Trustee of Solvay interests during the Second World War; Belgian delegate to the Purvis–Monnet Committee in 1940; financial adviser of Gutt 1940–1; counsellor of the Belgian government on temporary basis 1941–4; member of the Belgian delegations to Bretton Woods and Savannah conferences in 1944 and 1946.

Bolton, Sir George (1900–82): British banker. Adviser to the Bank of England 1941–8; member of the BIS board 1949–57.

Boris, Georges (1888–1960): French economist and journalist. Chief of Cabinet of Leon Blum 1938–9; director within the Free French administration; chief of Cabinet of Mendès France 1954–5.

Bradbury, Sir John (1872–1950): British civil servant. Private secretary to Asquith 1905–8; head of Treasury finance division 1908–13; joint permanent of Treasury 1913–19; British representative to the Reparation Commission 1919–25.

Briand, Aristide (1862–1932): French statesman. French prime minister 1909–13; 1915–17; 1921–22; 1925–26; Noble Peace prize winner jointly with Gustav Stresemann in 1926.

Broek, van den, Johannes (1882–1946): Dutch businessman and minister. President of the Dutch Purchasing Commission in New York 1941–2; Dutch finance minister 1942–5.

Budd, Sir Cecil Lindsay (1865–1945): International metals dealer. Founder of the British Metals Corporation.

Cadogan, Sir Alexander (1884–1968): British diplomat; entered the Foreign Office in 1908. Permanent undersecretary at the Foreign Office 1938–46; British permanent representative to the United Nations 1946–50.

Campenhout, André van (1908–87): Belgian lawyer and civil servant. Private secretary of Prime Minister Janson 1937–8; chief of Cabinet at the Ministry of Economic Affairs and deputy-head of the Belgian Economic Mission to London 1940–4; general counsel of the IMF 1946–53; executive director, 1954–73.

Cassel, Gustav (1866–1945): Swedish economist. Professor of political economy, University of Stockholm from 1924; member of the Gold Delegation of the League of Nations 1919–32; Swedish delegate to the London World Monetary and Economic Conference in 1933.

Cattier, Félicien (1869–1946): Belgian businessman. Entered the Board of the Banque d'Outremer in 1916, then the Board of the Société Générale de Belgique 1928–39; was one of the key figures with Sengier in the Colonial activities of the Société Générale de Belgique during the interwar period.

Cauwelaert, Franz van (1880–1961): Belgian Catholic politician. Industry minister 1934; agriculture minister 1934–5; president of the Chamber of Representatives 1939–54; in charge of Belgian propaganda in South America during the Second World War.

Chlepner, Boris-Serge (1890–1964): Belgian economist. Specialist of monetary and financial questions and professor at the Free University of Brussels; found refuge in New York during the Second World War where he worked for the Brookings Institution; adviser to the Belgian delegation at the Bretton Woods conference in 1944.

Churchill, Winston (1874–1965): British statesman. Prime minister 1940–5 and 1951–5.

Clayton, William (1888–1966): American businessman. Assistant secretary of state 1944–5; undersecretary of state for economic affairs 1945–7.

Coudenhove-Kalergi, Richard (1894–1972): Austrian-born aristocrat, founder of the Pan-Europa Movement in 1922 he became a Czech national after the collapse of the Austria–Hungarian Empire, and was later naturalized French; found refuge in the US during the Second World War.

Couve de Murville, Maurice (1907–99): French minister and civil servant. Director of External Finances of Vichy regime 1940–3; Commissioner of Finance of the French Committee of National Liberation in 1943–4.

Crena de Iongh, Daniël (1888–1970): Dutch banker and Minister. Economic adviser to the Dutch government during the Second World War; head of the Dutch delegation to the Bretton Woods conference in 1944.

Creveling, Guy Franklin (1890–1944): American businessman and financial journalist. Vice-president of the African Metals Corporation 1926–44.

Cripps, Sir Richard Stafford (1889–1952): British Labour politician. Member of Churchill's wartime Cabinet; president of the Board of Trade 1945–7; chancellor of the Exchequer 1947–50.

Curie, Marie (1867–1934): French (Polish born) physicist. Pioneer in the field of radioactivity; Nobel Prize in Physics in 1903 and in Chemistry in 1911.

Daladier, Edouard (1884–1970): French statesman. Prime minister 1934; defence minister 1936–8; defence minister and foreign affairs minister 1938–40; arrested and tried by Vichy in 1942; deported by the Germans in 1943, was liberated in 1945.

Darland, François (1881–1942): French admiral and minister. Chief of staff of the French Navy 1937–40; Navy minister in the Vichy regime 1940–2; assassinated in 1942 in Algiers.

Dawes Charles, G. (1865–1951): American politician. Republican. vice-president in the Coolidge administration 1925–9; US ambassador to Britain 1929–32; head of the International Finance Reconstruction in 1932; winner of the Nobel Peace Prize in 1925; retired from politics after Roosevelt's victory of 1933.

Dewey, Thomas (1902–71): American politician, Republican. Governor of New York 1943–54; Republican candidate for President in 1944 and 1948.

Dielthem, André (1896–1954): French civil servant. Entered the French Finance Ministry in 1919; national commissioner for Finance and the Economy 1940–43; member of the French Committee of National Liberation in charge of Relief and 1943–44 and War in 1944.

Dulles, John Foster (1888–1959): American lawyer and politician. Head of the law firm Cromwell & Sullivan by 1927; legal counsel to the US delegation to the Versailles Peace conference in 1919 and member of the Reparation Commission; US secretary of state 1953–9.

Eden, Anthony (1897–1977): Conservative British politician. Foreign Secretary 1935–38 and 1941–5.

Einstein, Albert (1879–1955): German-born physicist. Nobel prize in Physics in 1921, Einstein settled in the US in 1933.

Empain, Edouard (1852–1929): Belgian businessman. Also known as the *General*; responsible for the coordination of Belgian war purchasing during the First World War and Theunis's boss, particularly active in the electricity, tramway and railways business activities, built the Métropolitain in Paris in 1900.

Eyskens, Gaston (1905–88): Belgian Catholic politician. Belgian finance minister in 1945 and 1947–9 and prime minister subsequently.

Feis, Herbert (1893–1972): American economist and author. Economic adviser to the State Department 1931–43; economic adviser to the War Department 1943–7.

Francq, Louis (1868–1937): Belgian lawyer and liberal politician. Member of Parliament 1906–26; colonies minister 1918–24; governor of the National Bank of Belgium 1926–37.

Francqui, Emile (1863–1935): Belgian businessman and minister. Member of the Board of directors of the Société Générale de Belgique 1912–23; vice-governor 1923–32; governor 1932–5; minister without portfolio 1926 and 1934–5.

Frère, Maurice (1890–1970): Belgian financier and diplomat. Director of the Economic Service of the reparation commission 1920–4; economic counsellor, Belgian embassy in Berlin 1930–2; close collaborator of Paul van Zeeland 1937–8; governor of the National Bank of Belgium 1945–57; BIS chairman 1947–58.

Frick, Charles (1830–1930): lawyer and local liberal political figure in Brussels. Owner of the newspaper *La Chronique* and Camille Gutt's father-in-law.

Funck, Walther (1890–1960): German minister. Reich minister of trade and commerce and plenipotentiary for the war economy 1938–45; president of the Reichsbank 1939–45; sentenced for life imprisonment at Nuremberg in 1946 and released on health grounds in 1957.

Gaulle, Charles de (1890–1970): French statesman and General. Under-secretary for defence in 1940; leader of the Free French during the Second World War; president of the French Committee of National Liberation in 1943 with Giraud, alone afterwards; president of the French provisional government 1944–6.

Gérard, Max-Léo (1879–1955): Belgian finance minister and businessman. Secretary of King Albert I of the Belgians 1919–24; finance minister 1935–6 and 1938.

Giraud, Henri-Honoré (1879–1949): French General. Co-chairman of the French Committee of National Liberation June–October 1943; commander-in-chief of the French army 1943–4.

Groves, Leslie R. (1896–1970): American general and engineer. Head of the Manhattan Project 1942–7.

Gruben, Hervé de (1894–1967): Belgian diplomat. Counsellor at the Belgian embassy in Washington 1938–45; director of political affairs and secretary general of the Ministry 1945–53.

Guindey Guillaume (1909–89): French civil servant. In charge of international affairs in the French Finance Ministry in Algiers and then in Paris 1943–53.

Gutt, Claire (1886–1948) née Claire Frick: wife of Camille Gutt. First Belgian swimmer to hold a world record and only Belgian representative to the Olympic Games of 1912; remained in Brussels during the Second World War where she headed a charity called Secours d'Hiver.

Gutt, Etienne (1922–): Camille Gutt's third son and Belgian lawyer. Studied in Britain during the Second World War, first at Rugby College, then at Oxford (Magdalen College); joined the RAF in 1944.

Gutt, François (1916–44): Camille Gutt's second son. Joined the RAF during the Second World War and died in service in June 1944.

Gutt, Hélène (1879–1944): Camille Gutt's half sister. Returned to France after First World War where she worked at the Institute of the Globe in Strasbourg.

Gutt, Jean-Max (1914–41): Camille Gutt's first son. Joined the RAF during the Second World War and died in action in August 1941.

Guttenstein, Max (1836–91): Austrian-born and naturalized Belgian journalist. Married first to Marie Schweitzer and then to Philomène Briers as a second wife; Camille Gutt's father.

Halifax, Edward, Lord (1881–1959): British political figure and diplomat. Foreign secretary 1938–1941; ambassador of Britain to the US 1941–6.

Hambro, Carl, J. (1885–1964): Norwegian politician. President of the Assembly of the League of Nations 1939–40; 1946; president of the Norwegian Parliament 1935–45.

Harriman, Averell (1891–1986): American politician, Democrat, businessman and diplomat. US ambassador and special representative to the British prime minister 1941–3; US ambassador to the Soviet Union, 1943–6; US commerce secretary 1946–8; US coordinator, European Recovery Program 1948–50.

Hayek, Friedrich (1899–1992): Austrian-born economist, naturalized British in 1938. Taught economics at: the London School of Economics 1931–50; the University of Chicago 1950–62; and at the University of Freiburg 1962–68.

Heinemann, Dannie (1872–1962): American businessman. Vice-president of the SOFINA 1905–19; President of the CHADE during the Second World War.

Hoffman, Paul G. (1891–74): American businessman. President of Studebaker 1935–48; head of the European Cooperation Administration 1948–50.

Hoover, Herbert (1874–1964). American businessman and politician, Republican. Founder of the Commission for Relief in Belgium during the First World War; secretary of commerce 1921–8; President of the US 1929–33; active opponent to Roosevelt's policies during the Second World War.

Hull, Cordell (1871–1955): American politician, Democrat. US secretary of state 1933–44.

Hymans, Paul (1865–1941): Belgian liberal political figure; foreign minister 1918–20, 1927–34, 1934–35.

Istel, André (1878–1966): French banker. Founder in 1919 with Schlumberger and Noyer, the Bank Schlumberger, Istel and Noyer and president of his American branch established just before the Second World War as the Bank André Istel & Co.; financial adviser of the French Committee of National Liberation during the Second World War and member of French delegation at the Bretton Woods conference.

Janssen, Albert-Edouard (1883–1966): Belgian lawyer. Director at the NBB 1919–25; finance minister 1925–6, 1938–9; member of the Financial Committee of the League of Nations 1921–40; expert for the Dawes Plan 1924–30; president of the League of Nations Commission for the Study of the Gold Question 1929–33; also private banker since 1934.

Janssen, Georges (1892–1941): Belgian banker and businessman. Administrator of the bank Mutuelle Solvay 1928–31; vice-governor of the NBB 1937–8; governor 1938–41.

Jaspar, Henri (1870–1939): Belgian Catholic politician. Foreign affairs minister 1920–4; prime minister 1926–31; finance minister 1932–4: Foreign affairs minister in 1934.

Jaspar, Marcel-Henri (1901–82): Belgian liberal politician. Minister of transport 1936–7; minister of health 1939–40; Belgian ambassador to the Czechoslovakian government in exile in London 1941–4, then in Prague in 1945, and numerous other postings until 1968.

Joliot-Curie, Frédéric (1900–58): French physicist. Co-winner in 1935 of the Nobel Prize in chemistry, with his wife Irène.

Jonnard, Charles (1857–1927): French politician and diplomat. President of the Reparations Commission 1919–20.

Kerstens, Petrus (Piet), Adrianus (1896–1958): Dutch politician. Minister of trade and industry 1942–4; Speaker of the Dutch Upper-House 1946–52.

Keynes, John Maynard (1883–1946): British economist and civil servant. Fellow of King's College, Cambridge 1909–46; member of the Treasury's Committee on Finance and Industry 1919–31; H.M. Treasury 1914–19 and 1940–6; editor of the Economic Journal 1911–44.

Kleffens, Eelco Nicolaas van (1894–1983): Dutch diplomat and minister. Dutch foreign minister 1939–45.

Knudsen, William (1879–1948), American businessman. Vice-president of General Motors 1933–6; president of General Motors 1937–40; head of the office for production management at the War Department during the Second World War.

Kronaker, Paul (1897–1994): Belgian businessman and politician. Minister for relief 1944–5.

Leith-Ross, Sir Frederick (1887–1961): British civil servant. Treasury official and chief economic adviser to the Government 1931–46; director-general of the Ministry of Economic Warfare 1939–42; chairman of the Inter-Allied Post-War Requirements Committee 1941–3; deputy director-general, UNRRA 1944–6.

Leopold II (1835–1909): King of the Belgians 1865–1909.

Leopold III (1901–83): King of the Belgians 1934–40; 1950–1. He abdicated in 1951 in favour of his son, Baudouin, facing mounting criticism about his attitude during the Second World War when he decided to remain in occupied Belgium, officially as a 'prisoner'.

Lie, Trygve (1896–1968): Norwegian politician and diplomat. Foreign affairs minister in the Norwegian government-in-exile 1940–4; first secretary-general of the United Nations 1946–52.

Lindberg, Charles S. (1902–74): American aviator; leader of the anti-war movement America First before the US entered the Second World War.

Lithiby, John Stewart (1892–1967): British economist. Assistant adviser to the Bank of England 1940–4; deputy adviser 1944–46; adviser to governors 1946–55.

Lloyd George, David (1863–1945): British statesman. Prime minister 1916–22.

Loucheur, Louis (1838–1929): French politician. Minister of labour and social affairs 1926–30.

Lyttleton Oliver, 1st Viscount Chandos (1893–1972): non-metals dealer and British political figure. Recruited by Cecil Budd at the British Metal Corporation; board member of the Société Générale des Minérais 1924–39; controller of non-ferrous metals 1939–40; president of the Board of Trade 1940–1; minister of state in the Middle East and member of the Cabinet 1941–2; minister of production and member of the War Cabinet (1942–5); Conservative MP for Aldershot 1945–51.

Man, Henri de (1883–1953): Belgian Socialist politician. Minister of public transports 1935–6; minister of finance 1936–8; minister without portfolio 1939–40; condemned for treason at the end of the Second World War found refuge in Switzerland where he died.

Mannheimer, Fritz (1890–1939): Dutch banker. Director of the Dutch branch of the Berlin-based investment bank Mendelssohn & Co. 1920–39.

Massigli, René (1888–1988): French diplomat. Commissioner in charge of foreign affairs within the CNF, the CFLN and the provisional French government 1943–4; French ambassador to Britain 1944–51.

Mayer, René (1875–1972): French politician; Commissioner of Communications and of the Merchant Marine 1943–4.

McFadyean, Andrew, Sir (1887–1974): British civil servant, businessman and politician. Entered the Treasury in 1910; secretary of the British delegation to the Reparation Commission 1920–2; general secretary to the Reparation Commission 1922–4; secretary to the Dawes Committee in 1924; embarked on a career in the city as chairman of S. G. Warburg & Co. 1934–52.

Meade, James (1907–95): British economist. Nobel prize-winner in Economics in 1977; served in the Economic Section of the War Cabinet 1940–7.

Mendès France, Pierre (1907–82): French statesman. Finance Commissioner within the French Committee of National Liberation 1943–4 and then minister of the national economy within the French provisional government 1944–5; French prime minister in 1954–5.

Mises, Ludwig (1891–1979): American-Austrian born economist. Professor in economics at the University of Vienna 1913–38; New York University 1945–69.

Mladek, Jan (1912–89): Czechoslovak economist. Vice-chairman of the Czechoslovakian delegation to Bretton Woods in 1944; Czechoslovakian executive director to the IMF 1946–8; Director of the IMF's European Office 1953–9.

Monnet, Jean (1888–1979): French industrialist and businessman. Head of the Coordination Committee (Purvis-Monnet Commitee) 1939–40; sent in 1940 by Churchill to the US to supervise British war purchases; commissioner in charge of supplies and armaments within the French provisional government 1943–5; head of French economic planning authority; head of the High Authority of the European Coal and Steel Community 1951–4.

Morgan, John Pierpont (1867–1943): American banker. Chairman of J. P. Morgan & Co. Inc. New York; member of Young Expert Committee in 1929.

Morgenthau, Henry Jr (1891–1967): American politician. Governor of the Farm Credit Administration in 1933; Acting undersecretary of the US Treasury 1933–34; secretary of the Treasury 1934–45.

Nelson, Donald M. (1880–1959): American businessman. Vice-president of Sears Roebuck 1931–41; director of office production management 1941–2; chairman of the War Production Board 1942–4.

Niemeyer, Otto (1883–1971): Civil servant and banker. Entered the Treasury in 1906; executive director of the Bank of England 1938–49; chairman of the Committee of Post-War Domestic Finance 1943–4.

Nisot, Joseph (1894–1974): Belgian lawyer and diplomat. Member of the Belgian delegation to the UNRRRA conference in November 1943 and to the Bretton Woods conference in July 1944. Belgian permanent representative to the United Nations 1948–59.

Norman, Lord Montaigu (1871–1950): British banker. Governor of the Bank of England 1920–44.

Nothomb, Pierre (1887–1966): Belgian Caholic political figure and writer. During the First World War he worked for the Belgian government and founded the Great Belgium Movement.

Oliphant, Sir Lancelot (1881–1965): British diplomat. Ambassador of Britain to Belgium and minister-plenipotentiary to Luxembourg 1939–40 and to the Belgian and Luxembourger governments-in-exile 1941–4.

Overby, Andrew (1909–84): American banker and Treasury official. Joined the Federal Reserve Bank of New York in 1942, then the US Treasury in 1946; US executive director to the IMF 1947–9; deputy managing director 1949–52; returned to the US Treasury and joined the First Boston Corporation until retirement in 1974.

Perry, Percival Lee Dewhurst, Lord Perry of Stock Harvard (1878–1956): British motor vehicle manufacturer. Head of Ford Motor Cy (England) Ltd; founder of Ford Motor Co. Belgium.

Pierlot, Hubert (1883–1963): Belgian statesman and Catholic political figure. Home Office minister 1934–5; minister for agriculture 1936–9; prime minister 1939–45.

Pisart, Fernand (1877–1942): Belgian engineer and businessman. Close friend associate of Gutt in the Tin and Copper business sectors; worked with Theunis in New York where he died in 1942.

Pleven, René (1901–93): French minister; national commissioner for the economy, finance, the colonies and foreign affairs with the French National Committee 1941–4; minister of economy and finance in the French provisional government 1945–6.

Poincaré, Raymond (1860–1934): French politician. Prime minister and foreign affairs minister 1912–13, 1922–4; French finance minister and prime minister 1926–9.

Purvis, Arthur (1890–1941): British businessman. Head of the Anglo-French (subsequently Purchasing Board) and first chairman of the British Supply Council 1939–41.

Ramadier, Paul (1888–1961): French politician. Prime minister January–November 1947.

Raminski, Louis (1908–98): Canadian economist. Chairman of the Foreign Exchange Control Board 1940–51; member of the Canadian delegation at the Bretton Woods conference in July 1944.

Rathenau, Walter (1867–1922): German statesman and industrialist. Head of the Allgemeine-Elektrizitäts-Gesellschaft (AEG) 1914–22; minister of reconstruction 1921–2; foreign affairs minister, 1921–2; assassinated by right-wing fanatics in 1922.

Rens, Joseph, known as Jeff (1905–85): Belgian trade unionist. Adviser of Spaak during the Second World War.

Richard, Raoul (1885–1962): Belgian businessman and minister. Minister of economic affairs in 1939; undersecretary of state in charge of relief 1943–4.

Reynaud, Paul (1878–1961): French statesman. Prime minister and foreign affairs minister 1940; finance minister 1938–9; arrested and jailed by the Vichy regime during the Second World War.

Rioust de Largentaye, Jean (1903–71): French engineer and civil servant. Joined the French Finance Ministry in 1931; translator of Keynes's *General Theory* in French; served as a senior adviser at Commissariat in charge of finance in Algiers 1943–4; member of the French delegation at the Bretton Woods conference; alternate executive director to the IMF in 1946; executive director 1946–64.

Rolin-Jacquemyns, Guillaume (1918–80): Belgian banker. Resistant during the war, liberated from Dachau in June 1944; secretary of the Belgian delegation to the Savannah conference in March 1946; worked at the IMF and then returned to banking in Belgium.

Roosevelt, Franklin Delano (1882–1945): American statesman; President of the US, 1933–45.

Sachs, Alexander (1893–1973): American banker and economist. Vice-president of Lehman Corporation 1931–43; board member 1943–73; close friend to President Roosevelt to whom he delivered the letter written by Slizard and Einstein to Roosevelt in October 1939.

Salter, Sir Arthur (1881–1975): British civil servant and politician. General secretary of the Reparations Commission 1920–2; director of the Economic Section of the League of Nations 1922–31.

Schuman , Robert (1886–1963): French politician. Finance minister 1946–7; prime minister 1947–8; foreign affairs minister 1948–53.

Schweizer, Marie-Pauline (1853–1937): Max Guttenstein's first wife and Camille Gutt's mother; returned to France after the First World War.

Schyver, August de (1893–1952): Belgian Catholic politician. Minister of justice and economic affairs 1939–40; arrived in London in August 1942; minister of interior 1943–4.

Selliers de Moranville, Ernest de (1911–64): Belgian diplomat. Secretary at the Belgian Legation in Ottawa 1936–41; chief of Cabinet at the Finance Ministry 1941–4; general secretary of the Belgian delegation to the Bretton Woods conference; Belgian alternate-executive director 1946–54; senior partner with of Gutt at the Bank Lambert 1954–64.

Sengier, Edgar (1879–1963): Belgian businessman. Managing director of the Union Minière du Huat-Katanga 1924–46, president 1946–60; member of the board of directors of the Société Générale de Belgique 1932–40; based in New York and in charge of Union Minière's interests in the Free World during the Second World War.

Siepmann, Arthur (1889–1963): British economist. Former collaborator of Keynes during the First World War; counsellor to the governor of the Bank of England 1926–45 and then executive director 1945–54.

Silvercruys, Robert (1893–1953): Belgian diplomat. Belgian ambassador to Canada during the Second World War; Belgian ambassador to the US 1945–59.

Smuts, Jan (1870–1950): South African statesman. Prime minister of South Africa 1919–24; 1939–48.

Southard, Frank Jr (1907–89): American economist and Treasury official. Assistant director of the US Treasury division of monetary research 1941–2; special assistant to the secretary of Treasury and executive director to the IMF 1949–62; deputy managing director of the IMF 1962–74.

Spaak, Paul-Henri (1899–1972): Belgian Socialist political figure. Prime minister and foreign affairs minister 1938–9; minister of foreign affairs 1939–45; prime minister and foreign affairs minister 1946–9; chairman of the UN General Assembly in 1945; foreign affairs minister 1961–6; NATO general secretary 1957–61.

Stavisky, Alexandre (1888–1934): French financier and swindler. His death triggered a right-wing agitation resulting in a major crisis in the history of the Third Republic.

Stettinius, Edward Jr (1900–49): American businessman. Vice-president of General Motors 1931–40; president of US Steel 1938–40; US undersecretary of state 1943–4; US secretary of state 1944–5.

Straeten Ponthoz (van der), Robert (1879–1962): Belgian ambassador to the US 1935–45.

Stresemann Gustav (1878–1929): German statesman. German chancellor and foreign minister in 1923; foreign minister 1923–9; Nobel Peace Prize winner with Aristide Briand in 1926.

Strong, Benjamin (1878–1928): American banker. Governor of the Federal Reserve Bank of New York 1914–28.

Szilárd, Leon (1898–1964): Hungarian-born physicist. Pioneer in the field of nuclear energy; co-author with Albert Einstein of the letter warning President Roosevelt of the importance of uranium in the coming war.

Taft, Robert (1889–1953): American senator, Republican. Senator from 1933 to 1953; leading figure of the isolationists in US politics.

Theunis, Georges (1873–1966): Belgian statesman and businessman. Minister of finance 1920–1; prime minister and minister of finance 1921–5; defence minister in 1932; prime minister 1934–5; member of the Board of directors of the Société Générale de Belgique 1928–31; ambassador-at-large of Belgium to the US 1939–44; governor of the National Bank of Belgium 1942–4.

Tizard, Sir Henry Thomas (1885–1959): British scientist. Rector of Imperial College 1929–42; formed in March 1940 the Maud Committee under George Thomson to investigate the feasibility of an atomic bomb.

Towers, Graham (1897–1965): Canadian banker. Governor of the Bank of Canada 1934–54.

Truman, Harry S. (1884–1972): American politician. President of the US 1945–53.

Vandervelde, Emile (1866–1938): Belgian statesman. Leader of the Belgian Socialist Party 1928–38; foreign affairs minister 1925–7.

Vanlangenhove Fernand (1889–1982): Belgian diplomat. General secretary of the Belgian Ministry of Foreign Affairs 1929–46; specialized in economic and trade questions, he became a close adviser of Spaak during the Second World War. Also known as van Langenhove.

Vinson, Frederick (1890–1953); American lawyer. Secretary of the US Treasury 1945–6.

Vleeschauwer, Albert de (1897–1971): Belgian Catholic politician; Colonies Minister 1938–39; 1939–45; Home Office Minister 1949–50; Minister for Agriculture 1958–60.

Voghel, Franz de (1903–95): Belgian banker and finance minister. Secretary and director of the Belgian Banking Commission 1934–44; director of the NBB in 1944; finance minister 1945–6; vice-governor of the NBB 1957–70.

Waley, David, Sigismund (1887–1962): Deputy-secretary to the Treasury 1924–9; undersecretary to the Treasury 1939–46.

Warburg, James P. (1896–1969): American banker and financier. President of the Bank of Manhattan 1931–2; vice-chairman 1932–5; at first a staunch opponent to the New Deal, he assumed a key position in supervising American propaganda aimed at the Axis powers during the Second World War.

White Harry Dexter (1898–1948). American economist and public servant. Assistant director of Research, US Treasury 1934–8; director of monetary research 1938–45.

Wood, Sir John Kingsley (1880–1969). British Conservative politician. Chancellor of the Exchequer 1940–3.

Young, Owen D. (1874–1962): American businessman and international negotiator. Vice-president of General Electric 1913–22; chairman 1922–39; chairman of the Expert Committee on Reparations, 1929.

Zeeland, Marcel van (1897–1972): Manager of the BIS Banking Department 1930–47; head of banking department 1947–62; first manager 1948–62.

Zeeland, Paul van (1893–1973): Economist and Belgian Catholic politician. Director at the NBB 1926–34; vice-governor 1934–5; Belgian prime minister 1935–7; resigned and joined the SOFINA during the Second World War; head of the CEPAG during the Second World War 1940–4; Belgian foreign affairs minister 1935–6 and 1949–54.

NOTES

The following abbreviations have been used throughout the notes:

ABOE   Archives of Bank of England
AEF   Archives économiques et financières
AIMF   Archives of International Monetary Fund
AGR   Archives Générales du Royaume
CEGES   Centre d'Etudes et de Documentation Guerres et Sociétés
           Contemporaines
FEA   Foreign Economic Administration
FO   Foreign Office
GP   Gutt Papers
MF   Ministère des Finances
ML   Mudd Library, University of Princeton
NARA   National Archives and Records Administration
PRO   Public Records Office (UK)
RP   Richard Papers
TP   Theunis Papers
WP   White Papers

Introduction

1.   'Gutt of the Fund', *Fortune Magazine*, 3 (1946), pp. 115–44 [pages discontinued].
2.   C. Gutt, *Pourquoi le franc belge est tombé* (Bruxelles: Editions nouvelles, 1935); C. Gutt, *La Belgique au carrefour* (Paris: Editions Fayard, 1971).
3.   Y. Cassis and L. Cottrell, 'Financial History', *Financial History Review*, 1 (1994), pp. 5–22; P. Fridenson, 'Business and History', in G. Jones and J. Zeitlin (eds), *The Oxford Handbook of Business History* (Oxford: Oxford University Press, 2007), pp. 37–66; G. Kurgan-van Hentenryk, 'Finance and Financiers in Belgium 1880–1940', in Y. Cassis (ed.), *Finance and Financiers in European History 1880–1960* (Cambridge: Cambridge University Press, 1992), pp. 317–35.
4.   J. Fear, 'Cartels', in Jones and Zeitlin (eds), *The Oxford Handbook of Business History*, pp. 268–92, on p. 278.

5. D. Hudson and D. Lee, 'The Old and the New Significance of Political Economy in Diplomacy', *Review of International Studies*, 30 (2004), pp. 343–60.

6. L. W. Pauly, *The League of Nations and the Foreshadowing of the International Monetary Fund*, Essays in International Finance Series, 201 (Princeton, NJ: International Finance Section, 1997); L. W. Pauly, *Who Elected the Bankers?: Surveillance and Control in the World Economy* (Ithaca, NY: Cornell University Press, 1997).

7. E. Helleiner, *Nation-States and Money: The Past, Present and Future of National Currencies* (London: Routledge, 1999).

8. P. Clavin, *The Failure of Economic Diplomacy: Britain, Germany, France and the United States, 1931–36* (Basingstoke: Macmillan, 1996); P. Clavin and J.-W. Wessels, 'Another Gold Idol? The League of Nations's Gold Delegation and the Great Depression', *International History Review*, 26:4 (2004), pp. 765–95.

9. Z. Steiner, *The Lights that Failed: European International History, 1919–1933* (Oxford: Oxford University Press, 2005); P. O. Cohrs, *The Unfinished Peace after World War I: America, Britain and the Stabilization of Europe, 1919–1932* (Cambridge: Cambridge University Press, 2006).

10. P. Einzig, *World Finance since 1914* (London: K. Paul, Trench, Trubner & Co., 1935), pp. 116–22.

11. E. Helleiner, 'When Finance is the Servant: International Capital Movement in the Bretton Woods Order', in Ph. G. Cerny (ed.), *Finance and World Politics: Markets, Regimes and States in the Post Hegemonic Era* (Aldershot: Elgar, 1993), pp. 20–30.

12. R. H. Meyers, *Bankers' Diplomacy: Monetary Stabilization in the 1920s* (New York: Columbia University Press, 1970), pp. 165–70.

13. In this case, Francqui as French national expert, see Cohrs, *The Unifinished Peace*, p. 532.

14. M. MacMillan, *Peacemakers: The Paris Conference of 1919 and its Attempts to End War* (London: John Murray, 2001), pp. 285–6; S. Marks, *Innocent Abraod: Belgium at the Paris Peace Conference of 1919* (Chapel Hill, NC: The University of North Carlolina Press, 1981), pp. 292–402

15. P. Clavin, 'Defining Transnationalism', *Contemporary European History*, 14:4 (2005), pp. 421–39.

16. Steiner, *The Lights that Failed* pp. 285–6, also see pp. 13–15 of this book.

17. One of the few books written on the subject is J. Helmreich's, *Belgium and Europe: A Study in Small Power Diplomacy* (The Hague: Mouton & Co., 1976).

18. Ibid., pp. 380–92; J. Gotovitch, 'Projets européens dans la résistance et à Londres durant la guerre', in M. Dumoulin (ed.), *La Belgique et les débuts de la construction européenne. De la guerre aux traités de Rome* (Ciaco Editeurs: Louvain-la-Neuve, 1987), pp. 38–47.

19. M. Conway and J. Gotovitch (eds), *Europe in Exile: European Exile Communities in Britain 1940–1945* (New York and Oxford: Bergham Books, 2001).

20. M. Conway, 'Legacies of Exile: The Exile Governments in Exile during the Second World War during the Second World War and the Politics of Postwar Europe', in Conway and Gotovitch (eds), *Europe in Exile*, pp. 255–74.

21. E. Mandel, *The Meaning of the Second World War* (London: Verso, 1986).

22. A. S. Milward, *War, Economy and Society 1940–1945* (Penguin: Harmondsworth, 1987); N. Ferguson, *The Pity of War* (London: Allen Lane, Penguin Press, 1998).

23. J. F. Crombois, *Camille Gutt: Les finances et la guerre 1940–1945* (Brussels: CEGES/ Quorum, 1999).

24. H. van der Wee and M. Verbeyt, *Oorlog en monetarire politiek: de National Bank van Belgïe, de Emissiebank te Brusse en the Belgische regering, 1939–1945* (Brussels: National

Bank van Belgïe, 2005); for an English shorter version of this book: H. van der Wee and M. Verbeyt, *A Small Nation in the Turmoil of the Second World War: Money, Finance and Occupation* (Leuven University Press: Leuven, 2009); R. Brion and J.-L. Moreau, *La politique monétaire dans une Europe en reconstruction (1944–1958)* (Bruxelles: Banque Nationale de Belgique, 2005).

25. See Works Cited.
26. See Manuscript Sources section of Works Cited.

1 Camille Gutt, Finance and Politics (1919–40)

1. File 190153, Police des Etrangers, AGR, ff. 1–3.
2. Helen Gutt (1879–1944) returned to live in Strasbourg with her mother after the First World War where she worked for the Atronomical Institute.
3. For biographical information on Camille Gutt, see: J. F. Crombois, 'Camille Gutt', in *Nouvelle Biographie Nationale*, 9 vols (Bruxelles: Académie Royale de Belgique, 1988–), vol. 6, pp. 228–32.
4. Interview donnée par Camille Gutt à Charles d'Ydewalle (Radio Belgique), 1958, AGR, TP, 1150, f. 2.
5. A copy of the manifesto can be found in R. Collinet, *L'annexion d'Eupen et de Malmédy à la Belgique en 1920* (Verviers: Librairie La Dérive, 1986), p. 7.
6. 'Nous causâmes ... Mais la conversation n'était pas finie. Elle a duré exactement cinquante ans', Interview donnée par Camille Gutt à Charles d'Ydewalle (Radio Belgique), 1958, AGR, TP, 1150, f. 3.
7. 'J'ai toujours pensé que ces divergences, au lieu de nous écarter l'un l'autre, avaient établi entre nous la complémentarité qui nous avait unie', in 'Première rencontre entre le Commandant Theunis et le Sous-Lieutenant Gutt', 23 May 1966, AGR, TP, 1, f. 2.
8. Y. Toussaint, *Les barons Empain* (Paris: Fayard, 1996), pp. 173–208; A. Duchesne, 'Un général pas comme les autres. Le baron Empain durant la guerre 1914–1918', *Revue belge d'histoire militaire*, 24:1 (1985), pp. 156–95.
9. G. Kurgan-van Hentenryk, 'La Société Générale 1850–1934', in H. van der Wee (ed.), *La Générale de Banque 1822–1997* (Bruxelles: Editions Racine, 1997), pp. 63–285, on pp. 246–8.
10. Following the Senate's rejection of the Treaty of Versailles, the American delegates had to leave the Commission, although they stayed in Paris as observers.
11. R. Depoortere, *La question des réparations allemandes dans la politique extérieure de la Belgique 1919–1925* (Bruxelles: Académie Royale de Belgique, 1998), pp. 281–4.
12. Crombois, *Camille Gutt*, p. 21.
13. Kurgan-van Hentenryk, 'La Société Générale', pp. 63–285.
14. R. Depoortere, 'Theunis, Georges', *Nouvelle Biographie Nationale*, 9 vols (Bruxelles: Académie Royale de Belgique, 1988–), vol. 5, pp. 327–31.
15. On Francqui, see: L. Ranieri, *Emile Francqui ou l'intelligence créatrice 1863–1935* (Bruxelles: Duculot, 1985); and G. Kurgan-van Hentenryk, *Gouverner la Générale de Belgique: Essai de biographie collective* (Bruxelles: De Boeck, 1996), pp. 102–7, 122–5.
16. 'Le bonheur suprême de Francqui était de renverser et de constituer des ministères. Je pense qu'il l'avait fait souvent par intérêt national, souvent par intérêt personnel, mais qu'il l'aurait fait aussi bien sans intérêt, pour le plaisir', Un an de gouvernement Van Zeeland (1936), CEGES, GP, 70, f. 3.

17. D. Wallef, 'Les collusions politico-financières devant l'opinion' (MA dissertation, Université Libre de Bruxelles année académique 1969–1970), pp. 221–2.
18. 'Gutt to Theunis, 30 April 1925', AGR, TP, 109, p. 2.
19. G. Vanthemsche, 'De val van de regering Pouillet-Vandervelde: een samenzwering der bankiers', *Revue Belge d'Histoire contemporaine*, 9:1–2 (1978), pp. 167–8.
20. B. Eichengreen, *Golden Fetters: The Gold Standard and the Great Depression 1919–1939* (Oxford: Oxford University Press, 1992), pp. 33–6.
21. Kurgan-van Hentenryk, 'La Société Générale', p. 253; Vanthemsche, 'De val van de regering Pouillet-Vandervelde', pp. 167–8.
22. Ranieri, *Emile Francqui*, pp. 223–6.
23. E. Bussière, 'Economics and Franco-Belgian Relations in the Interwar Period', in R. Boyce (ed.), *French Foreign and Defence Policy 1918–1940* (Routledge: London, 2005), pp. 71–88.
24. 'Grands hommes vus de près (conférence 9 janvier 1938)', CEGES, GP, 70, p. 24.
25. Theunis was finance minister between 1920 and 1921.
26. 'Gutt to Theunis', 8 August 1926, AGR, TP, 109, f. 1.
27. K. Tavernier and H. van der Wee, *La Banque nationale de Belgique et l'histoire monétaire entre les deux guerres mondiales* (Bruxelles: Banque Nationale de Belgique, 1975), p. 184.
28. Kurgan-van Hentenryk, 'La Société Générale', p. 256.
29. See n. 56.
30. L. H. Dupriez, *Les réformes monétaires en Belgique* (Bruxelles: Office international de librairie 1948), p. 83.
31. G. Jones, *Multinationals and World Capitalism: From the Nineteenth to the Twenty First Century* (Oxford: Oxford University Press, 2004), p. 46. The *Metallgesellschaft* was established in 1881. In 1912, the Metallegesllschaft opened a refinery in Belgium. See n. 34.
32. O. Lyttleton [Viscount Chandos], *The Memoirs of Lord Chandos* (London: Bodley Head, 1962), pp. 128–9.
33. A. Walters, 'The International Copper Cartel', *Southern Economic Journal*, 11:2 (1944), pp. 133–56.
34. S. Ball, 'The German Octopus: The British Metal Corporation and the Next War 1914–1939', *Enterprise and Society*, 5:3 (2004), pp. 451–90.
35. Lyttleton, *The Memoirs*, pp. 309–10.
36. 'Belgian Metal Group in Consolidation Here', *New York Times*, 17 February 1926, p. 28.
37. Walters, 'The International Copper Cartel', pp. 135–6.
38. Jones, *Multinationals*, p. 58.
39. 'Copper Men Gather for World Parley', *New York Times*, 29 November 1932, p. 27.
40. 'Rapport définitif. Société des Nations, Conférence économique international Genève, Mai 1927', AGR, TP, 993, f. 12.
41. Walters, 'The International Copper Cartel', p. 135.
42. 'Dans la complexité actuelle de la vie économique, où tous les problèmes se touchent, où l'international réagit sur le national et financier sur l'économique, ces associations sont des régulateurs nécessaires et il est indispensable que leur rôle soit exactement connu du public', in 'Les problèmes des matières premières et les ententes industrielles, Conférence faite à la Chambre de Commerce de Verviers le 18 janvier 1938', AGR, TP, 1150, f. 23.
43. 'Gutt to Van Langenhove, 19 November 1932', AGR, TP, 1134, ff. 1–4.
44. H. Bonin, Th. Grosbois, N. Hetzfeld, J.-L. Laudet, *Ford en France et en Belgique 1903–2003* (Paris: P.L.A.G.E, 2004), p. 134.

45. Crombois, *Camille Gutt*, p. 36.
46. 'Gutt to Vasseur', 10 July 1936, AGR, TP, 929, f. 1.
47. Interview donnée par Camille Gutt à Charles d'Ydewalle (Radio Belgique), 1958, AGR, TP, 1150, f. 5.
48. Depoortere, *La question*, p. 137.
49. Ibid., pp. 223–5.
50. P. Hymans, *Mémoires*, 2 vols (Bruxelles: Institut de Sociologie Solvay, 1958), vol. 2, p. 819
51. G. Toniolo, *Central Bank Cooperation at the Bank for International Settlements, 1930–1973* (Cambridge: Cambridge University Press, 2005), pp. 33–48.
52. Ibid., pp. 127–31.
53. 'Depuis 1919, en effet, il n'y a pas de Commissions interalliées ou de conférences internationales auxquelles il n'ait représenté la Belgique et où il ne soit fait remarquer par sa connaissance approfondie des questions, la justesse de ses vues, et en cas de difficultés, par les trouvailles de son imagination'. This article was re-published by a Belgian local newspaper, see extract from *Le Courrier du Soir de Verviers*, 22 October 1929, AGR, TP, 1134.
54. Depoortere, *La question*, pp. 331–6.
55. H. Spender, 'Some Notes of the London Conference', *Fortnightly Review* 116:693 (1924), pp. 323–32, on p. 324.
56. 'Grands hommes', AGR, TP, 1, ff. 23–4.
57. I. Cassiers, *Croissance, crise et régulation en économie ouverte. La Belgique entre les deux guerres* (Bruxelles: De Boeck université, 1988), pp. 122–6; R. L. Hogg, *Structural Rigidities and Policy Inertia in Inter-War Belgium* (Brussels: Koninklijke Academie voor Wetenschappen, Letteren en Schone Kunsten van België 1986), pp. 21–3.
58. M.-R. Desmed-Thielemans, *La grande crise et le gouvernement des banquiers. Essai* (Bruxelles: Institut belge de Sciences politiques, 1979), p. 2.
59. Tavernier and van der Wee, *La Banque nationale*, pp. 252–78.
60. G. Vanthemsche, 'L'élaboration de l'AR sur le contrôle bancaire (1935)', *Revue Belge d'Histoire contemporaine*, 11 (1980), pp. 389–437.
61. On the political aspects, see: J. Vanwelkenhuyzen, *Le gâchis des années 30, 1933–1937*, tome I (Bruxelles Editions Racine, 2007), pp. 233–42.
62. Desmed-Thielemans, *La grande crise*, p. 24.
63. 'President Greets Belgian Mission', *New York Times*, 17 May 1934, p. 27.
64. Tavernier and van der Wee, *La Banque nationale*, p. 234.
65. V. Dujardin and M. Dumoulin, *Paul van Zeeland 1893–1973* (Bruxelles: Editions Racine, 1997), pp. 46–7.
66. 'Le government des banquiers', in Desmed-Thielemans, *La grande crise*, p. 29–35.
67. 'Le mur d'argent'; French expression first used in 1920s to describe the opposition of the French bankers to the policy of social and economic reforms advocated by the governing leftist coalition led by Prime Minister Herriot.
68. 'Pourquoi sommes-nous partis? (25 March 1935)', AGR, TP, 929, f. 2.
69. See n. 67.
70. On the Note, see n. 59. On the meeting with the King Leopold III: Gutt to Theunis, 11 April 1935, AGR, TP, 929, f.1.
71. Ibid., p. 8.
72. Gutt, *Pourquoi le franc belge est tombé*.
73. 'Gutt to Vandervelde', 19 June 1935, AGR, TP, 929, f. 1.

74. G. Kurgan-van Hentenryk, *Max-Léo Gérard: Un ingénieur dans la cité (1879–1955)* (Bruxelles: Editions de l'Université de Bruxelles, 2010), pp. 149–52.

75. Dujardin and Dumoulin, *Paul van Zeeland*, pp. 43–58; It is not uninteresting to notice that in his book, Gutt also singled out the articles of the Belgian economists and columnist, Fernand Baudhuin, while in his note, Gutt put most of the blame on van Zeeland; Gutt, *Pourquoi le franc belge est tombé*, pp. 57–61, 101–104, see n. 55.

76. Ranieri, *Emile Francqui*, p. 327.

77. S. Tilman, 'Les banquiers et la politique: incompatibilités? Le cas de la Belgique (XIXème–XXème siècles)', in S. Jaumain and K. Bertrams (dir.), *Patrons, gens d'affaires et banquiers. Hommages à Ginette Kurgan-van Hentenryk* (Bruxelles: Le Livre Timperman, 2004), pp. 357–80.

78. 'Hommes et choses que j'ai vues (1936)', AGR, TP, 1, ff. 29–30.

79. 'Hommes et choses que j'ai vues (1936)', AGR, TP, 1, ff. 33–4.

80. 'Je suis essentiellement écrivain, Van Zeeland est essentiellement un économiste. Le mots m'attirent, les concepts le charment. Je suis sceptique, et enthousiaste: il est croyant et calme', in 'Grands hommes', f. 28.

81. J. M. Keynes, *Activities 1931–1939: World Crisis and Policies in Britain and America*, The Collected Writings of J. M. Keynes Series, vol. 21: Activities 1939–1945: Internal War Finance, ed. D. Moggridge (Cambridge: Cambridge University Press: 1982), p. 356.

82. Tavernier and van der Wee, *La Banque nationale*, pp. 307–12.

83. Dujardin and Dumoulin, *Paul van Zeeland*, pp. 90–5.

84. Van der Wee and Verbeyt, *Oorlog en monetaire*, p. 592.

85. M. van Zeeland, *L'expérience van Zeeland en Belgique* (Lausanne: Payot, 1940).

86. Cassiers, *Croissance*, pp. 165–6, 200–1.

87. G. Vanthemsche, 'De mislukking van een verniewed economische politiek in Belgïe voor de tweede wereloorlog', *Revue Belge d'Histoire contemporaine*, 13: 2–3 (1982), pp. 339–89.

88. 'Pourquoi nous sommes partis 26 mars 1935', AGR, TP, 929, f. 1.

89. 'Un an de gouvernement Van Zeeland' (1936), AGR, TP, 929, ff. 5–8.

90. 'Précédemment, le roi s'était conduit très proprement avec moi, au moment, ou, après avoir quitté le gouvernement en 1935, j'avais été l'objet d'attaques abominables ... Je l'avais assuré de mon total dévouement. C'est à ce dévouement qu'il fit appel et je du bien m'incliner', in 'Exposé de Mr. Gutt devant le Conseil consultatif, 5 mai 1942', CEGES, GP, 7, f. 4.

91. J. F. Crombois, 'Finance, économie et politique en Belgique à la veille de la Seconde Guerre mondiale 1939–1940', *Cahiers d'Histoire du Temps Présent*, 5 (1998), pp. 171–206.

92. Tavernier and van der Wee, *La Banque nationale*, pp. 300–20.

93. Germany that followed suit later in October 1937. F. van Langenhove, *L'élaboration de la politique étrangère de la Belgique entre les deux guerres mondiales* (Bruxelles: Académie Royale de Belgique, 1980), pp. 271–6; M. Dumoulin, *Spaak* (Bruxelles: Editions Racine, 1999), p. 74–85.

94. 'Grands hommes', f. 24.

95. 'Le pays doit se préparer à vivre dans une économie de guerre', Crombois, 'Finance économie et politique', p. 195

96. Crombois, *Camille Gutt*, pp. 65–6.

97. J. M. Keynes, *How to Pay for the War, A Radical Plan for the Chancellor of the Exchequer* (London: Macmillan, 1940).

98. Crombois, *Camille Gutt*, p. 69.

2 Belgian War Financial Diplomacy

1. Dumoulin, *Spaak*; Dujardin and Dumoulin, *Paul van Zeeland*; Th. Grosbois, *Pierlot 1930–1950* (Bruxelles: Editions Racine, 2007).

2. On economic collaboration during the Second World War, see: P. Nefors, *La collaboration industrielle en Belgique 1940–1945* (Bruxelles: Editions Racine, 2006); On Leopold III see note below.

3. Or 'Question royale': after the war, King Leopold III and his family went to Switzerland. In 1949, a non-mandatory referendum was held on the question of a possible return of Leopold III to Belgium. Comforted by the results that showed a majority in his favour, Leopold III came back to Belgium in July 1949. However, facing the division of the country between French- and Flemish-speaking Belgians that put the country on the brink of a potential civil war, king Leopold III decided, in 1951, to abdicate to his son, the Royal Prince Baudouin, future King of the Belgians. See as main references: J. Stengers, *Aux origines de la question royale. Léopold III et le gouvernement. Les deux politiques belges* (Gembloux: Duculot, 1980); and H. van Goethem and J. Velaers, *Leopold III, de koning, het land, de Oorlog* (Tielt: Lannoo, 1994).

4. Cabinet Council Minutes, 18 June 1940, AGR, microfilm 2081/1, ff. 380–1.

5. 'Gutt to Theunis', 14 July 1940, AGR, TP, 21, f. 3.

6. 'juif, banquier et liberal', AGR, TP, 21, f. 3.

7. 'déclarent juif qui ils veulent', AGR, TP, 21, f. 3.

8. 'Vilain to Gutt (Lisbon)', 22 May 1943, CEGES, GP, 130, f.1.

9. 'Gutt to Theunis', 14 July 1940, AGR, TP, f. 2.

10. 'Où est le gouvernement? Pourquoi ne vient-il pas ici?', in 'Séjour à Londres (Non-dated note signed by De Vleeschauwer)', CEGES, RP, 128, f. 4.

11. 'Gutt to Leopold', 13 July 1940, CEGES, GP, 4, f. 1.

12. 'Gutt to Theunis', 28 July 1940, CEGES, GP, 4, f. 1.

13. 'Gutt to Theunis', 28 July 1940, CEGES, GP, 4, f. 2.

14. On these events, see J. F. Crombois and J. Gotovitch, 'Gouvernement belge de Londres', in P. Aron and J. Gotovitch (eds), *Dictionnaire de la Second Guerre mondiale de Belgique* (Bruxelles: André Versailles, 2008), pp. 211–16.

15. Van der Wee and Verbeyt, *A Small Nation*, pp. 47–60.

16. Stengers, *Aux origines*, pp. 154–5.

17. 'Broadcast of Gutt', 3 October 1940, CEGES, GP, 61, p. 2.

18. E. Roussel, *Jean Monnet (1888–1979)* (Paris: Editions Fayard, 1996), p. 254.

19. On these aspects, see: Crombois, *Camille Gutt*, pp. 247–9.

20. MacFadyean helped Gutt during the war, especially with respect to the education of his third son, Etienne, who went to Rugby College before going to Oxford.

21. P. Hennessy, *Whitehall* (London: Fontana, 1990), pp. 69–79.

22. F. van Langenhove, *La Belgique et ses garants. L'été 1940. Contribution à l'histoire de la période 1940–1950* (Bruxelles: Académie Royale de Belgique, 1995), pp. 110–13.

23. 'Conversation tenure le 26 août 1940 au 10 Downing Street entre M. Winston Churchill, Premier Ministre de Grande-Bretagne d'une part, et MM. De Vleeschauwer and Gutt, Ministre des Colonies et Ministre des Finances, d'autre part', CEGES, GP, 26, ff.1–3.

24. R. Sayers, *Financial Policy 1939–1945*, History of the Second World War United Kingdom Civil Series (London: Her Majesty's Stationary Office, 1956), pp. 366–72.

25. 'Appel aux garants du 10 May 1940', 10 May 1940, CEGES, GP, 26, f.1.

26. 'Demandes d'ordre économique à présenter au gouvernement britannique (Londres 10 September 1940)', CEGES, GP, 148, ff.1–2.

27. 'Kingsley Wood to Halifax', 12 October 1940, PRO, FO 371/24286, f. 1.
28. 'Note sur les demandes à présenter au gouvernement britannique (Londres 16 October 1940)', CEGES, GP, 26, ff. 1–2.
29. 'Gutt to Kingsley Wood', 16 October 1940, CEGES, GP, 26, ff. 1–3.
30. 'Waley to Gutt', 18 October 1940, CEGES, GP, 26, f. 1.
31. Van Langenhove, *La Belgique*, pp. 153–6.
32. 'Halifax to Cartier de Marchienne', 22 October 1940, CEGES, GP, 26, f. 1.
33. 'C'est une occasion dont il faut profiter. Faire aboutir ces conservations serait faire plus qu'aucun gouvernement n'a fait depuis 1919', in 'Gutt to Spaak', 28 November 1940, CEGES, GP, 26, f. 1.
34. 'Baudewijns to Gutt', 29 December 1940, CEGES, GP, 26, f. 2.
35. 'Note Treasury Department', December 1940, PRO, FO 371/26338/43, ff. 5–6.
36. 'Agreement between the Government of the United Kingdom and the Belgian Government respecting God', 4 March 1941, PRO, FO 371/26332, ff. 90–4.
37. 'Political and Economic Relations with Belgium. Memorandum for the Secretary of State for Foreign Affairs (draft memorandum for the Cabinet)', PRO, FO 371/26332, f. 42.
38. 'Spaak to Cadogan', 20 February 1941, PRO, FO 371/26332, f. 43.
39. *Agreements between the Government of the United Kingdom and the Belgian Government relating to the Belgian Congo in respect of Finance and the Purchase of Commodities, London 21 January 1941*, Treaty Series, 1 (London: His Majesty's Stationery Office, 1941), ff. 1–8.
40. 'Note: Congo Financial and Purchase Agreement', PRO, FO 371/26337/20, f. 136.
41. 'Statement for the Press by M. Gutt', 21 January 1941, PRO, FO 371/26337/19, ff. 138–9.
42. G. Vanthemsche, 'La Banque de 1934 a nos jours', in H. Van der Wee (ed.), *La Générale de Banque 1822–1997* (Bruxelles: Editions Racines, 1997), pp. 303–66, on p. 360.
43. G. Vanthemsche, *La Belgique et le Congo: empreinte d'une colonie 1885–1980* Nouvelle Histoire de Belgique Series, 4 (Brussels: Editions Complexe, 2007), pp. 135–42; Crombois, *Camille Gutt*, pp. 228–33.
44. On these questions, see: Crombois, *Camille Gutt*, pp. 276–7.
45. Ibid., pp. 270–2.
46. Steiner, *The Lights that Failed*, pp. 38–9.
47. 'Theunis to Gutt', 1 June 1942, CEGES, GP, 151, f. 7.
48. Other suggestions were also made but without results. See Th. Grosbois, 'Les relations diplomatiques entre le gouvernement Belge de Londres et les Etats-Unis (1940–1944)', *Guerres mondiales et conflits contemporains*, 2 (2001), pp. 167–87.
49. J. Hoff, *American Business and Foreign Policy. Business Views and Foreign Policy 1920–1933* (Boston, MA: Beacon Press, 1948), pp. 65–7; and J. A. Schwartz, *The New Dealers: Power Politics in the Age of Roosevelt* (New York: Knopf, 1993), pp. 138–53.
50. B. Catton, *The War Lords of Washington* (New York: Harcourt, 1948), p. 124.
51. 'Les dictateurs de la vie économique aux Etats-Unis', in 'Theunis to Spaak', 2 February 1943, CEGES, GP 148, f. 1.
52. Schwartz, *The New Dealers*, pp. 47–53, 212.
53. D. Fromkin, *In the Time of the Americans: FDR, Truman, Eisenhower, Marshall, MacArthur* (London: MacMillan, 1995), p. 538.
54. C. Hull, *The Memoirs of Cordell Hull*, 2 vols (New York: Macmillan Company, 1948), vol. 2, p. 1052.

55. Gutt, *La Belgique*, p. 149.
56. On these attempts, see: Crombois, *Camille Gutt*, p. 287.
57. 'Gutt to Dulles', 27 January 1945, ML, John Foster Dulles Papers, f. 1; R. Pruessen, *John Foster Dulles: The Road to Power* (New York: Free Press, 1982), pp. 250–308.
58. Grosbois, 'Les relations diplomatiques', pp. 177.
59. 'Theunis to Gutt', 17 November 1941', CEGES, GP, 149, f. 2.
60. F. van Langenhove, *La sécurité en Belgique. Contributions à l'histoire de la politique extérieure de la Belgique pendant la Seconde Guerre mondiale* (Académie Royale de Belgique: Bruxelles, 1972), pp. 94–6.
61. Grosbois, 'Les relations diplomatiques', pp. 167–87.
62. 'General Ruling 13. Trading with the Enemy Act as Amended by the First War Powers relating to Foreign Funds Control (Treasury Department)', 21 April 1942, CEGES, GP, 33, f. 1.
63. R. M. Littauer, 'The Unfreezing of Foreign Funds', *Columbia Law Review*, 45:2 (March 1945), pp. 132–74; and 'Boël to Gutt', 13 April 1943, CEGES, GP, 33, f. 1.
64. 'Federal Reserve Bank of New York', 11 August 1942, NARA, 855.516/58, f. 1.
65. 'Boël to Gutt', 3 January 1942, CEGES, GP, 33, f. 1.
66. 'Gutt to Theunis', 2 June 1942, CEGES, GP, 151, ff. 1–2.
67. 'Department of State. Memorandum of Conversation', 12 May 1942, NARA 855.5034/32, ff. 1–2.
68. 'Van Campenhout to Gutt', 18 May 1942, CEGES, GP, 46, ff. 3–4.
69. 'Summary of my conversation with Mr. White, Assistant to the Secretary of the Treasury, Washington', 2 June 1942, f. 3, and 'Memorandum of my conversation between the Assistant to the Secretary of State Acheson, Mr. Gutt and Mr. De Gruben', 3 June 1943, CEGES, GP, 93, ff. 1–4.
70. 'Il me semble invraisemblable qu'après une guerre faite pour le triomphe du droit et de la revanche de l'individualisme contre la dictature, les Etats-Unis omettent des droits individuels aussi flagrants que ceux consisteraient à ne pas restituer immédiatement à leurs propriétaires les biens belges réfugiés aux Etats-Unis', in 'Note sur les biens belges aux Etats-Unis (8 juin 1943)', 8 June 1943, CEGES, GP, 46, f.1.
71. 'Conversation entre Mr. Pehle (Chief of Foreign Funds Control) et son Assistant, M. Fox, d'une part, et le conseiller de l'Ambassade, d'autre part, le 8 novembre 1943', 8 November 1943, CEGES, GP, 46, ff.1–2.
72. W. Kimball, *The Most Unsordid Act: Lend-Lease, Weapons for Victory* (Baltimore, MD: Johns Hopkins Press, 1969), pp. 10–25.
73. For a good description of the Lend-Lease mechanisms see: C. Valensi, *Un témoin sur l'autre rive 1943–1949* (Paris: Comité pour l'histoire économique et financière de la France Ministère des Finances, 1994), pp. 139–48.
74. 'Theunis to Gutt', 24 October 1941, CEGES, GP, 147, ff. 1–2.
75. 'Theunis to Gutt'. 24 December 1941, AGR, TP, 241, f. 2.
76. 'Résumé de la politique belge concernant le Lend-Lease pour le Département des Affaires étrangères (Londres, 20 octobre 1942)', J. Gotovitch, *Documents diplomatiques belges, 1941–1960. De l'indépendance à l'interdépendance* (Bruxelles: Académie Royale de Belgique, 1998), pp. 371–3.
77. 'Belgium and the Belgian Congo (draft, 1943)', NARA, FEA, 2974, ff. 3–4.
78. J. E. Helmreich, *Gathering Rare Ores: The Diplomacy of Uranium Acquisition 1943–1954* (Princeton, NJ: Princeton University Press, 1986), pp. 15–41.

79. P. Buch and J. Vanderlinden, *L'uranium. La Belgique et les puissances. Marché de dupes ou chef d'œuvre diplomatique* (Brussels: De Boek, 1995), pp. 20–6.
80. 'Gutt to Theunis', 9 February 1942, CEGES, GP, 139, f. 2.
81. 'Sengier to Gutt', 13 February 1941, CEGES, GP 105, ff. 1–2.
82. 'Gutt to Sengier', 25 September 1942, CEGES, GP, 105, f. 3.
83. 'Sengier to Gutt', 28 April 1942, CEGES, GP, 205, f. 2.
84. 'Preliminary Report of the *Société Générale de Belgique* and *African Metals Corporation*', September 1943, NARA, FEA 150/040, ff. 40–1.
85. Buch and Vanderlinden, *L'uranium*, p. 14.
86. V. C. Jones, *Manhattan: The Army and the Atomic Bomb* (Washington, DC: Center of Military History, 1985), p. 25.
87. Buch and Vanderlinden , *L'uranium*, p. 14.
88. 'La radium a pris une importance spéciale aux yeux des Américains, due aux usages des matières premières lumineuses nécessaires à l'appareillage de guerre et à l'usage de la radiographie industrielles. Les besoins en radium son assurés par les minerais raffinés au Canada et aux Etats-Unis. Les fournitures ont lieu aux Etats-Unis et en Angleterre', in 'Note pour Mr. Paul-Henri Spaak, ministre des Affaires étrangères de Belgique (1 Novembre 1943)', CEGES, GP, 105, ff. 3–4.
89. Jones, *Manhattan*, p. 297.
90. Hennessy, *Whitehall*, pp. 560–4.
91. 'Gutt to Sengier', 30 March 1944, CEGES, GP, 105, f. 1.
92. 'Notes sur ma conversation avec le Chancelier de l'Echiquier au sujet des gisements d'uranium du Congo belge (25 mars 1944)', 25 March 1944, CEGES, GP, 105, f. 1.
93. 'Notes sur ma conversation avec le Chancelier de l'Echiquier au sujet des gisements d'uranium du Congo belge (25 mars 1944)', 25 March 1944, CEGES, GP, 105, f. 1.
94. 'Tout ce que je me rappelle c'est qu'on m'avait dit qu'une quantité infime de ce métal rem-placerait – si les expériences réussissaient- tout le charbon nécessaire à la Queen Mary pour 50 voyages', CEGES, GP, 105, note, f. 2.
95. 'Gutt to Anderson', 25 March 1944, CEGES, GP, 105, f. 1.
96. See n. 88.
97. 'Mémorandum signé Sengier, 3 mai 1944', 3 May 1944, CEGES, GP 105, ff.1–5.
98. 'Conversation avec Sir John Anderson, Chancelier de l'Echiquier 4 mai 1944', 4 May 1944, CEGES, GP, 105, ff. 1–5.
99. 'Note pour Gutt (signée Sengier)', 28 June 1944, CEGES, GP, 105, ff. 4–6.
100. 'Agreement between the United States and the United Kingdom and between the United States, the United Kingdom and Belgium regarding the Acquisition and Con-trol of Uranium', *Foreign Relations of the United States, Diplomatic Papers (1944)*, vol. 2: General: Economic and Social Matters (Washington DC: US Government Printing Office, 1967), pp. 1026–30.

3 Financial Diplomacy in London During the Second World War

1. 'Pendant la dernière guerre, tout le monde n'avait qu'une seule idée: rétablir la situa-tion existant avant 1914. A présent, plus personne ne croit à la possibilité de restaurer la situation d'avant-guerre. Il y au contraire, une incontestable volonté de faire du neuf', in 'Note sur le diner de M. Gutt, au Berkeley Hotel, Londres le 17 juin 1942', 17 June 1942, CEGES, Rens Papers, 241, f. 2.

2. R. Skidelsky, 'Keynes's Road to Bretton Woods', in M. Flandreau and H. James (eds), *International Financial History in the Twentieth Century: Systems and Anarchy* (Cambridge: Cambridge University Press, 2003), p. 129.

3. D. E. Traynor, *International Monetary and Financial Conferences in the Inter-War Period* (Washington, DC: Catholic University of America Press, 1949), pp. 171–5.

4. S. Pollard, 'Economic Interdependence and Economic Protectionism: From the Conference of Genoa (1922) to the Conference of London (1933)', in R. Ahmann, A. M. Birke and M. Howard (eds), *The Quest for Stability: Problems of West European Security 1918–1957* (Oxford: Oxford University Press, 1993), pp. 157–71.

5. B. Eichengreen, 'International Coordination in Historical Perspective: A View for the Interwar Years', in B. Eichengreen (ed.), *Elusive Stability: Essays in the History of International Finance 1919–1939* (Cambridge: Cambridge University Press, 1993), pp. 113–52, on pp. 130–1.

6. P. L. Cotrell, 'Norman, the Bank of England and Europe since the 1920s: Case-Studies of Belgian and Italian Stabilisations', in E. Bussiere and M. Dumoulin (eds), *Milieux économiques et intégration européenns en Europe occidentale au XX siècle* (Arras: Artois Presses Université, 1998), pp. 37–84.

7. Eichengreen, *Golden Fetters*, p. 396.

8. Eichengreen, 'International Coordination', p. 116.

9. C. P. Kindleberger, 'Commercial Policy Between the Wars', in P. Matthias and S. Pollard (eds), *The Cambridge Economic History of Europe*, vol. 8: The Industrial Economies: The Development of Economic and Social Policies (Cambridge: Cambridge University Press, 1989), pp. 161–96.

10. C. F. Feinstein, P. Temin and G. Toniolo, *The World Economy between the World Wars* (Oxford: Oxford University Press, 2008), pp. 93–5.

11. Eichengreen, *Golden Fetters*, pp. 330–5.

12. Feinstein et al., *World Economy*, pp. 135–59.

13. D. E. Moggridge, 'The Gold Standard and National Economic Policies', in P. Matthias and S. Pollard (eds), *The Cambridge Economic History of Europe*, vol. 8: The Industrial Economies (Cambridge: Cambridge University Press, 1989), pp. 250–314.

14. I. A. Drummond, *London, Washington and the Management of Franc 1936–1939* Princeton Studies in International Finance Series, 45 (Princeton, NJ: Princeton University Press, 1979), pp. 3–10.

15. Clavin, *The Failure of Economic Diplomacy*, p. 192; M. Dumoulin, 'La mission Van Zeeland. Essai de clearing diplomatique de l'appeasement', *Relations Internationales*, 39 (1984), pp. 355–72.

16. M. Suetens, 'The Van Zeeland Report', *Contemporary Review*, 153 (1938), pp. 316–23.

17. C. P. Kindleberger, *The World in Depression 1929–1939* (Berkeley, CA and Los Angeles, CA: University of California Press, 1986), pp. 288–303.

18. A. Wyatt-Walker, 'The United States and Western Europe: The Theory of Hegemonic Stability', in N. Woods (ed.), *Explaining International Relations since 1945* (Oxford: Oxford University Press, 1996), pp. 126–54.

19. Clavin, *The Failure of Economic Diplomacy*, pp. 200–1.

20. Eichengreen, *Golden Fetters*, p .396.

21. F. Cesarano, *Monetary Theory and Bretton Woods: The Construction of an International Monetary Order* (Cambridge, Cambridge University Press, 2006), pp. 120–40.

22. D. Markwell, *John Maynard Keynes and International Relations: Economic Paths to War and Peace* (Oxford: Oxford University Press, 2006), pp. 123–4.

23. C. Fink, *The Genoa Conference: European Diplomacy 1921–1922* (Chapel Hill, NC: University of North Carolina Press, 1984), pp. 303–7.

24. 'Mémorandum pour Mr. Theunis sur ce qui s'est passé depuis la précédente session du Comité préparatoire (avril 1926)', AGR, TP, 984, ff. 1–3.

25. Clavin, *The Failure of Economic Diplomacy*, pp. 38–49.

26. Traynor, *International Monetary*, pp. 171–3.

27. On the CEPAG, see n. 4.

28. 'La Commission des illusions', this expression was often used by Gutt in his letters to Theunis, see: 'Gutt to Theunis', 17 January 1941, CEGES, GP, 128, f. 2.

29. Dumoulin and Dujardin, *Paul van Zeeland*, pp. 124–5.

30. A. B. Polonsky, 'Polish Failure in Wartime London: Attempts to Forge a European Alliance 1940–1944', *International History Review*, 7:4 (1965), pp. 176–91.

31. Ibid., p. 176.

32. 'Notes préliminaires sur quelques points importants, relatifs à la reconstruction économique de l'Europe après la guerre', Gotovitch, *Documents diplomatique belges*, pp. 202–8.

33. Ibid., p. 204.

34. Ibid., p. 206.

35. C. Navari, 'David Mitrany and International Functionalism', in D. Long and P. Wilson (eds), *Thinkers of the Twenty Years' Crisis* (Oxford: Clarendon Press, 1995), pp. 214–46.

36. Kurgan-van Hentenryk, 'La Société Générale', pp. 124–6.

37. 'Van Zeeland Report', CEGES, GP, 47, ff. 2–3.

38. 'Theunis to Gutt', 15 Janunary 1943, CEGES, GP, 153, f. 1.

39. 'Theunis to Gutt', 4 March 1943, CEGES, GP, 155, f. 2.

40. 'Van Zeeland to Aghnides', 21 August 1943, CEGES, Van Zeeland Papers, f. 3.

41. J. K. Horsefield, *The International Monetary Fund 1945–1965: Twenty Years of International Monetary Cooperation*, vol. 1: Chronicles (Washington DC: International Monetary Fund, 1969), pp. 12–13.

42. 'Gutt to Theunis', 26 January 1942, CEGES, GP, 139, f. 3.

43. R. Skidelsky, *John Maynard Keynes 1883–1946: Economist Philosopher, Statesman* (London: Penguin Books, 2005), pp. 640–2.

44. Skidelsky, 'Keynes's Road', pp. 144–5.

45. See n. 33.

46. On the Clearing Union, see: J. K. Horsefield, *The International Monetary Fund 1945–1965: Twenty Years of International Monetary Cooperation*, vol. 3: Documents (Washington DC: International Monetary Fund, 1969), pp. 3–19; Skidelsky, *John Maynard Keynes* (2003), pp. 679–82.

47. Skidelsky, 'Keynes's Road', pp. 132–3.

48. J. A. Boughton, 'Why White? Inventing the Post-War Monetary System', *IMF Working Papers*, 52 (2002), pp. 1–23.

49. 'Gutt to Theunis', 12 February 1941, CEGES, GP, 142, f. 3

50. Skidelsky, *John Maynard Keynes*, pp. 672–3.

51. Ibid., pp. 197–8.

52. 'Gutt to Theunis', 12 February 1941, CEGES, GP 142, f. 3.

53. F. Leith-Ross, *Money Talks, Fifty Years of International Finance: The Autobiography of Sir Frederick Leith-Ross* (London: Huchinson, 1968), pp. 279–87.

54. 'Post War Currency Situation of the Allies', July 1942, PRO, T160/1161/34325, ff. 1–2.

55. 'Frazer to Gutt', 30 April 1942, CEGES, GP, 16, ff. 1–2.

56. The so-called French plan was published in the *New York Times* in May 1943, see: Horse-field, *The International Monetary Fund*, vol. 3, pp. 97–102.

57. R. Frank, *La Hantise du déclin. Le rang de la France en Europe 1920–1960. Finances, défense, et identité nationale* (Paris: Belin, 1994), pp. 196–7.

58. 'Meeting at Treasury', 24 July 1942, PRO, T160/34329, ff. 1–2.

59. 'Meeting at Treasury', 24 July 1942, PRO, T160/34329, f. 3.

60. 'Meeting at Treasury', 24 July 1942, PRO, T160/34329, f. 3.

61. Eventually, the two plans were released by the two governments on 7 April 1943, see: R. Skidelsky, *John Maynard Keynes 1883–1946*, 3 vols(London: Macmillan, 1983–2000), vol. 3, pp. 152–253.

62. 'Meeting of Finance Ministers', 26 February 1943, PRO, T160/1161/F18181/3, f. 2.

63. 'Meeting of Finance Ministers', 26 February 1943, PRO, T160/1161/F18181/3, f. 2.

64. 'Meeting of Finance Ministers', 26 February 1943, PRO, T160/1161/F18181/3, f. 2.

65. 'Meeting of Finance Ministers', 26 February 1943, PRO, T160/1161/F18181/3, ff. 3–4.

66. Skidelsky, *John Maynard Keynes*, vol. 2, pp. 216–17.

67. 'J'ai la vague impression qu'on enterrera le plan Keynes sans les fleurs', in 'Gutt to Theunis 16 March 1943', CEGES, GP, 144, f.1.

68. 'A mon sens une machine universelle comme celle-ci [ou le plan Keynes] n'ira pas parce qu'universelle. Ca me ramène a mon accord hollando-belge, anglo-hollando-belge, puis atlantique', in 'Gutt to Theunis', 26 March 1943, CEGES, GP 144, f. 2.

69. See: R. F. Harrod, *The Life of John Maynard Keynes* (London: MacMillan, 1951), pp. 632, 635; D. E. Moggridge, *Maynard Keynes, an Economist Biography* (London, Routledge, 1992), p. 835; Skidelsky, *John Maynard Keynes*, vol. 2, pp. 467–8.

70. J. M. Keynes, 'The Savannah Conference and the Bretton Woods Final Act 27 March 1946', in *The Collected Writing of John Maynard Keynes*, vol. 26: Activities 1941–1946: Shaping the Post-War World. Bretton Woods and Reparations, ed. D. Moggridge (London: MacMillan, 1980), pp. 237–8, on p. 238.

71. 'Meeting of Finance Ministers', 26 February 1943, PRO, T160/1161/F18181/3, f. 4.

72. Crombois, *Camille Gutt*, pp. 458–9.

73. Markwell, *John Maynard Keynes and International*, pp. 120–4.

74. 'Gutt to Spaak', 12 October 1943, CEGES, GP, 108, f. 2.

75. Markwell, *John Maynard Keynes and International*, pp. 120–4.

76. B. W. Bateman, 'Keynes and Keynesianism', in Backhouse and Bateman (eds), *The Cambridge Campanion to Keynes*, pp. 271–90, on pp. 283–6.

77. J. M. Keynes, *The General Theory of Employment, Interest and Money* (London: Macmillan, 1936).

78. G. C. Peden, 'Sir John Hopkins, the Keynesian Revolution in Employment Policy 1929–1945', *Economic History Review*, 36:2 (1986), pp. 281–95.

79. J. M. Keynes, *Théorie générale de l'emploi, de l'intérêt et de la monnaie*, translated from English edition by Jean de Largentaye, 2nd edn (Paris: Payot 1969).

80. On Keynes's influence in France, see: J. Wolff, 'Pierre Mendès-France et J. M. Keynes. Un premier repérage', in *Pierre Mendès France et l'économie. Pensée et action sous la direction de M. Margairaz. Actes du Colloque organisé par l'Institut Mendès France à l'Assemblée nationale les 11 et 12 janvier 1988 sous la présidence de Mr Claude Cheysson* (Paris: Odile Jacob, 1989), pp. 57–79; P. Rosanvallon, 'The Development of Keynesianism in France', in P. Hall (ed.), *The Political Power of Economic Ideas: Keynesianism across Nations* (Princeton, NJ: Princeton University Press, 1989), pp. 171–94.

81. Cassiers, *Croissance*, pp. 173–83.
82. D. Herremans and K. Tavernier, 'De evolutie van de monetaire denkbeelden in Belgie 1914–1940', *Revue de la Banque*, 8–9 (1980), pp. 117–33.
83. Jeff Rens considered Keynes as 'the greatest economist in the world'. See n. 1.
84. On Keynes's influence in Belgium, see: I Maes, 'The Spread of Keynesian Economics: A Comparison of the Belgian and the Italian Experience 1945–1970', *Journal of the History of Economic Thought*, 30:4 (2008), pp. 491–509.
85. 'Un an de gouvernement Van Zeeland', CEGES, GP, 75, f. 8.
86. M. J. Flanders, *International Monetary Economics, 1870–1960: Between the Classical and the New Classical* (Cambridge: Cambridge University Press, 1989), pp. 65, 87–8.
87. 'World Group Asks Stabilized Money', *New York Times*, 26 March 1934, p. 27.
88. Clavin and Wessels, 'Gold Idol?', pp. 765–95.
89. B. Eichengreen and P. Temin, 'The Gold Standard and the Great Depression', *Contemporary European History*, 9 (2000), pp. 183–207, p. 207.
90. Flanders, *International Monetary Economics*, pp. 121–41.
91. F. Cesarano, 'The Bretton Woods Agreements: A Monetary Theory Perspective', in L. Cottrell, G. Notaras and G. Totella (eds), *Studies in European Monetary Integration* (London: Ashgate, 2007), pp. 113–37.
92. Keynes, *How to Pay for the War*, pp. 1–15.
93. G. C. Peden, 'Keynes and British Economic Policy', in Backhouse and Bateman (eds), *The Cambridge Companion*, pp. 108–112.
94. R. Skidelsky, 'Hayek versus Keynes: the road to reconciliation', in E. Feser (ed.), *The Cambridge Companion to Hayek* (Cambridge: Cambridge University Press, 2006), pp. 82–110, on p. 97.
95. 'Pour revenir à Keynes, je lui ai reproché dans le temps d'être fort théoricien mais il a beaucoup changé à cet égard. C'est d'ailleurs lui, vous vous en souvenez, qui juste au début de la guerre, a lancé le drive contre l'inflation et c'est son procédé de voluntary and unvoluntray savings qui est mis en pratique avec le succès que vous connaissez', in 'Gutt to Theunis', 26 March 1943, CEGES, GP, 144, f.1.

4 Extending the Benelux Agreements

1. T. Grosbois, 'La naissance du Benelux (1941–1944)', *Cahiers* [Centre de Recherches et d'Etudes historique sur la Seconde Guerre Mondiale], 15 (1992), pp. 53–101; T. Grosbois, 'Les négociations de Londres pour une Union Douanière Benelux (1941–1944)', in H. Baltahazar, M. Dumoulin and A. Postma, *Regards sur le Benelux. 50 Ans de coopération* (Bruxelles: Edition Racine, 1994), pp. 31–63; T. Grosbois, 'Benelux', in P. Gerbet (dir.), *Dictionnaire historique de l'Europe unie. Préface d'Elie Barnavi* (Bruxelles: André Versailles, 2009), pp. 110–18; B. Zeeman and C. Wiebes, 'The Netherlands and Alliances 1940–1949' (PhD dissertation, Rijksuniversiteit te Leiden, 1993), pp. 46–8.
2. W. Lipgens (ed.), *Documents on the History of European Integration*, vol. 2: Plans for European Union in Great Britain and in Exile 1939–1945 (Berlin: Alter de Gruyter, 1986), pp. 786–824.
3. 'Note de Franz Van Cauwelaert: il n'y a plus d'Europe', Gotovitch, *Documents diplomatiques*, pp. 197–200.
4. 'un fou dangereux en ce sens que tous ses plans de fédération européenne sont contraires à l'intérêt des petites', in 'Theunis to Gutt, 28 January 1943', CEGES, GP, 153, f. 2.

5. 'En conclusion, il me semble donc qu'une fédération européenne est impossible au lendemain de la guerre, mais que l'idée fédérale est une idée juste', Gotovitch, *Documents diplomatiques*, pp. 209–13.

6. On the 'pre-history' of the Benelux agreements, see: G. van Roon, 'Rapprochement en vagues successives. La préhistoire du Benelux', in Balthazar et al., *Regards sur le Benelux*, pp. 13–38.

7. E. Bussière, *La France, la Belgique et l'organisation économique de l'Europe, 1918–1935* (Paris: Ministère de l'Economie, des Finances et du Budget, 1992), pp. 393–413.

8. Ibid.

9. Zeeman and Wiebes, 'The Netherlands', pp. 46–8.

10. Grosbois, 'La naissance', pp. 53–101

11. Ibid., p. 65.

12. 'Gutt to Theunis', 12 February 1941, CEGES, GP, 142, f. 3.

13. 'J'ai quitté Keynes vers minuit, il est 9 heures et je vous dicte vite cela pour que ma lettre parte par l'avion: c'est vous dire que je me pose des questions sans avoir le temps d'y répondre ni même d'y penser suffisamment', in 'Gutt to Theunis', 12 February 1941, CEGES, GP, 142, f. 4.

14. Gutt, *La Belgique*, pp. 153–4.

15. P. H. Spaak, *Combats inachevés. De l'indépendance a l'alliance* (Paris: Fayard, 1969), p. 150.

16. 'L. Nemry, ambassadeur de Belgique près du gouvernement néerlandais à Londres, Londres le 27 mars 1941', Gotovitch, *Documents diplomatiques*, pp. 390–2.

17. 'Cabinet Council Minutes 26 June 1941', AGR, microfilm 2081/1, f. 223.

18. 'D'habitude, lorsqu'il s'agissait d'une question économique et financière, mes collègues me faisaient confiance. Cette fois-là, l'accueil que je reçus fut inattendu; ma proposition fut rejetée à l'unanimité de mes trois collègues: Pierlot, Spaak, De Vleeschauwer ! ... J'écrivis à Vandenbroeck que j'avais échoué, mais ne me tenais pas pour battu et reviendrais à la charge', Gutt, *La Belgique*, p. 155

19. 'Note de F. van Langenhove, secrétaire général du ministère des affaires étrangères sur les conditions dont dépendent la conclusion et le fonctionnement d'une union douanière hollando-belge, Londres le 2 juillet 1941', Gotovitch, *Documents diplomatiques*, pp. 395–6.

20. 'Van den Broeck to Sengier', 30 November 1942, CEGES, GP, 105, f. 1.

21. 'De Schryver to Gutt', 7 January 1943, CEGES, GP, 104, f. 1.

22. 'Note de F. van Langenhove, secrétaire général du ministère des affaires étrangères au sujet d'une union douanière hollando-belge-luxembourgeoise (Londres, le 22 mars 1943)', Gotovitch, *Documents diplomatiques*, pp. 401–3.

23. 'Ce que l'on veut principalement éviter par l'accord, ce sont les manipulations de la monnaie d'un des deux pays par l'autre', in 'Cabinet Meeting Minutes', 15 April 1943, AGR, microfilm 2081/2, f. 129.

24. Crombois, *Camille Gutt*, pp. 415–16.

25. Grosbois, 'La naissance', p. 52.

26. 'Gutt to Pierlot', 24 May 1943, CEGES, GP, 102, f. 3.

27. 'Gutt to Pierlot', 24 May 1943, CEGES, GP, 102, f. 3.

28. Grosbois, 'La naissance', pp. 54–5.

29. Grosbois, 'Benelux', pp. 110–18.

30. 'Keynes, la Treasury et la Banque d'Angleterre suivent cela de très près', in 'Gutt to Theunis', 26 March 1943, CEGES, GP, 140, f. 3.

31. Grosbois, 'Les négociations', p. 52.
32. 'Note from Waley to Phillips', undated, PRO, FO 271/34323, f. 34.
33. 'Gutt to Rens', 29 October 1943, CEGES, Rens Papers, f. 2.
34. 'Conversation tenue avec le Chancelier de l'Echiquier le 16 octobre 1943', 16 October 1843, CEGES, GP, 18, f. 1.
35. 'Parliamentary Question', 2 November 1943, PRO, FO 371/34323/C 14211, f. 1.
36. 'Parliamentary Question', 2 November 1943, PRO, FO 371/34323/C 14211, f. 1.
37. 'Secret. Proposed Monetary Agreement between the Dutch and the Belgian Governments: Comparison with United Kingdom Payments Agreements', Overseas and Foreign Office, Trade and Payment Group, 4 November 1943, ABOE, OV 88/A, f. 1.
38. Cabinet Council Minutes, 4 May 1944, AGR, PVCM 2081/2, f. 123.
39. 'Note sur une conversation tenue le 6 avril 1944 entre le Chancelier de l'Echiquier, Sir John Anderson, et M. Gutt, ministre des Finances', CEGES, GP, 19, f. 1.
40. A. Eden, *The Eden Memoirs*, 3 vols (London: Cassel, 1960), vol. 1, p. 444; A. Dumoulin and E. Remacle, *L'Union de l'Europe occidentale. Phénix de la défense européenne* (Bruxelles: Bruylandts, 1998), pp. 4–27.
41. 'Notes on the Anglo-Belgian Monetary Agreement', 5 February 1945, ABOE, OV 11, f. 2.
42. 'C'est vraiment un home lucide, maître de lui, ne perdant pas de temps en phrases, voyant bien les grandes lignes de la politique', in 'Gutt to Theunis', 11 December 1941, CEGES, GP, 138, f. 2.
43. Interview of Etienne Gutt on 15 April 1997, CEGES.
44. Cabinet Council Minutes, 2 October 1941, AGR, microfilm 2081/2, f. 203.
45. 'Gutt to Theunis', 9 November 1943, CEGES, GP, 140, f. 1
46. Roussel, *Jean Monnet 1888–1979*), pp. 275–80.
47. 'Note sur l'or belge 13 février 1943', 13 February 1943, MF, AEF, ff. 1–2.
48. Van der Wee and Verbeyt, *A Small Nation*, pp. 410–11; For a more detailed account see: Van der Wee and Verbeyt, *Oorlog en monetarie politiek*, pp. 426–47.
49. 'Cable sent to Theunis', 17 November 1942, CEGES, GP, 18, f. 1.
50. 'Minutes of the Second Meeting of the Sub-Committee on Post-War Currency Requirements held at the Treasury on 18 November 1942', PRO T160/1161/34329, ff. 3–4.
51. 'Conversations avec MM. Pleven (18 november), Dielthelm (20 novembre), Waley and Frazer (21 novembre)', CEGES, GP, 18, ff. 1–4.
52. 'Conversations avec MM. Pleven (18 november), Dielthelm (20 novembre), Waley and Frazer (21 novembre)', CEGES, GP, 18, ff. f. 2.
53. 'Conversations avec MM. Pleven (18 november), Dielthelm (20 novembre), Waley and Frazer (21 novembre)', CEGES, GP, 18, ff. f. 4.
54. 'Baudewijns to Gutt', 21 November 1942, CEGES, GP, 16, ff. 2–3.
55. 'Conversation avec Mr. Pleven 18 novembre 1942', 18 November 1942, CEGES, GP, 18, f. 2.
56. P. Margairaz, *L'Etat, les finances et l'économie. Histoire d'une conversion 1932–1952*, 2 vols (Paris: Comité pour l'histoire économique et financière de la France, 1991), vol. 2, pp. 742–5.
57. On these aspects: R. F. Kuisel, *Capitalism and the State in Modern France: Renovation and Economic Management in the Twentieth Century* (Cambridge: Cambridge University Press: Cambridge, 1981), pp. 159–63, 191–201.
58. 'Premier mémoire sur l'organisation économique de l'Europe d'après-guerre (Note Blum-Picard)', 1 December 1943, MF, AEF, B 33002, f. 15.

59. Margairaz, *L'Etat*, vol. 2, p. 755
60. 'Boël to Gutt', 8 November 1943, CEGES, GP, 81, ff. 3–4.
61. 'Cable n° 168', 18 November 1943, CEGES, GP, 18, f. 1.
62. 'Boël to Gutt', 11 November 1943, CEGES, GP, 92, f. 3.
63. Margairaz, *L'Etat*, vol. 2, p. 723.
64. 'Entretien avec André Istel à Washington 18 Décembre 1943', 18 December 1943, CEGES, GP, 18, ff. 1–3.
65. 'Note signed Hervé de Gruben', December 1943, CEGES, GP, 18, ff. 1–3
66. 'Réunion à la Trésorerie américaine 5 janvier 1944', 5 January 1944, CEGES, GP, 19, ff. 1–2.
67. Meeting at the US Treasury, 13 January 1944, CEGES, GP, 19, ff. 1–3.
68. Margairaz, *L'Etat*, vol. 2, pp. 723–4, 749–71.
69. 'Cable n° 168, 18 novembre 1943', 18 November 1943, CEGES, GP, 18, f. 1.
70. 'Cable Monnet to Massigli', undated, MF, AEF, B 19857, f. 2.
71. 'Je connais depuis vingt ans son intelligence. Je connais la situation qu'il a acquise auprès des Anglais , puis des Américains. D'autre part, je le crois loyal', in 'Gutt to Spaak (New York)', 19 January 1944, CEGES, GP, 108, f. 1.
72. 'Gutt to Spaak (New York)', 19 January 1944, CEGES, GP, 108, ff. 2–3.
73. 'Mémorandum d'une conversation tenue dans le cabinet de Monsieur Gutt 4 avril 1944', 4 April 1944, CEGES, GP, 19, ff. 1–2.
74. 'Gutt to Spaak', Bretton Woods, 21 July 1944, in Gotovitch, *Documents Diplomatiques*, pp. 347–8.
75. Van der Wee and Verbeyt, *A Small Nation*, pp. 403–11.

5 The Birth of a Monetary System

1. Boughton, 'Why White not Keynes?', pp. 1–24.
2. J. G. Ikenberry, 'A World Economy Restored: Expert Consensus and the Anglo-American Post-War Settlement', in P. M. Hass (ed.), *Knowledge, Power, and International Policy Coordination* (Cambridge MA: MIT Press, 1992), pp. 289–321.
3. H. James, *International Monetary Cooperation since Bretton Woods* (Oxford: Oxford University Press, 1996), pp. 33–57; N. Woods, *The Globalizers: The IMF, the World Bank, and their Borrowers* (Ithaca, NY: Cornell University Press, 2006), pp. 16–22.
4. J. S. Odell, 'From London to Bretton Woods. Sources of Change in Bargaining Strategies and Outcomes', *Journal of Public Policy*, 8:3–4 (1988), pp. 287–315.
5. E. Helleiner, *States and the Reemergence of Global Finance: From Bretton Woods to the 1990s* (Ithaca, NY: Cornell University Press, 1996), pp. 26–33.
6. Horsefield, *The International Monetary*, vol. 1, pp. 89–118; A. van Dormael, *Bretton Woods: Birth of a Monetary System* (London: Macmillan, 1978), pp. 168–223.
7. J. A. Boughton, 'American in the Shadows: Harry Dexter White and the Design of the International Monetary Fund', *IMF Working Papers*, 6 (2006), pp. 1–14, on p. 14.
8. Dormael, *Bretton Woods*, pp. 69–70; Horsefield, *International Monetary*, vol. 1, pp. 21–5.
9. 'le premier est rédigé par une poète, le second par un avocat américain. En d'autres termes, le plan Keynes est pensé avec tout l'art, la finesse et la clarté d'une vieille civilisation, le plan White avec l'absence d'expériences, de nuances et de sens du relatif que l'on trouve aussi bien chez les jeunes nations que chez les jeunes individus. Le plan Keynes fait paraître simple les choses de nature assez compliquées. Le plan White a l'air compliqué, de par

sa présentation, alors qu'il est brutalement simple', in 'Note de Camille Gutt à propos des plans Keynes et White 13 avril 1943', 13 April 1943, AGR, TP, 62, f. 2.

10. 'Note de Camille Gutt à propos des plans Keynes et White 13 avril 1943', AGR, TP, 62, f. 3.

11. 'Theunis to Gutt', 20 October 1943, CEGES, GP, 155, f. 2.

12. Cabinet Council Minutes, 15 April 1943, AGR, microfilm 2081/2, f. 129.

13. Cabinet Council Minutes, 3 May 1943, AGR, microfilm 2081/2, f. 139.

14. Skidelsky, *John Maynard Keynes*, vol. 2, p. 300; Van Dormael, *Bretton Woods*, pp. 80–3.

15. 'Résumé de mon entretien avec M. White, Assistant to the Secretary of Treasury (Washington 2 Juin 1943)', CEGES, GP, 17, f. 1.

16. 'Résumé de mon entretien avec M. White, Assistant to the Secretary of Treasury (Washington 2 Juin 1943)', CEGES, GP, 17, f. 2.

17. 'Résumé de mon entretien avec M. White, Assistant to the Secretary of Treasury (Washington 2 Juin 1943)', CEGES, GP, 17, f. 3.

18. 'Le jour où leur antagonisme se sera manifesté, où la lutte aura lieu, où les adversaires se seront fatigués, alors nous pourrons intervenir', in 'Gutt to Pierlot 13 June 1943', CEGES, GP, 102, f. 2.

19. 'Boël to White', 27 October 1943, ML, WP, ff. 2–3; and S. Black, *A Levite Amongst the Priest: Edward Bernstein and the Origins of the Bretton Woods System* (Boulder, CO: Westview, 1991), pp. 3–5.

20. 'Gutt to Boël 17 November 1943', CEGES, GP, 92, f. 2.

21. D. Kapur, J. P. Lewis and R. Webb, *The World Bank: Its First Half Century*, vol. 1: History (Washington DC: Brookings Institution Press, 1997), pp. 58–70; R. W. Oliver, *International Economic Cooperation and the World Bank* (London: MacMillan, 1996), pp. 128–52.

22. Tavernier and van der Wee, *La Banque nationale*, p. 264.

23. Meeting in M. White's Office, 7 January 1944, ML, WP, 9, ff. 1–3.

24. Cabinet Council Minutes, 4 May 1943', AGR, microfilm 1/2, f. 149.

25. Crombois, *Camille Gutt*, p. 461.

26. For a detailed overview of the discussions, see: Crombois, *Camille Gutt*, pp. 464–73; Van der Wee and Verbeyt, *Nationale Bank*, pp. 592–8.

27. 'Aucune force humaine n'enlèvera des jambes à un cul-e-jatte', in 'Grands hommes', CEGES, GP, 75, f. 13.

28. 'Theunis to Gutt', 27 November 1942, CEGES, GP, 143, f.. 3.

29. 'Note by Lord Keynes', 6 December 1942, CEGES, GP, 16, f. 1.

30. Van der Wee and Verbeyt, *Oorlog en monetaire politiek*, pp. 593–4.

31. 'Gutt to Spaak', 13 May 1943, CEGES, GP, 17, ff. 1–2.

32. 'Conversation avec Sir John Anderson, Chancelier de l'Echiquier (26 octobre 1943)', 26 October 2943, CEGES, GP, 16, ff. 1–3.

33. 'Conversation avec Mr. White', 7 December 1943, CEGES, GP, 18, f. 1.

34. 'Theunis to Spaak', 14 January 1944, CEGES, GP, 19, f. 1.

35. 'Gutt to Anderson', 13 April 1943, CEGES, GP, 19, f. 2; and 'Gutt to Morgenthau', 13 April 1943, CEGES, GP, 19, f. 1.

36. Skidelsky, *John Maynard Keynes*, vol. 2, pp. 335–6.

37. 'Exposé sur le Fonds de Stabilisation par Mr. Gutt (19 juin 1944)', 19 June 1944, CEGES, GP, 13, f. 3.

38. R. B. Woods, *A Changing of the Guard: Anglo-American Relations, 1941–1946* (Chapel Hill, NC: University of North Carolina Press, 1990), pp. 128–9.

39. Oliver, *International Economic Cooperation*, pp. 159–61; Woods, *A Changing of the Guard*, pp. 128–9.
40. M. Kahler, 'Bretton Woods and its Competitors: The Political Economy of Institutional Choice', in D. M. Andrews, C. R. Henning and L.W. Pauly (eds), *Governing the World's Money* (Ithaca, NY: Cornell University Press, 2002), pp. 38–59, on pp. 53–4.
41. 'Il y a une ressemblance frappante entre les arguments présentés récemment par Lord Keynes et les arguments du Président Roosevelt lors de la conférence de Londres, en 1933. Dans le message du Président à cette époque, message qui est tombé comme une bombe sur la conférence et l'a ruinée, le Président disait qu'un système économique sain est plus important pour le bien-être d'un pays que la valeur de sa monnaie par rapport aux autres monnaies. La future conférence devra répondre à la question claire suivante: croyons-nous vraiment à des monnaies stables et des taux de change stables, ou bien devons-nous retourner à al situation de 1933, après la bombe lancée par Roosevelt', in 'Theunis to Gutt', 22 June 1944, CEGES, GP, 156, f. 2
42. 'Gutt to Pierlot', 29 June 1944, CEGES, GP, 141, f. 1.
43. 'Gutt to Theunis', 17 March 1943, CEGES, GP, 140, f.1.
44. 'Theunis to Gutt', 15 June 1944, CEGES, GP, 156, f. 2.
45. 'Gutt to Pierlot', 7 July 1944, CEGES, GP, 102, f. 1
46. Van Dormael, *Bretton Woods*, pp. 176–93. Skidelsky, *John Maynard Keynes*, vol. 2, pp. 361–4.
47. A. Mantez, 'Pierre Mendès France. Expert International 1944–1953', *Pierre Mendes – France et l'économie* (Paris: Editions Odile Jacob, 1989), pp. 119–42; Dormael, *Bretton Woods*, pp. 186–91.
48. 'Theunis to Spaak', 21 and 22 July 1944, AGR, TP, 102, ff. 2–3.
49. Skidelsky, *John Maynard Keynes*, pp. 353–4; Van Dormael, *Bretton Woods*, pp. 198–9.
50. Keynes, *The Collected Writings*, vol. 26, p. 100
51. Remarks of Georges Theunis, Delegate of Belgium at the Executive Plenary Session, July 21, 1944, in *United Nations Monetary and Financial Conference. Proceedings and Documents, vol. II* (Washington DC: United States Government Printing Office: 1948), pp. 1217–22.
52. 'Cette conférence était [en moins bien à certains points de vue] la reproduction exacte, dans ses grandes lignes , dans son déroulement er dans son épilogue, d'une dizaine de grandes conférences auxquelles j'ai assisté de 1920 à 1944 ... Même tendance.. à se mettre d'accord sur un texte ambigu que chacun pourra rapporter chez soi comme une succès en l'interprétant à sa façon ... Mêmes efforts pour escamoter les réserves faites par certains membres et donner au monde une impression illusoire d'unanimité ... Mêmes interventions des grandes puissances, négociant dans la coulisse et imposant soudainement leur volonté aux autres ... Mêmes appels à l'intérêt général dans les discours', in 'Note de Mr Gutt devant le Conseil consultative sur la Conférence de Bretton Woods 16 août 1944', 16 August 1944, CEGES, GP, 13, ff. 1–2.
53. 'Deux fois, j'ai causé quelques minutes avec l'un d'eux, et deux fois il a rompu visiblement en vitesse la conversation pour ne pas se compromettre. Tout le monde a eu la même expérience. Parfois, c'est un Russe qui vient tirer par la manche le délégué en danger', in 'Theunis to Spaak', 21 and 22 July 1944, AGR, TP, 102, f. 2
54. See n. 48.
55. F. Perroux, *Textes complementaires sur la coexistence pacifique* (Grenoble: Presses Universitaires de Grenoble, 1992), pp. 90–5.

6 Camille Gutt, First Managing Director of the International Monetary Fund

1. 'Rapport au Comité ministériel économique sur la négociation du Lend-Lease à Washington (20 avril 1945)', CEGES, GP, 30, ff. 1–2.
2. Woods, *Changing of the Guard*, pp. 314–20.
3. 'Rapport au Comité ministériel économique sur la négociation du Lend-Lease à Washington (20 avril 1945)', CEGES, GP, 30, f. 2.
4. G. Bossuat, *La France, l'aide américaine à la construction européenne 1944–1954*, 2 vols (Paris: Comite pour l'Histoire économique et financière de la France, 1992), vol. 1, pp. 301–32.
5. 'Rapport au Comité ministériel économique sur la négociation du Lend-Lease à Washington (20 avril 1945)', CEGES, GP, 30, ff. 3–4.
6. 'Spaak to Acheson', 14 September 1945, CEGES, GP, 30, ff. 1–2.
7. 'Rapport au Ministre des Finances (décembre 1945)', December 1945, CEGES, GP, 32, ff. 4–6.
8. Data taken from: Brion and Moreau, *La politique monétaire*, p. 125.
9. 'Gutt to De Voghel, 19 October 1945', CEGES, GP, 32, ff. 1–2.
10. 'Agreemnent between the Kingdom of Belgium and the Export-Import Bank of Washington, 20 October 1945', CEGES, GP, 30, ff. 1–3.
11. *Articles of the Agreement. International Monetary Fund and International Bank for Reconstruction and Development, Article XX* (Washington DC: United States Treasury, 1944), p. 34
12. Crombois, *Camille Gutt*, p. 493.
13. Van Dormael, *Bretton Woods*, pp. 284–6.
14. Memorandum, 24 January 1946. 'Conversation with Lord Keynes at the British Treasury', ML, WP, box 27, f. 2.
15. Van Dormael, *Bretton Woods*, pp. 288–9.
16. 'Gutt to Eyskens', 11 February 1946, CEGES, GP, 60, f. 1.
17. 'Silvercruys to Selliers', 25 January 1946, CEGES, GP, 60, f. 1.
18. Van Dormael, *Bretton Woods*, p. 290.
19. Horsefield, *International Monetary Monetary Fund*, vol. 1, pp. 235–6.
20. E. Deshormes, 'Camille Gutt – Premier Directeur général du Fonds Monétaire International 1946–1951', *Revue de la Banque* [supplément historique], 3 (1986), pp. 3–63, on p. 18.
21. Keynes, *The Collected Writings*, vol. 26, pp. 237–8.
22. Brion and Moreau, *La politique monétaire*, p. 145.
23. 'International Monetary Fund, Cable Address InterFund', undated, CEGES, GP, 73, f. 1.
24. 'Gutt Named Head of Monetary Fund', *New York Times*, 7 May 1946, p. 35
25. G. Bossuat, 'La France et le FMI au lendemain de la Seconde Guerre mondiale: les raisons de la tension', in *La France et les institutions de Bretton Woods 1944–1994. Actes du Colloque tenu à Bercy les 30 juin et 1er juillet 1994* (Paris: Comité pour l'Histoire économique et financière de la France, 1998), pp. 15–34, on pp. 17–21.
26. See, n. 20.
27. C. P. Kindleberger, 'Bretton Woods Reappraised', *International Organization*, 5:1 (1951), pp. 32–47, p. 37.
28. C. P. Kindleberger, *Marhsall Plan Days* (Boston, MA: Allan & Uwin, 1987), p. 57.

29. A. S. Milward, *The Reconstruction of Western Europe 1945–1951* (London: Routledge, 1984), p. 44

30. B. Eichengreen, 'Institutions and Economic Growth: Europe after World War II', in N. Crafts and G. Toniolo (eds), *Economic Growth in Europe since 1945* (Cambridge: Cambridge University Press, 1996), pp. 56–7.

31. James, *International Monetary Cooperation*, p. 83.

32. Skidelsky, 'Keynes Road, pp. 150–1.

33. Skidelsky, *John Maynard Keynes* (2003), p. 703.

34. Meeting, 17 August 1947, AIMF, Executive Board Minutes, f. 5.

35. Staff Memo 109, June 1947: Scarce Currency Provisions, AIMF, ff. 1–4.

36. 'The Monetary Fund and the Dollar Scarcity', [author unidentified], 3 September 1947, AIMF, ff. 1–2.

37. R. Higgs, 'From Central Planning to the Market: The American Transition', *Journal of Economic History*, 59:3 (1999), pp. 599–623.

38. 'The Monetary Fund and the Dollar Scarcity', [author unidentified], 3 September 1947, AIMF, f. 2.

39. H. D. White, 'The Monetary Fund: Some Criticisms Examined', *Foreign Affairs*, 23 (January 1945), pp. 195–210, on p. 208.

40. C. Gutt, 'Exchange Rates and the International Monetary Fund', *Review of Economics and Statistics*, 30:2 (May 1938), pp. 81–90.

41. On the origins of the Schuman's financial plan, see: Bossuat, 'La France', vol.1, pp. 266–73.

42. These events are described in: 'Gutt to Ansiaux', 9 March 1948, CEGES, GP, 98, ff. 4–8.

43. Bossuat, 'La France', pp. 24–6.

44. Deshormes, 'Camille Gutt', p. 35.

45. 'Minutes of the 80th Meeting of the NAC on International Monetary and Financial Matters', 19 January 1948, in *Foreign Relations of the United States*, vol. 3: Western Europe (Washington DC: US Government Printing Office, 1974), pp. 598–601.

46. Minutes of the NAC, 20 January 1948, in *Foreign Relations of the United States*, vol. 2, pp. 594–5.

47. Meeting, 19 January 1948, AIMF, Executive Board Mimutes, f. 7.

48. Meeting, 24 January 1948, AIMF, Executive Board Minutes, f. 3.

49. Meeting, 24 January 1948, AIMF, Executive Board Minutes, f. 4.

50. Meeting, 19 January 1948, AIMF, Executive Board Minutes, f. 7.

51. Bossuat, 'La France', pp. 33–4.

52. 'Le sentiment général est que le Fonds a agi plus comme un tribunal en dernier ressort sur la base de principes rigides que comme un expert financier qui chercherait des solutions raisonnables et humaines', in 'Ansiaux to Gutt', 16 February 1948, CEGES, GP, 98, f.2.

53. 'Le monde a vécu longtemps sur la solidité de trois monnaies clés. Avant la guerre de 1914 le franc français, la livre sterling et un peu moins solidement le dollar. Après la Grande Guerre, le dollar, un peu moins solidement le franc français. Pour le moment le franc français est écarté. Le dollar a gardé sa primauté (dans le royaume des aveugles les borgnes sont rois, et l'Angleterre si vous voulez joue le rôle du borgne en ce sens que la livre est secouée mais qu'elle est restée dans une certaine mesure une monnaie mondiale). Avons-nous intérêt à précipiter son effondrement ? Personnellement, je ne le crois pas', in 'Gutt to Ansiaux', 9 March 1948, CEGES, GP, 98, f.1.

54. S. Lepage, 'Chronique d'un malentendu: la direction des finances extérieures et le Fonds Monétaire International, 1944–1948', in *La France et les institutions de Bretton Woods*

1944–1994. Actes du Colloque tenu à Bercy les 30 juin et 1er juillet 1994 (Paris: Comité pour l'Histoire Economique et Financière de la France, 1998), pp. 35–67, on p. 46.

55. On the Marshall Plan, see: Milward, *Reconstruction*; M. J. Hogan, *The Marshall Plan: America, Britain and the Reconstruction of Western Europe* (Cambridge, Cambridge University Press, 1987).

56. H. Arkes, *Bureaucracy, the Marshall Plan and the National Interest* (Princeton, NJ: Princeton University Press, 1972), pp. 224–8.

57. C. Maier, *In Search of Stability: Explorations in History Economy* (Cambridge: Cambridge University Press, 1987), pp. 95–139.

58. C. Gutt, 'Les accords de Bretton Woods and les institutions qui en sont issues' *Recueil des Cours. Académie de Droit International*, 72:1 (1948), pp. 71–162, on p. 91.

59. 'Gutt to Spaak', 21 June 1947, CEGES, GP, 136, f. 1.

60. 'Gutt to Spaak', 21 June 1947, CEGES, GP, 136, f. 2.

61. It should be pointed out that the Americans tried unsuccessfully in 1948 to appoint Spaak as a possible position of Managing Director of the OEEC in order to re-launch their attempts to promote European integration, see: G. Kurgan-van Hentenryk, 'La Belgique et le Plan Marshall ou les paradoxes des relations belgo-américaines', *Revue Belge de Philologie et d'Histoire*, 71:2 (1993), pp. 290–354; Dumoulin, *Spaak*, pp. 423–5; 'Gutt to Spaak', 21 June 1947, CEGES, GP, 136, f. 2.

62. Material for Summarisation of the Marshall Plan Discussions, AIMF, ff. 8–9.

63. Meeting, 21 January 1948, AIMF, Executive Board Minutes, f. 4.

64. J. K. Horsefield and G. Lovasy, 'Evolution of the Fund's Policy on Drawings', in de Vries and Horsefield (eds), *The International Monetary Fund 1945–1965*, vol. 2, pp. 415–27, on p. 424.

65. Meeting, 21 January 1948, AIMF, Executive Board Minutes, f. 4.

66. Meeting, 1 September 1948, AIMF, Executive Board Minutes, f. 5.

67. F. Block, *The Origins of International Economic Disorder: A Study of United States International Monetary Policy from World War II to the Present* (Berkeley, CA and London: University of California Press, 1977), pp. 99–102.

68. A. Caincross, *Years of Recovery: British Economic Policy 1947–1951* (London: Methuen, 1987), pp. 176–80; J. Fforde, *The Bank of England and Public Policy 1941–1958* (Cambridge: Cambridge University Press, 1992), pp. 280–311.

69. Meeting, 20 March 1949, AIMF, Executive Board Minutes, f. 4.

70. Caincross, *Years of Recovery*, pp. 180–6.

71. Ibid., pp. 186–8.

72. 'Devaluation and the Consequences', *Economist*, 24 September 1949, pp. 680–5.

73. 'Les méthodes qui ont été suivies n'ont pas été celles que l'on aurait pu souhaiter', in 'Gutt to Spaak', 28 September 1949, CEGES, GP, 108, f. 1

74. 'International cooperation should be more than words [undated]', CEGES, GP, 57, f. 5

75. 'Même avec cette conception, les Anglais auraient pu agir autrement', in 'Gutt to Spaak', 3 October 1949, CEGES, GP, 108, f. 4.

76. 'Devaluation and the Consequences', *Economist*, p. 683.

77. 'Gutt to Spaak', 3 October 1949, CEGES, GP, 108, f. 3.

78. J. Polak, 'Contribution of the September 1949 Devaluations to the Solution of Europe's Dollar Problem', *IMF Staff Papers*, 2:1 (1951), pp. 1–32.

79. Block, *The Origins*, pp. 103–8.

80. J. F. Crombois, 'International Organizations and Regional Integration: The IMF and the EPU (1946–1958)', in E. Remacle and P. Winand (eds), *America, Europe, Africa 1943–1973* (Oxford: Peter Lang, 2009), pp. 67–82, on pp. 76–9.

81. Brion and Moreau, *La politique monétaire*, pp. 171–2.

82. Report on the Inter-European Negotiations Associated with the Marshal Plan, 16 October 1947, AIMF, ff. 1–2.

83. Report on the Inter-European Negotiations Associated with the Marshal Plan, 16 October 1947, AIMF, ff. 4–5.

84. Meeting, 12 November 1948, AIMF, Executive Board Minutes, f. 8.

85. In Bretton Woods, a resolution aimed at suppressing the BIS was agreed. But at Savannah, the American delegation did not push for the decision to be implemented, see: James, *International Monetary Cooperation*, pp. 48–50.

86. Fforde, *The Bank of England*, pp. 177–8; Brion and Moreau, *La politique monétaire*, pp. 153–4.

87. S. Lepage, 'Chronique d'un malentendu', pp. 43–6.

88. 'Gutt to Ansiaux', 19 May 1948, CEGES, GP, 98, ff. 3–4.

89. 'Gutt to Ansiaux', 2 January 1948, CEGES, GP, 98, f.2.

90. Meeting, 12 November 1948, AIMF, Executive Board Minutes, f. 4.

91. Meeting, 12 November 1948, AIMF, Executive Board Minutes, f. 4.

92. J. Kaplan and G. Schleiminger, *The European Payments Union: Financial Diplomacy in the 1950s* (Oxford: Clarendon Press, 1989), pp. 340–1.

93. EPU and Ansiaux Plan 15 May 1950, IMF Secretariat, AIMF, f.13.

94. Idem, f. 15.

95. Kaplan and Schleiminger, *The European Payments*, p. 52.

96. Meeting, 15 May 1950, AIMF, Executive Board Minutes, f. 6.

97. *Agreement for the Establishment of a European Payment Union (with Annexes and Protocol of Provisional Applications, Paris, 19 Sept. 1950* (Paris: Organisation européenne de coopération économique, 1950), p.15.

98. 'Meeting on 25 January 1951 in Mr Gutt's office. Subject: Fund's relations with Europe', AIMF, ff. 1–3.

99. 'Note for the statement made by the Managing Director M. Camille Gutt to the Executive Board of the International Monetary Fund at the meeting 652', 19 March 1951, CEGES, GP, 35, ff. 1–3.

100. Deshormes, 'Camille Gutt', p. 30.

101. 'Gutt to Frère', 12 March 1951, CEGES, GP, 90, f. 2.

102. 'Dilemmas of Leadership', *Economist*, 22 July 1951, pp. 213–14.

WORKS CITED

Manuscript Sources

Archives Générales du Royaume.
    Police des Etrangers.
    Theunis Papers.
    Cabinet Council Minutes.
Archives of the Bank of England, UK.
    Series OV/88.
    Belgium (1938–46).
Archives of the International Monetary Fund.
    Executive Board Minutes.
    EPU and Ansiaux Plan 15 May 1950, IMF Secretariat.
    Material for Summarisation of the Marshall Plan Discussions.
    Meeting on 25 January 1951 in Mr Gutt's office. Subject: Fund's relations with Europe.
    Report on the Inter-European Negotiations Associated with the Marshal Plan, 16 October 1947.
    Staff Memo 109, June 1947: Scarce Currency Provisions.
    'The Monetary Fund and the Dollar Scarcity' [author unidentified].
Centre d'Etudes et de Documentation Guerres et Sociétés Contemporaines, Belgium.
    Gutt Papers.
    Rens Papers.
    Richard Papers.
    Van Zeeland Papers.
    Interviews of Etienne Gutt.
Ministère des Finances.
    Archives économiques et financières.
Mudd Library, University of Princeton, New Jersey.
    John Foster Dulles Papers.
    Harry Dexter White Papers.
National Archives and Records Administration, Washington DC.
    Foreign Economic Administration.
    Department of State.
Public Records Office, UK.
    Foreign Office Series.
    Belgium and Luxembourg.
    Series T 160.
    Overseas Finance Division.

Published Sources

Agreements between the Government of the United Kingdom and the Belgian Government relating to the Belgian Congo in respect of Finance and the Purchase of Commodities. London 21 January 1941, Treaty Series, 1 (London: His Majesty's Stationery Office, 1941).

Agreement for the Establishment of a European Payment Union (with Annexes and Protocol of Provisional Applications, Paris, 19 Sept. 1950 (Paris: Organisation européenne de coopération économique, 1950).

Arkes, H., *Bureaucracy, the Marshall Plan and the National Interest* (Princeton, NJ: Princeton University Press, 1972).

Articles of the Agreement. International Monetary Fund and International Bank for Reconstruction and Development, Article XX (Washington DC: United States Treasury, 1944).

Backhouse, R. F., and B. W. Bateman (eds), *The Cambridge Campanion to Keynes* (Cambridge: Cambridge University Press, 2006).

Ball, S., 'The German Octopus: The British Metal Corporation and the Next War 1914–1939', *Enterprise and Society*, 5:3 (2004), pp. 451–90.

Bateman, B. W., 'Keynes and Keynesianism', in Backhouse and Bateman (eds), *The Cambridge Campanion to Keynes*, pp. 271–90.

'Belgian Metal Group in Consolidation Here', *New York Times*, 17 February 1926, p. 28.

Black, S., *A Levite Amongst the Priest: Edward Bernstein and the Origins of the Bretton Woods System* (Boulder, CO: Westview, 1991).

Block, F., *The Origins of International Economic Disorder: A Study of United States International Monetary Policy from World War II to the Present* (Berkeley, CA and London: University of California Press, 1977).

Bonin, H., T. Grosbois, N. Hetzfeld and J.-L. Laudet, *Ford en France et en Belgique 1903–2003* (Paris: P.L.A.G.E., 2004).

Bossuat, G., *La France, l'aide américaine à la construction européenne 1944–1954*, 2 vols (Paris: Comite pour l'Histoire économique et financière de la France, 1992).

—, 'La France et le FMI au lendemain de la Seconde Guerre mondiale: les raisons de la tension', in *La France et les institutions de Bretton Woods 1944–1994. Actes du Colloque tenu à Bercy les 30 juin et 1er juillet 1994* (Paris: Comité pour l'Histoire Economique et Financière de la France, 1998), pp. 15–34.

Boughton, J. A., 'Why White? Inventing the Post-War Monetary System', *IMF Working Papers*, 52 (2002), pp. 1–24.

—, 'American in the Shadows: Harry Dexter White and the Design of the International Monetary Fund', *IMF Working Papers*, 6 (2006), pp. 1–14.

Brion, R., and J. L. Moreau, *La politique monétaire dans une Europe en reconstruction (1944–1958)* (Bruxelles: Banque Nationale de Belgique, 2005).

Buch, P., and J. Vanderlinden, *L'uranium. La Belgique et les puissances. Marché de dupes ou chef d'œuvre diplomatique* (Bruxelles: De Boeck, 1995).

Bussière, E., *La France, la Belgique et l'organisation économique de l'Europe, 1918–1935* (Paris: Ministère de l'Economie, des Finances et du Budget, 1992).

—, 'Economics and Franco-Belgian Relations in the Interwar Period', in R. Boyce (ed.), *French Foreign and Defence Policy 1918–1940* (Routledge: London, 2005), pp. 71–88.

Caincross, A., *Years of Recovery: British Economic Policy 1947–1951* (London: Methuen, 1987).

Cassiers, I., *Croissance, crise et régulation en économie ouverte. La Belgique entre les deux guerres* (Bruxelles: De Boeck Université, 1988).

Cassis, Y., and L. Cottrell, 'Financial History', *Financial History Review*, 1 (1994), pp. 5–22.

Catton, B., *The War Lords of Washington* (New York: Harcourt, 1948).

Cesarano, F., *Monetary Theory and Bretton Woods: The Construction of an International Monetary Order* (Cambridge: Cambridge University Press, 2006).

—, 'The Bretton Woods Agreements: A Monetary Theory Perspective', in L. Cottrell, G. Notaras and G. Totella (eds), *Studies in European Monetary Integration* (London: Ashgate, 2007), pp. 113–37.

Clavin, P., *The Failure of Economic Diplomacy: Britain, Germany, France and the United States, 1931–36* (London: MacMillan, 1996).

—, 'Defining Transnationalism', *Contemporary European History*, 14:4 (2005), pp. 421–39.

Clavin, P., and J.-W. Wessels, 'Another Gold Idol? The League of Nations's Gold Delegation and the Great Depression', *International History Review*, 26:4 (2004), pp. 765–95.

Cohrs, P. O., *The Unfinished Peace after World War I: America, Britain and the Stabilization of Europe, 1919–1932* (Cambridge: Cambridge University Press, 2006).

Collinet, R., *L'annexion d'Eupen et de Malmédy à la Belgique en 1920* (Verviers: Librairie La Dérive, 1986).

Conway, M., 'Legacies of Exile: The Exile Governments in Exile during the Second World War and the Politics of Postwar Europe', in Conway and Gotovitch (eds), *Europe in Exile*, pp. 255–74.

Conway, M., and J. Gotovitch (eds), *Europe in Exile: European Exile Communities in Britain 1940–1945* (Bergham Books: New York-Oxford, 2001).

'Copper Men Gather for World Parley', *New York Times*, 29 November 1932, p. 27.

Cotrell, L., 'Norman, the Bank of England and Europe since the 1920s: Case-Studies of Belgian and Italian Stabilisations', in E. Bussiere and M. Dumoulin (eds), *Milieux économiques et intégration européenns en Europe occidentale au XX siècle* (Arras: Artois Presses Université, 1998), pp. 37–84.

Crombois, J. F., 'Finance, économie et politique en Belgique à la veille de la Seconde Guerre mondiale 1939–1940', *Cahiers d'Histoire du Temps Présent*, 5 (1998), pp. 171–206.

—, *Camille Gutt: Les finances et la guerre 1940–1945* (Brussels: CEGES/Quorum, 1999).

—, 'Camille Gutt', in *Nouvelle Biographie Nationale*, 9 vols (Bruxelles: Académie Royale de Belgique, 1988–), vol. 6, pp. 228–32.

—, ' International Organizations and Regional Integration: The IMF and the EPU (1946–1958)', in E. Remacle and P. Winand (eds), *America, Europe, Africa 1943–1973* (Oxford: Peter Lang, 2009), pp. 67–82.

Crombois. J. F., and J. Gotovitch, 'Gouvernement belge de Londres', in P. Aron and J. Gotovitch (eds), *Dictionnaire de la Second Guerre mondiale de Belgique* (Bruxelles: André Versailles, 2008), pp. 211–16.

Depoortere, R., *La question des réparations allemandes dans la politique extérieure de la Belgique 1919–1925* (Bruxelles: Académie Royale de Belgique, 1998).

—, 'Theunis, Georges', *Nouvelle Biographie Nationale*, 9 vols (Bruxelles: Académie Royale de Belgique, 1988–), vol. 5, pp. 327–31.

Deshormes, E., 'Camille Gutt – Premier Directeur général du Fonds Monétaire International 1946–1951', *Revue de la Banque* [supplément historique], 3 (1986), pp. 3–63.

Desmed-Thielemans, M.-R., *La grande crise et le gouvernement des banquiers. Essai* (Bruxelles: Institut belge de Sciences politiques, 1979).

'Devaluation and the Consequences', *Economist*, 24 September 1949, pp. 680–5.

'Dilemmas of Leadership', *Economist*, 22 July 1951, pp. 213–14.

Dormael, A. van, *Bretton Woods: Birth of a Monetary System* (London: Macmillan, 1978).

Drummond, I. A., *London, Washington and the Management of Franc 1936–1939*, Princeton Studies in International Finance Series, 45 (Princeton, NJ: Princeton University Press, 1979).

Duchesne, A., 'Un général pas comme les autres. Le baron Empain durant la guerre 1914–1918', *Revue belge d'histoire militaire*, 24:1 (1985), pp. 156–95.

Dujardin, V., and M. Dumoulin, *Paul Van Zeeland 1893–1973* (Bruxelles: Editions Racine, 1997).

Dumoulin, A., and E. Remacle, *L'Union de l'Europe occidentale. Phénix de la défense européenne* (Bruxelles: Bruylandts, 1998).

Dumoulin, M., 'La mission Van Zeeland. Essai de clearing diplomatique de l'appeasement', *Relations Internationales*, 39 (1984), pp. 355–72.

—, *Spaak* (Bruxelles: Editions Racine, 1999).

Dupriez, L. H., *Les réformes monétaires en Belgique* (Bruxelles: Office international de librairie 1948).

Eden, A., *The Eden Memoirs*, 3 vols (London: Cassel, 1960–5).

Eichengreen, B., *Golden Fetters: The Gold Standard and the Great Depression 1919–1939* (Oxford: Oxford University Press, 1992).

—, 'International Coordination in Historical Perspective: A View for the Interwar Years', in B. Eichengreen (ed.), *Elusive Stability: Essays in the History of International Finance 1919–1939* (Cambridge: Cambridge University Press, 1993), pp. 113–52.

—, 'Institutions and Economic Growth: Europe after World War II', in N. Crafts and G. Toniolo (eds), *Economic Growth in Europe since 1945* (Cambridge: Cambridge University Press, 1996), pp. 56–7.

Eichengreen, B., and P. Temin, 'The Gold Standard and the Great Depression', *Contemporary European History*, 9 (2000), pp. 183–207.

Einzig, P., *World Finance since 1914* (London: K. Paul, Trench, Trubner & Co., 1935).

Fear, J., 'Cartels', in Jones and Zeitlin (eds), *The Oxford Handbook of Business History*, pp. 268–92.

Feinstein, C. F., P. Temin and G. Toniolo, *The World Economy between the World Wars* (Oxford: Oxford University Press, 2008).

Ferguson, N., *The Pity of War* (London: Allen Lane, Penguin Press, 1998).

Fforde, J., *The Bank of England and Public Policy 1941–1958* (Cambridge: Cambridge University Press, 1992).

Fink, C., *The Genoa Conference: European Diplomacy 1921–1922* (Chapel Hill, NC: University of North Carolina Press, 1984),

Flanders, M. J., *International Monetary Economics, 1870–1960: Between the Classical and the New Classical* (Cambridge: Cambridge University Press, 1989).

Foreign Relations of the United States, Diplomatic Papers 1944 (1944), vol. 2: General: Economic and Social Matters (Washington DC: US Government Printing Office, 1967).

Foreign Relations of the United States, vol. 3: Western Europe (Washington DC: US Government Printing Office, 1974).

Frank, R., *La Hantise du déclin. Le rang de la France en Europe 1920–1960. Finances, défense, et identité nationale* (Paris: Belin, 1994).

Fridenson, P., 'Business History and History', in Jones and Zeitlin (eds), *The Oxford Handbook of Business History*, pp. 37–66.

Fromkin, D., *In the Time of the Americans: FDR, Truman, Eisenhower, Marshall, MacArthur* (London: MacMillan, 1995).

Goethem, H. van, and Velaers, J., *Leopold III, de koning, het land, de Oorlog* (Tielt: Lannoo, 1994).

Gotovitch, J., 'Projets européens dans la résistance et à Londres durant la guerre', in M. Dumoulin (ed.), *La Belgique et les débuts de la construction européenne. De la guerre aux traités de Rome* (Ciaco Editeurs: Louvain-la-Neuve, 1987), pp. 38–47.

—, *Documents diplomatiques belges, 1941–1960. De l'indépendance à l'interdépendance* (Bruxelles: Académie Royale de Belgique, 1998).

Grosbois, T., 'La naissance du Benelux (1941–1944)', *Cahiers* [Centre de Recherches et d'Etudes historique sur la Seconde Guerre Mondiale], 15 (1992), pp. 53–101.

—, 'Les négociations de Londres pour une Union Douanière Benelux (1941–1944)', in H. Balthazar, M. Dumoulin and A. Postma, *Regards sur le Benelux. 50 Ans de coopération* (Bruxelles: Edition Racine, 1994), pp. 31–63.

—, 'Les relations diplomatiques entre le gouvernement Belge de Londres et les Etats-Unis (1940–1944)', *Guerres mondiales et conflits contemporains*, 2 (2001), pp. 167–87.

—, *Pierlot 1930–1950* (Bruxelles: Editions Racine, 2007).

—, 'Benelux', in P. Gerbet (dir.), *Dictionnaire historique de l'Europe unie. Préface d'Elie Barnavi* (Bruxelles: André Versailles, 2009), pp. 110–18.

'Gutt of the Fund', *Fortune Magazine*, 3 (1946), pp. 115–44 [pages discontinued].

Gutt, C., *Pourquoi le franc belge est tombé* (Bruxelles: Editions nouvelles, 1935).

—, 'Exchange Rates and the International Monetary Fund', *Review of Economics and Statistics*, 30:2 (May 1938), pp. 81–90.

—, 'Les accords de Bretton Woods and les institutions qui en sont issues', *Recueil des Cours. Académie de Droit International*, 72:1 (1948), pp. 71–162.

—, *Le Belgique au Carrefour* (Paris: Editions Fayard, 1971).

'Gutt Named Head of Monetary Fund', *New York Times*, 7 May 1946, p. 35.

Harrod, R. F., *The Life of John Maynard Keynes* (London: MacMillan, 1951).

Helmreich, J., *Belgium and Europe: A Study in Small Power Diplomacy* (The Hague: Mouton & Co., 1976).

—, *Gathering Rare Ores: The Diplomacy of Uranium Acquisition 1943–1954* (Princeton, NJ: Princeton University Press, 1986).

Helleiner, E., 'When Finance is the Servant: International Capital Movement in the Bretton Woods Order', in Ph. G. Cerny (ed.), *Finance and World Politics: Markets, Regimes and States in the Post Hegemonic Era* (Aldershot: Elgar, 1993), pp. 20–30.

—, *States and the Reemergence of Global Finance: From Bretton Woods to the 1990s* (Ithaca, NY: Cornell University Press, 1996).

—, *Nation-States and Money: The Past, Present and Future of National Currencies* (London: Routledge, 1999).

Hennessy, P., *Whitehall* (London: Fontana, 1990).

Herremans D., and K. Tavernier, 'De evolutie van de monetaire denkbeelden in Belgie 1914–1940', *Revue de la Banque*, 8–9 (1980), pp. 117–33.

Higgs, R., 'From Central Planning to the Market: The American Transition', *Journal of Economic History*, 59:3 (1999), pp. 599–623.

Hoff, J., *American Business & Foreign Policy: Business Views and Foreign Policy 1920–1933* (Boston, MA: Beacon Press, 1948).

Hogan, M. J., *The Marshall Plan: America, Britain and the Reconstruction of Western Europe* (Cambridge, Cambridge University Press, 1987).

Hogg, R. L., *Structural Rigidities and Policy Inertia in Inter-War Belgium* (Brussels: Koninklijke Academie voor Wetenschappen, Letteren en Schone Kunsten van België 1986).

Horsefield, J. K. (ed.), *The International Monetary Fund 1945–1965: Twenty Years of International Cooperation*, vol. 1: Chronicle (Washington DC: International Monetary Fund, 1969).

— (ed.), *The International Monetary Fund 1945–1965: Twenty Years of International Monetary Cooperation*, vol. 3: Documents (Washington DC: International Monetary Fund, 1969).

Horsefield, J. K., and G. Lovasy, 'Evolution of the Fund's Policy on Drawings', in de Vries and Horsefield (eds), *The International Monetary Fund 1945–1965*, vol. 2, pp. 415–27.

Hudson, D., and P. Lee, 'The Old and the New Significance of Political Economy in Diplomacy', *Review of International Studies*, 30 (2004), pp. 343–60.

Hull, C., *The Memoirs of Cordell Hull*, 2 vols (New York: Macmillan Company, 1948).

Hymans, P., *Mémoires*, 2 vols (Bruxelles: Institut de Sociologie Solvay, 1958).

Ikenberry, J. G., 'A World Economy Restored: Expert Consensus and the Anglo-American Post-War Settlement', in P. M. Hass (ed.), *Knowledge, Power, and International Policy Coordination* (Cambridge MA: MIT Press, 1992), pp. 289–321.

James, H., *International Monetary Cooperation since Bretton Woods* (Oxford: Oxford University Press, 1996).

Jones, G., *Multinationals and World Capitalism: From the Nineteenth to the Twenty First Century* (Oxford: Oxford University Press, 2004).

Jones, G., and J. Zeitlin (eds), *The Oxford Handbook of Business History* (Oxford: Oxford University Press, 2007).

Jones, V. C., *Manhattan: The Army and the Atomic Bomb* (Washington, DC: Center of Military History, 1985).

Kahler, M., 'Bretton Woods and its Competitors: The Political Economy of Institutional Choice', in D. M. Andrews, C. R. Henning and L. W. Pauly (eds), *Governing the World's Money* (Ithaca, NY: Cornell University Press, 2002), pp. 38–59.

Kaplan, J., and G. Schleiminger, *The European Payments Union: Financial Diplomacy in the 1950s* (Oxford: Clarendon Press, 1989).

Kapur, D., J. P. Lewis and R. Webb, *The World Bank: Its First Half Century*, vol. 1: History (Washington DC: Brookings Institution Press, 1997).

Keynes, J. M., *The General Theory of Employment, Interest and Money* (London: Macmillan, 1936).

—, *How to Pay for the War, A Radical Plan for the Chancellor of the Exchequer* (London: Macmillan, 1940).

—, *Théorie générale de l'emploi, de l'intérêt et de la monnaie*, translated from English edition by Jean de Largentaye, 2nd edn (Paris: Payot 1969).

—, *The Collected Writing of John Maynard Keynes*, vol. 26: Activities 1941–1946: Shaping the Post-War World. Bretton Woods and Reparations, ed. D. Moggridge (Cambridge: Cambridge University Press, 1980).

—, *The Collected Writings of J. M. Keynes*, vol. 21: Activities 1939–1945: Internal War Finance, ed. D. Moggridge (Cambridge: Cambridge University Press, 1982).

Kimball, W., *The Most Unsordid Act: Lend-Lease, Weapons for Victory* (Baltimore, MD: Johns Hopkins Press, 1969).

Kindleberger, C. P., 'Bretton Woods Reappraised', *International Organization*, 5:1 (1951), pp. 32–47.

—, *The World in Depression 1929–1939* (Berkeley, CA and Los Angeles, CA: University of California Press, 1986).

—, *Marhsall Plan Days* (Boston, MA: Allan & Uwin, 1987).

—, 'Commercial Policy Between the Wars', in P. Matthias and S. Pollard (eds), *The Cambridge Economic History of Europe*, vol. 8: *The Industrial Economies: The Development of Economic and Social Policies* (Cambridge: Cambridge University Press, 1989), pp. 161–96.

Kuisel, R. F., *Capitalism and the State in Modern France: Renovation and Economic Management in the Twentieth Century* (Cambridge: Cambridge University Press: Cambridge, 1981).

Kurgan-van Hentenryk, G., 'Finance and Financiers in Belgium 1880–1940', in Y. Cassis (ed.), *Finance and Financiers in European History 1880–1960* (Cambridge: Cambridge University Press, 1992), pp. 317–35.

—, 'La Belgique et le Plan Marshall ou les paradoxes des relations belgo-américaines', *Revue Belge de Philologie et d'Histoire*, 71:2 (1993), pp. 290–354.

—, *Gouverner la Générale de Belgique: Essai de biographie collective* (Bruxelles: De Boeck, 1996).

—, 'La Société Générale 1850–1934', in H. van der Wee (ed.), *La Générale de Banque 1822–1997* (Bruxelles: Editions Racine, 1997), pp. 63–285.

—, *Max-Léo Gérard: Un ingénieur dans la cité (1879–1955)* (Bruxelles: Editions de l'Université de Bruxelles, 2010).

Kurgan-van Hentenryk, G., S. Jaumain, V. Montens, with J. Puissant and J.-J. Heirwegh (eds), *Dictionnaire des patrons en Belgique* (Bruxelles: De Boek, 1996).

Langenhove, F. van, *La sécurité en Belgique. Contributions à l'histoire de la politique extérieure de la Belgique pendant la Seconde Guerre mondiale* (Académie Royale de Belgique: Bruxelles, 1972).

—, *L'élaboration de la politique étrangère de la Belgique entre les deux guerres mondiales* (Bruxelles: Académie Royale de Belgique, 1980).

—, *La Belgique et ses garants. L'été 1940. Contribution à l'histoire de la période 1940–1950* (Académie Royale de Belgique: Bruxelles, 1995).

Leith-Ross, F., *Money Talks, Fifty Years of International Finance: The Autobiography of Sir Frederick Leith-Ross* (London: Huchinson, 1968).

Lepage, S., 'Chronique d'un malentendu: la direction des finances extérieures et le Fonds Monétaire International, 1944–1948', in *La France et les institutions de Bretton Woods 1944–1994. Actes du Colloque tenu à Bercy les 30 juin et 1er juillet 1994* (Paris: Comité pour l'Histoire Economique et Financière de la France, 1998), pp. 35–67.

Lipgens, W. (ed), *Documents on the History of European Integration*, vol. 2: Plans for European Union in Great Britain and in Exile 1939–1945 (Berlin: Alter de Gruyter, 1986).

Littauer, R. M., 'The Unfreezing of Foreign Funds', *Columbia Law Review*, 45:2 (March 1945), pp. 132–74.

Lyttleton, O. [Viscount Chandos], *The Memoirs of Lord Chandos* (London: Bodley Head, 1962).

MacMillan, M., *Peacemakers: The Paris Conference of 1919 and its Attempts to End War* (London: John Murray, 2001).

Maes, I., 'The Spread of Keynesian Economics: A Comparison of the Belgian and the Italian Experience 1945–1970', in *Journal of the History of Economic Thought*, 30:4 (2008), pp. 491–509.

Maier, C., *In Search of Stability: Explorations in History Economy* (Cambridge: Cambridge University Press, 1987).

Mandel, E., *The Meaning of the Second World War* (London: Verso, 1986).

Mantez, A., 'Pierre Mendès France. Expert International 1944–1953', *Pierre Mendes-France et l'économie* (Paris: Editions Odile Jacob, 1989), pp. 119–42.

Margairaz, P., *L'Etat, les finances et l'économie. Histoire d'une conversion*, 2 vols (Paris: Comité pour l'histoire économique et financière de la France, 1991).

Markwell, D., *John Maynard Keynes and International Relations: Economic Paths to War and Peace* (Oxford: Oxford University Press, 2006).

Marks, S., *Innocent Abraod: Belgium at the Paris Peace Conference of 1919* (Chapel Hill, NC: University of North Carlolina Press, 1981).

Meyers, R. H., *Bankers' Diplomacy: Monetary Stabilization in the 1920s* (New York: Columbia University Press, 1970).

Milward, A. S., *The Reconstruction of Western Europe 1945–1951* (Routledge: London, 1984).

—, *War, Economy and Society 1940–1945* (Penguin: Harmondsworth, 1987)

Moggridge, D. E., 'The Gold Standard and National Economic Policies', in P. Mathias and S. Pollard (eds.), *The Cambridge Economic History of Europe*, vol. 8: The Industrial Economies (Cambridge: Cambridge University Press, 1989), pp. 250–314.

Moggridge, D. E., *Maynard Keynes, an Economist Biography* (London, Routledge, 1992).

Navari, C., 'David Mitrany and International Functionalism', in D. Long and P. Wilson (eds), *Thinkers of the Twenty Years' Crisis* (Oxford: Clarendon Press, 1995), pp. 214–46.

Nefors, P., *La collaboration industrielle en Belgique 1940–1945* (Bruxelles: Editions Racine, 2006).

Odell, J. S., 'From London to Bretton Woods. Sources of Change in Bargaining Strategies and Outcomes', *Journal of Public Policy*, 8:3–4 (1988), pp. 287–315.

Oliver, R. W., *International Economic Cooperation and the World Bank* (London: MacMillan, 1996).

Pauly, L. W., *The League of Nations and the Foreshadowing of the International Monetary Fund*, Essays in International Finance Series, 201 (Princeton, NJ: International Finance Section, 1997).

—, *Who Elected the Bankers?: Surveillance and Control in the World Economy* (Ithaca, NY: Cornell University Press, 1997).

Peden, G. C., 'Sir John Hopkins, the Keynesian Revolution in Employment Policy 1929–1945', *Economic History Review*, 36:2 (1986), pp. 281–95.

—, 'Keynes and British Economic Policy', in Backhouse and Bateman (eds), *The Cambridge Companion to Keynes*, pp. 98–117.

Perroux, F., *Textes complementaires sur la coexistence pacifique* (Grenoble: Presses Universitaires de Grenoble, 1992).

Polak, J., 'Contribution of the September 1949 Devaluations to the Solution of Europe's Dollar Problem', *IMF Staff Papers*, 2:1 (1951), pp. 1–32.

Pollard, S., 'Economic Interdependence and Economic Protectionism: From the Conference of Genoa (1922) to the Conference of London (1933)', in R. Ahmann, A. M. Birke and M. Howard (eds), *The Quest for Stability: Problems of West European Security 1918–1957* (Oxford: Oxford University Press, 1993), pp. 157–71.

Polonsky, A. B., 'Polish Failure in Wartime London: Attempts to Forge a European Alliance 1940–1944', *International History Review*, 7:4 (1965), pp. 176–91.

Pollard, S., 'Economic Interdependence and Economic Protectionism: From the Conference of Genoa (1922) to the Conference of London (1933)', in R. Ahmann, A. M. Birke and M. Howard (eds), *The Quest for Stability: Problems of West European Security 1918–1957* (Oxford: Oxford University Press, 1993), pp. 157–71.

'President Greets Belgian Mission', *New York Times*, 17 May 1934, p. 27.

Pruessen, R., *John Foster Dulles: The Road to Power* (New York: Free Press, 1982).

Ranieri, L., *Emile Francqui ou l'intelligence créatrice 1863–1935* (Bruxelles: Duculot, 1985).

Roon, G. van, 'Rapprochement en vagues successives. La préhistoire du Benelux', in Balthazar et al., *Regards sur le Benelux* (Bruxelles: Edition Racine, 1994), pp. 13–38.

Rosanvallon, P., 'The Development of Keynesianism in France', in P. Hall (ed.), *The Political Power of Economic Ideas: Keynesianism across Nations* (Princeton, NJ: Princeton University Press, 1989), pp. 171–94.

Roussel, E., *Jean Monnet (1888–1979)* (Paris: Editions Fayard, 1996).

Sayers, R., *Financial Policy 1939–1945*, History of the Second World War, United Kingdom Civil Series (London: Her Majesty's Stationary Office, 1956).

Schwartz, J. A., *The New Dealers: Power Politics in the Age of Roosevelt* (New York: Knopf, 1993).

Skidelsky, R., *John Maynard Keynes 1883–1946*, 3 vols (London: Macmillan, 1983–2000).

—, *John Maynard Keynes 1883–1946: Economist, Philosopher, Statesman* (London: Penguin Books, 2003).

—, 'Keynes's Road to Bretton Woods', in M. Flandreau and H. James (eds), *International Financial History in the Twentieth Century: Systems and Anarchy* (Cambridge: Cambridge University Press, 2003), pp. 125–51.

—, 'Hayek versus Keynes: The Road to Reconciliation', in E. Feser (ed.), *The Cambridge Companion to Hayek* (Cambridge: Cambridge University Press, 2006), pp. 82–110.

Spaak, P. H., *Combats inachevés. De l'indépendance a l'alliance* (Paris: Fayard, 1969).

Spender, H., 'Some Notes of the London Conference', *Fortnightly Review*, 116:693 (1924), pp. 323–32.

Steiner, Z., *The Lights that Failed: European International History, 1919–1933* (Oxford: Oxford University Press, 2005).

Stengers, J., *Aux origines de la question royale. Léopold III et le gouvernment. Les deux politiques belges* (Gembloux: Duculot, 1980).

Suetens, M., 'The Van Zeeland Report', *Contemporary Review*, 153 (1938), pp. 316–23.

Tavernier, K., and H. van der Wee, *La Banque nationale de Belgique et l'histoire monétaire entre les deux guerres mondiales* (Bruxelles: Banque Nationale de Belgique, 1975).

Tilman, S., 'Les banquiers et la politique: incompatibilités ? Le cas de la Belgique (XIXème–XXème siècles), in S. Jaumain and K. Bertrams (dir.), *Patrons, gens d'affaires et banquiers. Hommages à Ginette Kurgan-van Hentenryk* (Bruxelles: Le Livre Timperman, 2004).

Toniolo, G., *Central Bank Cooperation at the Bank for International Settlements, 1930–1973* (Cambridge: Cambridge University Press, 2005).

Toussaint, Y., *Les barons Empain* (Paris: Fayard, 1996).

Traynor, D. E., *International Monetary and Financial Conferences in the Inter-War Period* (Washington, DC: Catholic University of America Press, 1949).

United Nations Monetary and Financial Conference. Proceedings and Documents, vol. II (Washington DC: United States Government Printing Office: 1948).

Valensi, C., *Un témoin sur l'autre rive 1943–1949* (Paris: Comité pour l'histoire économique et financière de la France Ministère des Finances, 1994).

Van der Wee, H., and M. Verbeyt, *Oorlog en monetaire politiek: de Nationale Bank van België, de Emissiebank te Brussel en de Belgische regering, 1939–1945* (Brussels: National Bank van België, 2005).

—, *A Small Nation in the Turmoil of the Second World War: Money, Finance and Occupation* (Leuven: Leuven University Press: 2009).

Vanthemsche, G., 'De val van de regering Pouillet-Vandervelde: een samenzwering der bankiers', *Revue Belge d'Histoire contemporaine*, 9:1–2 (1978), pp. 167–8.

—, 'L'élaboration de l'AR sur le contrôle bancaire (1935)', *Revue Belge d'Histoire contemporaine*, 9 (1980), pp. 389–437.

—, 'De mislukking van een verniewded economische politiek in Belgïe voor de tweede wereloorlog', *Revue Belge d'Histoire contemporaine*, 13:2–3 (1982), pp. 339–89.

—, 'La Banque de 1934 a nos jours', in H. van der Wee (ed.), *La Générale de Banque 1822–1997* (Bruxelles: Editions Racines, 1997), pp. 303–66.

—, *La Belgique et le Congo: empreinte d'une colonie 1885–1980*, Nouvelle Histoire de Belgique Series, 4 (Brussels: Editions Complexe, 2007).

Vanwelkenhuyzen, J., *Le gâchis des années 30, 1933–1937*, tome I (Bruxelles Editions Racine, 2007).

Vries, M. de, and J. K. Horsefield (eds), *The International Monetary Fund 1945–1965*, vol. 2: Analysis (Washington, DC: International Monetary Fund, 1969).

Wallef, D., 'Les collusions politico-financières devant l'opinion (1930–1936)' (MA dissertation, Université Libre de Bruxelles, année académique 1969–1970).

Walters, A., 'The International Copper Cartel', *Southern Economic Journal*, 11:2 (1944), pp. 133–56.

White, H. D., 'The Monetary Fund: Some Criticisms Examined', *Foreign Affairs*, 23 (January 1945), pp. 195–210.

Wolff, J., 'Pierre Mendes-France et J. M. Keynes. Un premier repérage', in *Pierre Mendès France et l'économie. Pensée et action sous la direction de M. Margairaz. Actes du Colloque organisé par l'Institut Mendes France à l'Assemblée nationale les 11 et 12 janvier 1988 sous la présidence de Mr Claude Cheysson* (Paris: Odile Jacob, 1989), pp. 57–79.

Woods, N., *The Globalizers: The IMF, the World Bank, and their Borrowers* (Ithaca, NY: Cornell University Press, 2006).

Woods, R. B., *A Changing of the Guard: Anglo-American Relations, 1941–1946* (Chapel Hill, NC: University of North Carolina Press, 1990).

'World Group Asks Stabilized Money', *New York Times*, 26 March 1934, p. 27.

Wyatt-Walker, A., 'The United States and Western Europe: The Theory of Hegemonic Stability', in N. Woods (ed.), *Explaining International Relations since 1945* (Oxford: Oxford University Press, 1996), pp. 126–54.

Zeeland, M. van, *L'expérience van Zeeland en Belgique* (Lausanne: Payot, 1940).

Zeeman, B., and C. Wiebes, 'The Netherlands and Alliances 1940–1949' (PhD dissertation, Rijksuniversiteit te Leiden, 1993).

INDEX

The following abbreviations have been used: 'f' indicates a figure; 't' indicates a table; 'g' indicates an entry in the glossary of names; and 'n' indicates a note.

For Product Safety Concerns and Information please contact our EU
representative GPSR@taylorandfrancis.com
Taylor & Francis Verlag GmbH, Kaufingerstraße 24, 80331 München, Germany

www.ingramcontent.com/pod-product-compliance
Ingram Content Group UK Ltd.
Pitfield, Milton Keynes, MK11 3LW, UK
UKHW021611240425
457818UK00018B/502